CROSS-NATIONAL RESEARCH METHODS IN THE SOCIAL SCIENCES

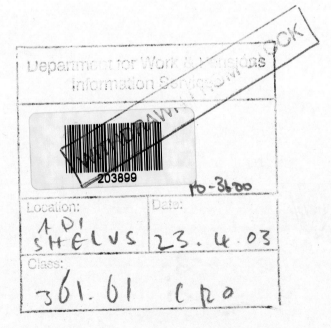

CROSS-NATIONAL RESEARCH METHODS IN THE SOCIAL SCIENCES

edited by

Linda Hantrais and Steen Mangen

PINTER
LONDON and NEW YORK

PINTER
A Cassell Imprint
Wellington House, 125 Strand, London WC2R 0BB
215 Park Avenue South, New York, New York 10003, USA

First published in 1996

British Library Cataloguing in Publication Data
A catalogue record for this book is available from The British Library

ISBN 1 85567 344 4 (H/B)
ISBN 1 85567 345 2 (P/B)

Printed in Great Britain by Biddles Ltd, Guildford and King's Lynn

Contents

List of Tables

Notes on Contributors

Robert Anderson is research manager at the European Foundation for the Improvement of Living and Working Conditions in Dublin, where he is responsible for research on older people, care issues and health at work. His publications include *Living with Chronic Illness* (1991) and *The Aftermath of Stroke* (1993).

Elfi Bendikat is a historian, working at the Historical Institute of the Humboldt University, Berlin, in a department specialising in comparative research on France and Germany. She was formerly assistant at the Historische Kommission zu Berlin, and assistant and associate professor at the Institute for Political Sciences at the Free University, Berlin. Her research interests include Imperialism, Liberalism and comparative electoral politics in Germany, Britain and France, and transport policies in Berlin and Paris.

Prue Chamberlayne is Principal Lecturer in European Social Policy at the University of East London and leads the 'Cultures of Care' project. Her publications cover neighbourhood networks in East Germany, women and social policy in Germany and welfare developments in Western Europe. Recent articles and chapters include 'Women and social policy' in J. Clasen and R. Freeman (eds), *Social Policy in Germany* (1994), and 'Gender and the private sphere – a touchstone of misunderstanding between Eastern and Western Germany, *Social Politics* (1995).

Paul Cheshire is Professor of Economic Geography at the London School of Economics, having previously been Professor of Urban and Regional Economics at the University of Reading. His research interests span European urban and regional economics and analysis. In the course of his work, he has built up an extensive database for European city-regions. He has published widely in the specialist literature, including a co-authored book, *Urban Problems in Western Europe: an Economic Analysis* (1989), with D. Hay.

Alain Desrosières is a member of the Research Department of the Institut National de la Statistiques et des Études Économiques (the French statistical office) in Paris. His research interests include the history and uses of statistical techniques from a comparative perspective, involving historical comparisons of social and demographic statistics in France, Germany, Great Britain, Russia and the United States. Amongst his many publications is a monograph entitled *La politique des grands nombres: histoire de la raison statistique* (1993).

Shirley Dex is Lecturer in Management Studies at the Judge Institute for Management Studies in Cambridge, following a secondment to the British Household Panel Study at the ESRC Centre for Micro-Social Change at the University of Essex. She has also been co-ordinator of a European Science Foundation network and a European Commission Human Capital and Mobility network. She has published widely on women's employment, ethnic minority employment and the use of longitudinal or work history data, including *British and American Women at Work* (1986), with L.B. Shaw, and *French and British Mothers at Work* (1993), with P. Walters and D. Alden.

Katherine Duffy is a researcher and lecturer in the Department of Corporate Strategy at De Montfort University. She has extensive experience of evaluation through her work with the European Commission's poverty programmes. She is Director of Research with the Council of Europe for a programme on Human Dignity and Social Exclusion.

Tony Eardley is a Senior Research Fellow in the Social Policy Research Centre at the University of New South Wales, Australia. Previously, he was a researcher at the Social Policy Research Unit at the University of York. His main interests are in comparative social security, labour markets and gender. He has used both qualitative and quantitative methodologies in his research, which has spanned the European Union and other OECD countries. His publications include *Low Income Self-Employment: Work, Benefits and Living Standards* (1995), with A. Corden, and *Social Assistance Schemes in the OECD Countries* (1996), with J. Ditch, J. Bradshaw, I. Gough and P. Whiteford.

Martin Evans is research officer with the Welfare State Programme in the Suntory Toyota International Centre for Economics and Related Disciplines (STICERD). His previous research has been into housing and social security benefits and the effects of the Social Security Act on family incomes in Britain.

Ana Furtado is a Portuguese doctoral student at the London School of Economics. Before coming to Britain, she worked in the Portuguese Ministry of Finance and the Bank of Portugal. Her research is on the analysis of inter-regional wage differentials in the European Union.

Judith Glover lectures in social policy in the Department of Sociology and Social Administration at Roehampton Institute, London. She has had experience of conducting a number of cross-national comparisons using large-scale databases. She has undertaken a collaborative Franco-British comparative study funded by the ESRC, looking at the occupational outcomes for women and men who have qualifications in science, engineering and technology.

Linda Hantrais is Professor of Modern Languages and Director of the European Research Centre at Loughborough University. Her research interests cover cross-national research theory, methodology and practice, with particular reference to public policy in the European Union. Her publications include *Social Policy in the European Union* (1995) and *Families and Family Policies in Europe* (1996), with Marie-Thérèse Letablier.

Alan Harding is Professor of Urban Policy and Politics at the European Institute for Urban Affairs, Liverpool John Moores University. He is co-author of *Urbanisation and the Functions of Cities in the European Community* (1993) and co-editor of *European Cities towards 2000: Profiles, Policies and Prospects* (1994).

Annette Jobert is a researcher in the CNRS Laboratory: Travail et Mobilités, directed by Georges Benguigui, at the University Paris-X Nanterre. Her research interests are in the area of training policy at enterprise, sector and regional level. She has conducted a comparative study of group negotiations and is examining European social policy from an industrial relations perspective. She is co-editor, of *Éducation et travail en Grande-Bretagne, Allemagne et Italie* (1995), with Catherine Marry and Lucie Tanguy.

Annette King worked as Research Officer for the 'Cultures of Care' project, led by Prue Chamberlayne at the University of East London, where she also conducted her own research for a doctorate on the analysis of care systems in Bremen.

Stefano Magrini is an Italian doctoral student at the London School of Economics, where he is conducting research on endogenous explanations of regional growth.

Steen Mangen lectures in European Social Policy at the London School of Economics. His main research interests are in inner city Europe and changing social policy responses, and the welfare state in post-Franco Spain. His publications include *Mental Health Care in the European Community* (1985) and *Spain after Franco: Regime Transition and the Welfare State* (forthcoming).

Helen Rainbird is Professor of Industrial Relations at Nene College, Northampton. She is a social anthropologist by training and was formerly Senior Research Fellow at the Industrial Relations Research Unit, University of Warwick, where she continues to be an Associate Fellow. Her main research interests are in industrial relations and vocational training. She has published on trade union policy, continuing training in companies and European policy on training.

Jill Rubery is Professor of Comparative Employment Systems at the Manchester School of Management, UMIST. Previously, while based in Cambridge, she worked on the ESRC Social Change and Economic Life Initiative and on a number of Employment Department projects concerned with women's employment and low-wage labour. Between 1991 and 1995, she was the co-ordinator of the European Commission's Network of Experts on the Situation of Women in the Labour Market. With Colette Fagan, she has produced regular reports, published in the *Social Europe* series, and the *Bulletin on Women and Employment in the EU*.

Michaela Schunk has written a doctoral thesis in Social Policy at Manchester University, having studied psychology, political science and philosophy at Heidelberg University in Germany. Her research interests include comparative social and public policy, health care, ageing and the lifecourse. She has prepared reports for a number of cross-national research projects, including 'Paying for Care: Lessons from Europe', co-ordinated by C. Glendinning and E. McLaughlin, and 'Social Assistance Schemes in OECD Countries' .

Bernard Simonin is a director of research at the Centre d'Études de l'Emploi in Paris, where he is leading a programme on the evaluation of employment policies. He has been a member of evaluation committees for European Commission programmes to combat unemployment and social exclusion and is engaged in an evaluation of the European Social Fund in France under Objective 3. His publications include a number of evaluation studies on French and European programmes.

Haluk Soydan is associate professor in social work at the University of Gothenburg and research director at the Centre for Evaluation of Social Services, National Board of Health and Welfare, Stockholm. He has published a number of articles on the vignette method in social work, and several books, including *Det sociala arbetets idéhistoria* [Social Work in the History of Ideas] (1993), and *Försäkringskassan och invandrarna* [The Social Insurance Office and Immigrant Clients] (1995).

Paul Spicker is Senior Lecturer in Social Policy at the University of Dundee. His research interests cover a wide range of social policy topics, including social security, housing and community care. Much of his writing has focused on the application of political and social theory to issues in social policy. His published work includes *Stigma and Social Welfare* (1984), *Principles of Social Welfare* (1988), *Poverty and Social Security: Concepts and Principles* (1993) and *Social Policy: Themes and Approaches* (1995).

Clare Ungerson is Professor of Social Policy at the University of Southampton. Her research interests cover cross-national studies of gender and welfare states, and she has used qualitative methods in small-scale, locally based, empirical research. Her publications include *Policy is Personal: Sex, Gender and Informal Care* (1987) and *Payments for Care: a Comparative Overview*(1994), with the European Centre and A. Evers and M. Pijl.

Robert Walker is Professor of Social Policy and Director of the Centre for Research in Social Policy at Loughborough University. He is an experienced analyst and evaluator of social policy in the British and international context and has published widely on social security issues, poverty dynamics and social research methods, including *Europe for Richer or for Poorer* (1993), with R. Simpson.

Preface

After the stimulus provided in the post-war period by the United Nations and its agencies, interdisciplinary and international collaboration and, more recently, networking have been consistently encouraged, especially since the 1980s, by funding bodies, the higher education sector, government departments and the European Union. The net result is that international comparisons are being used increasingly in the social sciences by researchers and policy makers.

Specifically, the large-scale Research and Development programmes launched by the European Commission in science and engineering have been a fundamental catalyst in encouraging teams from different countries working on similar topics to meet to exchange views and findings, or to spend some time in each other's laboratories, pooling ideas and equipment, with the aim of pushing back the frontiers of knowledge.

In the social sciences, the European Commission has initiated a number of large-scale European-wide programmes, such as those on poverty in the 1970s, which attempted to increase the level of political awareness of the problem of social exclusion. Observatories and networks have been set up to monitor social and economic developments: for example the European Observatory on National Policies to Combat Social Exclusion, on Ageing and Older People and on National Family Policies, or the Network on Childcare and Measures to Reconcile Employment and Family Responsibilities and the Network on the Situation of Women in the Labour Market. Their brief has been to monitor and report back to the Commission on developments in Member States. National representatives identify a common object of study and assemble materials from national datasets, which may or may not be analysed cross-nationally.

Many of the projects between East and West undertaken during the Cold War period by the European Coordination Centre for Research and Documentation in Social Sciences (known as the Vienna Centre), or those still being carried out by the European Foundation for the Improvement of Living and Working Conditions in Dublin afford further examples of this type of research, where large amounts of information are collected and collated, although often data may not be comparable.

The European Commission's Human Capital and Mobility Programmes have encouraged academic researchers to form multinational teams and to set up collaborative projects, which may involve researchers with little prior experience of international work. On a more modest scale, bilateral programmes have been established between EU member states to foster and promote international collaboration in the social sciences, with support from national research councils and government agencies.

Notwithstanding this impressive outburst of research activity, it remains true that few social scientists have been trained to conduct studies that cross national boundaries and compare different cultures. Those planning to embark on international projects are often unaware of the limitations of comparative research methods and of the problems that may arise due to an inadequate knowledge of the contexts in which comparisons are being conducted and the conceptual frameworks within which researchers from different countries are operating. A number of basic questions have still not received definitive answers and can profit from further exploration: What is cross-national comparative research and what distinguishes it from other comparative research? Why should social scientists do cross-national comparative research? What are the methodological approaches available for cross-national comparative research? What are the problems in doing cross-national comparative research and how can they be solved?

This edited collection is designed to provide an accessible resource book that remedies some of the deficiencies encountered in the literature, where the focus has often been on the presentation of empirical findings to the neglect of methodological problems and issues concerning the management of large-scale, multi-site international projects.

Our overarching aim is to contribute to the knowledge and understanding of the research process for social scientists engaged in cross-national comparative studies. The book is organised around four broad comparative methods and techniques: quantitative methods for collecting and analysing data cross-nationally using large-scale databases; qualitative methods; approaches adopted for accessing comparable information; and the evaluation of cross-national comparisons.

Analyses of methods devoid of context can make for dull reading. For that reason, the chapters emphasise the link between methods and conceptual problems within defined policy areas relating to the evolving labour market and social policy agenda of the European Union, which will extend into the next century. Each of the sections in the book covers the same themes: labour markets, training and mobility; demographic trends, ageing and family policy; social exclusion and related urban and social security issues.

The authors are experts working in various EU member states and, importantly, come from different disciplinary backgrounds. In their contributions, they examine critically the methodological and managerial issues that have arisen in their research. They are able to draw on their own experience of conducting comparisons to offer well-informed guidance on how to overcome the pitfalls and problems they have encountered.

We are grateful to the contributors for giving so generously of their time to reflect on their methods and to share their experience with others who are either new to the field or looking to extend and appraise their knowledge of cross-national comparative research.

Linda Hantrais and Steen Mangen
January 1996

Method and Management of Cross-National Social Research

Linda Hantrais and Steen Mangen

Even when individuals or groups of researchers from different countries work very closely together, they are not necessarily carrying out cross-national comparisons. They may simply be attempting to study a particular phenomenon in different national contexts. For the study to be cross-national and comparative, individuals or teams should set out to study particular issues or phenomena in two or more countries with the express intention of comparing their manifestations in different socio-cultural settings, using the same research instruments, either to carry out secondary analysis of national data or to conduct new empirical work.

Paradoxically, new technologies have been double-edged; they have made it possible to conduct extensive surveys and process enormous quantities of data that can be made available simultaneously to social scientists working in different countries, but much less progress has been recorded at the theoretical and conceptual levels, where the sophistication of data-handling techniques has not been matched by similar advances in methodology.

After briefly exploring some of the reasons for undertaking cross-national comparisons and the benefits that can be derived from international collaboration, the methodological and practical issues facing researchers who are seeking to cross national boundaries are examined in this introductory chapter, before looking at possible solutions to some of the problems raised by cross-national comparisons.

The unit of comparison

From the definitions given in the large body of literature on the subject, a study can be said to be cross-national and comparative if one or more units in two or more societies, cultures or countries are compared in respect of the same concepts and concerning the

1

systematic analysis of phenomena, usually with the intention of explaining them and generalising from them. The expectation is that the researchers gather data about the object of study within different contexts and, by making comparisons, gain a greater awareness and a deeper understanding of social reality.

Some authors distinguish between concepts such as cross-country, cross-national, cross-societal, cross-cultural, cross-systemic and cross-institutional; others substitute 'trans' for 'cross' to suggest that they are focusing on macro-structures, and yet others use the various terms as if they were synonymous (an issue discussed by Øyen, 1990, p. 7). National boundaries may be different from ethnic, cultural and social boundaries, and greater variation may occur within than between countries. Paul Cheshire *et al.* show in their contribution to this volume that the criteria used by Eurostat in its Nomenclature des Unités Territoriales Statistiques (NUTS) to define European regions are essentially political and do not produce a harmonised set of regional units.

Although 'cross-national' is the concept used in this book, it is becoming difficult to define in the context of changes in national boundaries and with the shift towards European political, economic and monetary union. 'Cross-cultural' comparative studies, which can often be no easier to delimit, imply regional or meso-level units of observation, providing the means of controlling and correcting for the cultural environment (institutions, customs, traditions, value systems, lifestyles, language, thought patterns) in which a particular phenomenon occurs (see for example Lisle, 1985; Samuel, 1989). This type of study has therefore been described as the equivalent of the controlled experiment in the natural sciences (Lisle *et al.*, 1984). The larger system is taken to influence the characteristics of the units examined, and at the same time it may be possible to generalise about the relations between variables from the analysis of the same concepts or phenomena in different national contexts.

The value of collaborative and cross-national research

As evidenced in this collection, the benefits are considerable when researchers from different backgrounds are brought together on collaborative or cross-national projects, enabling valuable personal contacts to be established. Indeed, they may sometimes be greater than the actual comparative results derived from the research. In international projects where researchers work in pairs or small teams, such collaboration is a valuable heuristic strategy capitalising on their experience and knowledge of different intellectual traditions. Collaborative projects provide opportunities to compare and evaluate different conceptual approaches.

A conventional wisdom has gradually emerged about the benefits and pitfalls of cross-national research. Comparisons can lead to fresh, exciting insights and a deeper understanding of issues that are of central concern in different countries. Cross-national projects may also point to possible directions that could be followed and about which the researcher may not previously have been aware. Questions need to be asked, for example, about the extent to which policies formulated in one national context could be applied elsewhere. For the Hungarian László Cseh-Szombathy (1985, p. 61), the great advantage of cross-national comparisons is that, at their best, they force researchers to look at a total context and enable them to discover the greatest number of factors that are interactive and interdependent. Cross-national comparisons may also help to sharpen the focus of analysis of the subject under study by suggesting new perspectives, as demonstrated by many of the contributions to the present volume. They can lead to the identification of gaps in knowledge which prevent effective cross-national comparisons, thereby suggesting useful avenues for future research.

Cross-national projects give researchers a means of confronting findings in an attempt to identify and illuminate similarities and differences, not only in the observed characteristics of particular institutions, systems or practices, but also in the search for possible explanations in terms of national likeness and unlikeness. Edmond Lisle (1985, p. 26) has argued persuasively that cross-national comparativists are forced to attempt to adopt a different cultural perspective, to learn to understand the thought processes of another culture and to see it from the native's viewpoint, while also reconsidering their own country from the perspective of a skilled observer from outside. This in itself might be considered as a sufficient justification for undertaking cross-national projects.

Approaches to cross-national research

It has become a truism that, in many respects, the methodology adopted in cross-national comparative research is no different from that used for within-nation comparisons or for other areas of sociological research. It can be descriptive, evaluative and/or analytical and is therefore subject to many of the same problems.

The descriptive, or survey, method, which will usually result in a state of the art review, is generally the first stage in any large-scale international comparative project, such as those carried out by the European Co-ordination Centre for Research and Documentation in Social Sciences (Vienna) and the Foundation for the Improvement of Living and Working Conditions (Dublin). A juxtaposition approach is often adopted at this stage: data gathered by individuals or teams, according to agreed criteria, and derived either from existing materials or new empirical work, are presented side by side. Many projects never go far beyond data collection and collation since analysis and evaluation are so costly in terms of time and funding and tend to give rise to problems which may be avoided if the study is confined to description. In this regard, the annual reports of the European observatories are intended to provide updates on national policies rather than comparisons, but they may subsequently be used for comparative purposes (see Simonin in this volume).

Some large-scale projects are intended to be explanatory from the outset: the aim is to determine and explain the degree of variability observed from one national sample to another. They draw on several methods: the inductive method, starting from loosely defined hypotheses and moving towards their verification; the deductive method, applying a general theory to a specific case in order to interpret certain aspects; and the demonstrative method, designed to confirm and refine a theory.

Rather than each researcher or group of researchers investigating their own national context and then pooling information, a single researcher or team of researchers may formulate the problem and research hypotheses and carry out studies in more than one country, using replication of the experimental design, generally to collect and analyse new data. The method is often adopted when a smaller number of countries is involved and where researchers are required to have intimate knowledge of all the countries under study. Where a single researcher or team from one country is carrying out research in two or more countries, it is generally described as the 'safari' approach. The safari method is used to look at a well-defined issue in two or more countries, as exemplified by Alan Harding, Michaela Schunk and Haluk Soydan in their contributions. The approach usually combines surveys, secondary analysis of national data, and also personal observation and an interpretation of the findings in relation to their wider social context.

Irrespective of the institutional organisation of the research, a shift is occurring in emphasis away from descriptive and 'culture-free' approaches back to a concern with critical case studies and other explanations of social phenomena that are rooted in their socio-cultural setting (Berting, 1987). The societal approach, which has perhaps been most fully explicated in relation to industrial sociology by Marc Maurice (1979) and is developed further by Michael Rose (1985), implies that the researcher sets out to identify the specificity of social forms and institutional structures in different societies to look for explanations of differences by referring to the wider social context. Since the collaborative framework in which more research is taking place today also requires a greater awareness of cultural diversity, the societal approach is becoming even more valuable and is often contrasted with convergence theory where researchers look for universal trends, particularly in comparisons of advanced industrial societies. Another result of the greater emphasis on contextualisation in comparative studies is their increasingly interdisciplinary and multidisciplinary character, since it is necessary to take into account such a wide range of factors at the lowest possible level of disaggregation, as illustrated by Annette Jobert's contribution to the present volume.

Problems in cross-national comparative research

Descriptive cross-national comparative research has tended to underestimate the impact of cultural differences. The shift in orientation towards a more interpretative approach means that quintessential linguistic and cultural factors can no longer be downplayed. As argued above, many of the problems that arise in cross-national comparisons are by no means peculiar to international research, but additional difficulties arise, which may be absent from single-nation studies, due to differences in research traditions and administrative structures. If these problems go unresolved, they are likely to affect the quality of the results of the whole project, since the researcher runs the risk of losing control over the construction and analysis of key variables.

Three main and interrelated problem areas are briefly examined here. They concern the management of research, availability of and access to comparable datasets and the definition of the research parameters and associated issues of equivalence of concepts.

Institutional and financial dimensions in the management of cross-national research

In ideal conditions, a project team manager will select the countries to be included in the study and researchers with appropriate knowledge and expertise to undertake the work. In small-scale bilateral comparisons, this may be feasible, but more often the reality is different, and participation may be determined by factors (sometimes political) which do not make for easy relationships between team members. European programmes may have to include all EU member states. With the entry of Greece, Portugal and Spain in the 1980s, and Austria, Finland and Sweden in the mid-1990s, the countries concerned represent very different stages of economic and social development. The mix of countries selected in comparative studies affects the quality and comparability of the data as well as the nature of the collaboration between researchers. For example, the Vienna Centre brought together countries with diverging intellectual traditions and ideological backgrounds (36 countries were, for instance, involved at the beginning of their project on the family); the studies conducted by Tony Eardley and the research team in the Social Policy Research Unit at York, reported in this volume, covered all the OECD countries. As an attempt at resolution of these problems, considerable advantages are offered by the managerial strategy adopted by international organisations such as the OECD, which directly employs its own experts rather than relying on extensive subcontracting, although it must be admitted that this option is not without its own constraints and is of limited feasibility in many research contexts.

Where the collection of secondary data is to be undertaken by researchers in their own country, the financial resources received and the amount of time that can be allocated to the research will differ considerably from one national context to another. The CNRS in France pays over 13,000 full-time researchers and does not, therefore, fund researchers' time for work on a specific project, whereas a large proportion of British researchers are academics who can devote only part of their time to research and employ contract staff to work on a project. Funding bodies have their own agenda: a topic that may attract interest in one country may not obtain funding elsewhere, as illustrated by Judith Glover's contribution. The ease with which reliable data can be obtained and the relative expense involved are also likely to affect the quality of the material for comparisons, as further exemplified below.

The problems of organising meetings that all participants in a project can attend, of negotiating a research agenda, of reaching agreement on approaches and definitions and of ensuring that they are observed are not to be underestimated, especially in projects involving participants from very different linguistic and cultural backgrounds, as reported by Helen Rainbird in her chapter and exemplified by many of the projects described in this collection. Jan Berting (1987) has argued that awareness of the effects of cultural boundaries on the research project is the first stage in being able to overcome them, and he therefore urges that they should be taken into account at the research design stage.

Linguistic and cultural affinity is central to an understanding of why researchers from some national groups find it easier to work together and to reach agreement on research topics, design and instruments. The language and cultural barriers existing between the members of an international research team are, however, rarely discussed in any detail as a major issue likely to affect the outcome of a project (Hantrais and Ager, 1985).

As Edmond Lisle (1985, pp. 24–5) has suggested, language is not simply a medium for conveying concepts, it is part of the conceptual system, reflecting institutions, thought processes, values and ideology, and implying that the approach to a topic and the interpretation of it will differ, according to the language of expression. The ability of members of a research team to communicate in a common tongue and to reach a common understanding of concepts, research methods and standards is far from being an automatic and straightforward process and may be an important factor determining not only the likelihood of collaboration between different combinations of countries but also the success of the outcome. The contribution by Prue Chamberlayne and Annette King is a convincing example of how the success of the biographical method is dependent on an intimate knowledge of the language and conceptual frame of reference of the country under study. In his chapter, Alan Harding demonstrates how linguistic barriers can be minimised.

Even within a single discipline, differences in the research traditions of participating countries remain substantial and may affect the results of a collaborative project and the quality of any joint publications, especially if they appear in languages in which all participants are not equally fluent.

Availability of and access to data for comparisons

If agreement can be reached on the management of the research and the method by which material will be collected, a major and sometimes insuperable obstacle, where secondary sources are to be used, is the availability of comparable data. Their source, the purpose for which they were gathered and the method of collection may vary considerably from one country to another. As Alain Desrosières shows in his chapter, data collection is strongly influenced by national conventions. Moreover, a recurring problem for the comparativist is that, all too frequently, official statistics are produced in too highly aggregate a form or are too imprecise in definition. Relatively few research areas benefit from time-series data, and the investigator must make the best of often crude cross-sectional analyses.

In some areas, national records may be non-existent or may not go back very far. For some topics, information may have been routinely collected in tailor-made surveys in a number of the participating countries, whereas in others information may be more limited because the topic has attracted less attention among policy-makers. Examples abound of the non-comparability of the available data due to differences in the timing and frequency of surveys, as well as in their nature and purpose, as demonstrated here by Judith Glover. Differences in the amount of information and detail that can be assembled may invalidate comparisons or make them extremely difficult. If the aim of a study is to locate trends in relation to the wider societal context, then data will be required about a range of background factors. Such information is often either not readily available or unlikely to have been collected according to common criteria. In many multinational studies, much time and effort can be expended on trying to reduce classifications to a common base, with the result that little of what is left may be truly comparable.

Conceptual links, research parameters and typologies

Although the problems of finding suitable collaborators and possible sources of comparable data may be overcome, difficulties remain in reaching agreement about research parameters, or units of comparison, and in achieving functional equivalence of concepts and terms.

Nicole Samuel (1985) has argued that, in cross-national comparisons, time and space are the main controlling variables. Yet, the definition of a country or society can be problematic, since there is no single identifiable, durable and relatively stable sociological unit equivalent to the total geographical territory of a nation, as noted earlier.

Although defining a time span may also appear to be a simple matter for a longitudinal study, innumerable problems can arise when national datasets are being used. In some countries, the criteria adopted for coding data may have changed over time, for example in the case of employment or socio-economic groupings. As a specific example, when new countries become members of the European Union, it may not be possible to produce harmonised datasets for them covering the period prior to membership.

Routine socio-demographic profiles of the age structure of the working population and unemployment rates may not be comparable, since the age groupings used in surveys vary from one national context to another, and different definitions of employment and unemployment may have been used, as pointed out by Annette Jobert and Jill Rubery in their contributions. These problems are compounded when comparisons are based on secondary analysis of existing national datasets, since it may not always be possible to apply agreed criteria uniformly.

Innumerable examples can be given of non-equivalence of terms and concepts, whatever the research topic. European comparisons of demographic statistics show clearly that definitions of unemployment or of part-time work, a household or family are problematic (Hantrais and Letablier, 1996). In the social policy area, examples abound of non-equivalence at the conceptual level: divergence in the understanding of terms such as harmonisation, solidarity and subsidiarity, marginalisation and poverty is at the heart of endless debates among members of European networks of researchers, as illustrated, in particular, by Katherine Duffy, Bernard Simonin and Paul Spicker in their contributions.

Many of these points apply to single-nation comparisons, but the problems are perhaps more acute in research which, by its nature, crosses cultural and linguistic boundaries and therefore involves not only issues of functional equivalence of concepts and terms but also the influence of the researcher's own cultural value system, assumptions and thought patterns. The problems are compounded according to the number of countries involved and their cultural diversity, which is demonstrated in some of the large-scale European programmes, where cultural rigidity and ethnocentrism may result in an inability to reach agreement over approaches to the research.

In his chapter, Martin Evans summarises the frustrations of data collection and interpretation in ever expanding cross-national situations: the problems of coping with context and the issue of episodic or ephemeral correlations; the consistency of data over time and space; the degree of comparability; and the challenge of interpreting complexity and diversity of situations. Problems are compounded, as many of the contributors bemoan, by the fact that a number of research contexts cannot rely on robust theoretical foundations. Given the imperatives imposed by the European Union to incorporate all member states or, at least, a broad mixture of them in many of its programmes, researchers have therefore been active in attempts to reduce the sorts of data problems alluded to above by refining typologies in advance of further development as models. Considerable research effort has been expended in the policy fields reviewed here, whether they be referred to as models, regimes or families. While this research strategy has undoubtedly contributed to conceptual development, a clear problem has emerged of downgrading specificity of variables and forcing them into uniform non-dynamic typologies or models, the majority of which have been elaborated in Anglo-Saxon and Scandinavian academic environments, as noted by Paul Spicker in his chapter. The same criticism of this reductionist approach applies to much evaluative research. In fact, if a northern dominance is perpetuated, the pressure to create what could be artificial typologies or standardised evaluative criteria may be intensified by the proliferation of research networks funded by the European Union.

Towards solutions to the problems of cross-national comparisons

Many solutions have been suggested to help researchers overcome the barriers to effective cross-national comparisons. The contributors to the present volume discuss the specific problems arising in their particular methodologies and their attempts to ensure an acceptable outcome. Most are in agreement that cross-national research by its very nature demands greater compromises in methods than a single country focus.

It goes without saying that there are no easy solutions: the problems of building and managing a research team can often be resolved only by a process of trial and error. Finding reliable collaborators with access to funding and data is no simple task, and the quality of the contributions to multinational projects is all too often depressingly uneven. The experience of the co-ordinators is critical in holding the team together, in obtaining material and in providing the comparative framework for the research, which requires a sound knowledge and understanding of other national contexts and their intellectual traditions, as well as analytical and management skills.

If re-analysis of existing large-scale data is the research method being used, then an attempt has to be made to re-establish comparable groupings from the most detailed information available. In studies comparing time-series data, the time span should not be set too rigidly, unless the research is centred on the impact of a particular historical event in different countries, as noted by Elfi Bendikat in her chapter. In secondary analysis, it may be useful to focus on the broader characteristics of the sample and to try to go back to the raw data wherever possible, as recommended by Judith Glover.

The solution to the problem of defining the unit of observation may be to carry out research into specific organisational, structural fields or sectors and to look at subsocietal units rather than whole societies. The problem of identifying comparable groups may be partly resolved by comparing categories, such as the 'young' or the 'retired', rather than trying to define narrow age groupings. Michaela Schunk, and Prue Chamberlayne and Annette King demonstrate how this may be achieved. The solution is not to disregard major demographic variables, for if age, social 'class', gender, ethnicity or geographical location are not taken into account, the researcher may be neglecting explanatory factors which indicate greater intranational than international differences, as shown by Jill Rubery with reference to gender.

Whatever the method adopted, the researcher must remain alert to the dangers of cultural interference (see Kinnear, 1987), to ensure that discrepancies are not forgotten or ignored and to be wary of using what may be a sampling bias as an explanatory factor. In interpreting the results, wherever possible, findings should be examined in relation to their wider societal context and with regard to the limitations of the original research parameters.

Where new studies are being carried out, it should, theoretically, be possible to replicate the research design and use the same concepts simultaneously in two or more countries on matched groups. Then the problem is mainly one of trying to reach agreement initially over parameters and functional equivalence. Whatever the solution adopted, it is essential always to be explicit about the nature of the data and their limitations and to guard against taking an artefact of the research design to explain similarities or differences.

Successful cross-national collaboration is often characterised by the variety of methodologies adopted and the range of disciplinary inputs applied to a common phenomenon. Clearly, any attempt to draw out meaningful conclusions from comparative work is, in part, dependent upon the degree to which the problems of collaboration can be resolved. Many of them are likely to remain insoluble, particularly if they have not been thoroughly discussed at the outset. While admitting that complete comparability of data is extremely difficult, if not impossible, to achieve, the irresistible impetus for cross-national collaborative projects in the present European research environment amply demonstrates that the challenge at the scientific and, equally important, human level will not go away.

Part One : Quantitative Methods

Shirley Dex

The four chapters in this section touch upon most of the issues which are raised by large-scale quantitative studies, from their inception, through to their final outputs and conclusions. The authors consider how national statistics have come to be defined and collected (Desrosières); the purposes and hypotheses which can be usefully generated and addressed through cross-national study (Glover, Eardley, Cheshire *et al.*); the issues raised by attempting to construct harmonised and commonly defined variables (Cheshire *et al.*, Eardley); the meanings of the statistics generated from cross-national research (Glover); and the realistic constraints, imposed by both funding bodies and the research process itself, which help to shape cross-national research.

Bradshaw (1994) has provided a framework for thinking about the tasks involved in researching cross-national comparisons; namely that the process can be seen as one of inputs and outputs. The descriptions of the differences and similarities between countries are part of the inputs. Explaining the variations are part of the outputs. Clearly a lot of effort is required to collect together the inputs. When analysis of large-scale survey data is being considered, the inputs are the questionnaire and the precise definitions, coding frames and interviewer instructions which lie behind the responses collected if they are from individuals. This detailed information may be difficult to get hold of where foreign surveys are concerned. As the authors note, the researcher ideally also needs to understand the motivation of those who constructed the questionnaires, the ideological context operating at the time when the data were collected and even epistemological issues.

The authors give numerous forceful reminders of the need to have a 'native' rather than a 'naive' perspective. The many statistics generated by the OECD and European Union give the impression that comparisons can be made from published data. Although harmonised, they still need to be interpreted with care, as can be seen in the examples described in the chapters.

The temptation to short-circuit the work required for a 'native' comparison is particularly acute when carrying out quantitative analyses of secondary data. Once the data are to hand, computers can easily generate seemingly comparative statistics, but erroneous conclusions may be drawn from them because of the lack of understanding of the context. Glover describes the temptation to undertheorise the questionnaire when doing secondary analysis. She quotes her experience of producing statistics on training in France and Britain which were easy to generate and yet were not comparable. As Glover also points out, more harmonised datasets are being transformed into single databases, with common variable names. It is growing easier to produce cross-national statistics without leaving one's office. The problems which this creates can be alleviated to some extent if the basic ground work on the context is covered before the computer churns out its products. Another aid is to have at least one non-national colleague able to check through the findings and interpretations made of the resulting statistics.

The chapters also demonstrate that the interaction of political, scientific and legal interests shapes the research agenda as well as influencing the outputs and their policy implications. The generation of occupational codes is a case which is discussed by Desrosières and Glover. Many dangers have to be faced in using published statistics for comparative analysis, even when they have been collected according to the same criteria.

Some interesting links can be found between information and action which may arise from policy-makers' interpretations of statistics, both within countries and between countries. This also means that survey questionnaires are themselves useful comparative data since they display society specific concerns and assumptions. Following on from Cheshire *et al.*, there are different interest groups within the EU who have their own view of what are appropriate spatial units of analysis, in some cases related to the incentives created by EU policies. The Union has set itself the aim of reducing spatial disparities. This policy has been generated in response to statistical differences, which in turn rest on a set of spatial categories. However, Cheshire *et al.* show that the choice of spatial units and the definitions of their boundaries can make crucial differences to whether inequalities are thought to be increasing, reducing or staying constant. Tightly drawn spatial boundaries give the impression that decentralisation has been occurring over time, whereas loosely drawn spatial boundaries provide evidence of recentralisation.

Cheshire *et al.* demonstrate repeatedly that the spatial aspects of all statistics are a very important and sometimes neglected dimension of their information content. It is easy to assume that subnational categories are comparable because they are part of a single classification system, but this will not always be the case.

All statistics are subject to measurement errors: interviewer errors, coding, punching, keying and routing errors. On the whole, these sorts of errors, which can be called statistical noise, might be expected to be of similar size across industrialised countries with a tradition of large-scale data collection. Variations in the definitions used will add another dimension of variation and will often be larger than other measurement errors. Methods are being adapted for use in quantitative comparative research which take account of statistical noise. For example, Bayesian statistics allow for a noise term which represents measurement error in the variables, thus capturing statistical noise (Dex and Sewell, 1995). Statistical techniques are being developed which recognise that measurement error enters into the observed values of statistics. Using Bayesian statistics allows the researcher to choose a level of noise appropriate for the variables in question. The more that measurement error and the lack of harmonisation are a problem, the higher the noise element that needs to be incorporated into the analysis. The noise level affects the significance of the results and, therefore, the conclusions which can be drawn from the analysis.

Cheshire *et al.*'s discussion of regional categories illustrates the problems of a further element of noise: conceptual noise. A number of concepts may lie behind subnational regional categories; they can be defined in terms of economic relationships, historical or political entities. If different concepts underlie the regional categories of countries, conceptual differences will enter the comparison as an element of noise. Cheshire *et al.* take the view that 'it is more important to have imperfect measures of a consistent conceptual definition than a perfect measure of different or inappropriate conceptual definitions'. Occasions may arise, for example in comparing the education systems of countries, where this prescription may not always be ideal. However, the points Cheshire *et al.* make about conceptual noise, as it affects regional or spatial categories, will have relevance to many other aspects of comparative research which uses large-scale data.

The chapters raise a number of methodological concerns which cut across the subject matter of each paper. They all consider the aims and purposes of comparative research in different but overlapping ways. While the same issues arise in small-scale qualitative research, researchers appear to worry more when they are doing large-scale quantitative analyses since the pitfalls and scope for misunderstandings appear so much greater. The chapters are all trying to reach 'an ideal': completely harmonised definitions of variables are being sought. Eardley's comparison of social assistance was clearly hoping to achieve consonant definitions by using the same questionnaire instruments. The questions were the same, but the underlying definitions varied in Glover's discussion of training and the Cheshire *et al.* discussion of regional categories, making the comparisons seemingly less meaningful. Striving always for harmonised definitions or measures may not necessarily be appropriate to the subject matter, as Desrosières points out; neither will harmonisation always be possible.

Political influence is another concern and is raised in all the chapters in this section. Eardley notes that political priorities influence the funding agenda. Desrosières describes how political criteria underlie definitions of official statistics and inform national traditions of statistical analysis. Cheshire *et al.* show how political criteria influence and define spatial categories. All contributors imply that political influence is at best a nuisance; at worst it is sinister and distorting.

There is a strong sociological tradition of viewing the methods of research as integral to the research itself (Roberts, 1981; Bell and Roberts, 1984). The documentation of specific issues provided by the chapters in this section has value for the next generation of researchers. It can help them to avoid certain pitfalls. The chapters offer solutions to some of the problems raised by regional analyses, social assistance comparisons and occupational comparisons. They provide useful management tips on organising cross-national research, and they raise further questions which need addressing.

Especially where secondary analyses of large-scale data sources are being undertaken, funders expect to award relatively small grants and to have short turn-around times because the data are already collected. Often, they will not wish to fund the time needed to develop a 'native' perspective, or to pay non-national researchers to check the interpretations. The chapters should help them to understand better what is required in obtaining good quality comparative research which has meaning when it is produced, what they can and cannot expect to get from such research, and how long and how much money it might realistically take to get quality outputs.

1 Statistical Traditions: an Obstacle to International Comparisons?

Alain Desrosières

Statistical descriptions of economic and social structures can be compared across countries using data on indicators such as the gross national product, price index, unemployment rates or socio-economic categories. These descriptions appear to be based on the assumption that the figures produced are measuring the same thing and are comparable. Users expect them to be reliable, except in so far as they are constrained by technical and financial factors. Closer scrutiny suggests, however, that statistical products are dependent on the history, culture and administrative structures specific to each country and are far from being identical, despite the costly efforts made by statisticians to harmonise methods, questionnaires and nomenclatures. The comparability of figures presented in cross-tabulations may, therefore, be of dubious value to the detriment of the user who expects to find truly comparable data as a result of ever greater international standardisation. However legitimate the aim of achieving general harmonisation of data collection, coding and the classification of basic information may be, it is only partially attainable.

The problems of achieving standardisation

The history of statistical institutions and techniques demonstrates that greater universality has not eliminated national specificity. As early as the mid-nineteenth century, within the framework of informal international organisations, attempts were made by official statisticians and scholars to find a common language and to unify statistical tools and methods of data presentation. Gradually, a universal professional language was developed. However, the tools for recording and analysing partially standardised data, still needed to be adapted when applied to different economic, social and

17

administrative structures. Two conflicting dimensions are apparent in comparisons of modern statistical systems: universalisation of techniques has to be set against specificity of national traditions. This contradiction is itself indicative of the peculiar position occupied by statistical agencies and administrations describing world phenomena since they are expected to combine two distinct forms of social legitimacy: science and the state. While science is universal, states differ from one country to another. The history and current status of comparisons of national statistical systems can be interpreted as the outcome of tensions between these two opposing poles and the distinctive way in which individual countries have managed the relationship between them.

The extent to which the production of statistics is linked to the organisation of the state and the functioning of society explains why standardisation is so difficult to achieve. The harmonisation of statistics involves standardisation of a variety of inputs, such as taxation and social protection systems, salary scales, and definitions of employment, and requires a very heavy input of resources. Statistical harmonisation appears to be a large enterprise, despite the efforts by statisticians to co-ordinate their work across EU member states.

Users of statistics – policy-makers, social scientists, social services – tend to refer to statistics as if they afforded a reliable source of information, but problems of harmonisation undermine reliability, as do issues such as political pressures. Statistics have been criticised for falling too readily under the influence of administrative and political structures in some countries, as for example when the apparatus of the state was seen as a source of oppression in Eastern Europe before 1989, and dictatorships used statistics to achieve ideological ends. In democracies, the production of statistics is also dependent on social structures, though for different reasons, as they provide the material which makes data recording possible.

Rather than being sceptical about variations in statistical tools and methods, because they compromise universality or prevent comparability, differences can be seen as a source of originality in comparisons. Europe of the early 1990s provides a case study of standardisation which is something of an exception. The political objective of establishing a single market and the difficulties associated with it reflect the problems surrounding the building of nation states. Statistical systems vary precisely because this process has followed different routes and because, even today, what is meant by a 'state' and its role in society is far from having the same meaning in countries which, in other respects, seem to be very similar to one another, such as Britain, France, Germany, Italy and the United States. The construction of Europe and of harmonised statistics brings out clear differences between the first four of these countries. The variations are even greater in the case of the United States where innovations introduced between 1930 and 1940 had an important impact on European statistical systems after 1945, for example through the use of sample surveys, computers, national accounting or econometric modelling which resulted in greater uniformity.

Creating a universal language of statistics

Statistics was one of the first scientific fields where efforts were made to achieve international normalisation of methods of observation. Quetelet, a Belgian statistician, and relentless supporter for the use of statistics in the conduct of human affairs, organised an international statistical congress in London in 1853, following the model created shortly before by an international meteorological congress. The idea of covering the entire planet with a network of standardised observations of population or commercial transactions, as was beginning to happen for climate, gained currency among scholars convinced that objective information about nations would help to reduce the tensions between them. States were involved not only in providing the resources which, as for meteorology, were required for the collection and analysis of harmonised statistics, but also as major users of the information gathered: for example as a basis for taxation or conscription into the armed forces, for determining policy on customs and excise and in the fight against epidemics. Statistics were needed both by scholars and by the state.

The attempt to reach agreement over standardisation through a series of congresses had to be abandoned. Some countries, chiefly the new German Empire, did not accept that their sovereignty should be compromised by decisions over normalisation taken by an assembly of scholars. Following this setback, a new international organisation was created in 1884 on the model of learned scientific or professional societies. The International Statistical Institute (ISI) was a grouping of independent individuals rather than of representatives nominated by states. Until the 1920s, it was concerned with the exchange of ideas about the problems of recording and classifying data. Its views on normalisation were not mandatory, but their official recognition meant that the ISI enjoyed a certain status which helped with dissemination. In the 1890s, two proposals for major nomenclatures were examined: one on occupations and the other on the causes of death. Both were used at the time as reference points for national nomenclatures. The International Classification of Diseases (ICD) has been revised every ten years and continues to play a vital role in the tables compiled by the World Health Organisation (WHO).

From 1920, when the League of Nations and the International Labour Organisation (ILO) were established, questions concerning statistical normalisation were gradually made the responsibility of international organisations concerned with economic affairs. In 1934, Neyman formalised methods for stratified sampling, making it possible to provide a scientific basis for sample surveys. The Federal Administration in the United States used the technique in the 1930s to measure unemployment and agricultural production. Gallup applied it commercially for carrying out market surveys, opinion polls and electoral forecasting. This new technology spread rapidly from the 1940s and made a contribution to the homogenisation of international standards and statistical surveys, as illustrated in particular by the labour force survey and surveys of family budgets, and patterns of consumer spending. Similarly, techniques for calculating indices, analysing prices, production or foreign trade have, to a large extent, been standardised.

The construction of national accounts (requiring an exhaustive and coherent macro-economic summary of data on income flows and the exchange of goods and services between nations) was the source of long and difficult negotiations. A common central core had to be defined to which countries would agree to be attached. The National Accounting System (NAS) was developed by the United Nations (UN), followed by the European Accounting System (EAS), which was more detailed and could be applied to the countries of the European Community. This framework for national accounting is one of the areas where international harmonisation is most advanced. By comparison, less progress has been made in the harmonisation of social statistics. Proposals for social indicators, which were developed in the 1970s by several international organisations based on the model of economic indicators, did not meet with the same success, most probably because the social institutions and social policies concerned (in the broadest sense) differ markedly from one country to another. In this area, statistical systems are still influenced by national traditions. National specificity can often be explained by the way in which the state has been constructed and has established its legitimacy, as illustrated by the following comparison of Britain, France and Germany.

English empiricism

In the second half of the seventeenth century, death certificates were used in England to provide the basis for mortality tables following epidemics. The work was carried out, not by the state but by academics, businessmen or members of Parliament. From 1688, the English monarchy was not under any real threat but it did want to allow civil society (the aristocracy and bourgeoisie) autonomy in the conduct of their affairs. The fact that the state was legitimate, but not omnipresent, acted as a brake on the development of exhaustive statistics as in national censuses (still considered in the eighteenth century as an infringement of individual freedom). It did allow scientific methods to develop freely, stimulated by the world of business. In this context, English 'political arithmetic' emerged as a technique for carrying out calculations and for making estimates in the absence of exhaustive counts. The first such count took place in 1801, leading to a long series of censuses every ten years.

The uncontrolled industrialisation and urbanisation of the nineteenth century and the associated poverty which it provoked, in conjunction with the recurring epidemics that decimated the working classes, brought about a philanthropic and reforming process concerned with the causes of these scourges as well as possible remedies. Since the apparatus of the central state had not yet acquired much weight, solutions were sought at local or parish level. Two forms of social description were developed. The General Register Office (GRO), which had been created in 1837, was changed into a statistical office. The detailed analysis of death certificates served as an important source of information on causes of death for local authorities trying to deal with epidemics and poverty. Starting from local health and social statistics, the GRO built up its legitimacy. Secondly, towards the end of the century, Booth and the wealthy chocolate baron Rowntree, and then economists like Bowley, launched social surveys on poverty and living conditions. The idea developed that these problems are not simply local: they require national solutions; they are not solely dependent on the charity of wealthy philanthropists, but on social action at national level. The welfare state and related forms of coding and statistical surveys were created at a national rather than local level.

Today's Office of Population Censuses and Surveys (OPCS) has inherited all these traditions: the central role of public health statistics, the importance of social surveys and their independence from economic statistics, which are managed by other institutions (Board of Trade). Unlike France and the Institut National de la Statistique et des Études Économiques (INSÉÉ), Britain does not have a centralised statistical institute. The Central Statistical Office (CSO) plays a co-ordinating, synthesising and analytical role, as distinct from the organisations responsible for conducting surveys and processing data. The resulting diversity in the statistics produced is less a source of concern for the British than it would be for the French.

In relation to other countries, the British statistical tradition is characterised by a less interventionist state; statistics are less codified and less formalised by law than in Germany. Thus, while in other countries the gross national product is calculated using co-ordinated and synthetic data within a single organisation, in Britain several variants are available, based on different methods of calculation. Nor are they as centralised as is France. Social surveys have been conducted for a long time with the aim of improving society or stimulating social reform. Although this empirical tradition has not been accompanied, as in Germany and France, by attempts at abstraction and the development of general social theories, the main mathematical techniques of statistical analysis were initiated in Britain: regression, correlation, hypothesis testing, analysis of variance. These tools were conceived in the context of eugenics, biometrics and experimentation in agriculture and were adopted by the social sciences in the United States from the 1930s. They have become a universal language, most often spoken and written in English.

German legalism

Even if it has moved closer to the Anglo-American tradition since 1950, the statistical tradition which has developed in Germany is rather different from that in Britain. The term 'statistics' was used in German in the eighteenth century to refer to all aspects of the formal description of states (law, institutions, customs, geography, climate, population, economy), without necessarily implying quantitative analysis. Building on political science and geography, this academic discipline was intended to help the princes in the many states that made up the Holy Empire to get to know their territory, to manage it and to resolve conflicts with their neighbours. For a long time, the German statistical tradition, as opposed to the political arithmetic of the English, was considered to be academic and formal, but by the early nineteenth century it had disappeared leaving only its name.

With the exception of the Nazi period, the West German state remained a federation in the twentieth century, allowing the *Länder* a certain amount of autonomy to develop their own statistical offices, administratively independent of the federal office in Wiesbaden. The legal framework regulating the relationship between the two is very specific, and the statistical system is both carefully co-ordinated and controlled by law. The legal framework was reinforced in the 1980s following the adverse publicity given to statistical surveys, both by firms complaining about the burden of official questionnaires and by ecological groups concerned about data protection. A campaign to boycott the 1980/81 census led to the questionnaire being revised and delayed for four years while a new law on privacy and data protection went through Parliament.

Modern statistics in Germany are therefore characterised by the autonomy of the *Länder*, offset by powerful co-ordinating techniques and a legal framework establishing the rights and duties of all individuals. Particular attention is paid to ensuring that the state and administration do not overstep clearly defined prerogatives (many German statisticians have legal training). The need to respect laws and rules to the letter can be attributed to the legacy of the regimes during which statistical traditions were established.

French centralism

The French statistical tradition, resulting from the peculiar history of the French state, distinguishes it from the two previous cases. The legitimacy of statistical institutions (about two-thirds of which are incorporated into the INSÉÉ) is very strong, and they are less often contested than in other countries. They have responsibility for a much larger and more concentrated range of tasks. Not only do they carry out censuses, household and industrial surveys and look after the cataloguing of data, they are also responsible for summarising macro-economic information, for conducting studies and regional surveys and for providing training. This last point is important: France is the only country where statisticians working in government offices and agencies receive a high level of training geared to meet their needs. They belong to a body of experts employed by the state and recruited for their scientific expertise. Statistical institutions are also geographically centralised and the regional offices are largely expected to execute decisions taken in Paris.

These four characteristics – legitimacy, range of areas of competence, existence of a corps of highly trained statisticians and centralisation – can be located in relation to a number of more general aspects of the French state, which, although already in existence before the Revolution and the Empire, were reinforced during this period: the decline of regionalism, the construction of a powerful central state, mediated by a body of civil servants organised into a number of corps renowned for their technical competence. The latter are incorporated into central administration through the status, which is peculiar to France, of *ingénieur d'État*. In this respect France is different from Germany or Anglo-Saxon countries, where this type of expertise and proficiency, at least in so far as the research component is concerned, is generally not part of the civil service. Rather, this role is reserved for academics or specialised agencies. Elsewhere, public administration is more narrowly concerned with the day-to-day running of the country than is the case in France.

The state and social taxonomies

Linkages have been made above between the construction of the state and the organisation of statistical systems. But when the users of the products from these systems are consulting tables of figures, they have the right to ask about the possible effects of national specificity. Social nomenclatures in Britain, France, Germany and the United States provide an example of the way in which the categories adopted can be shown to relate to the political and socio-philosophical history of the country concerned.

When socio-occupational status is examined, three categories of salaried workers can be distinguished, illustrating national specificity. The terms used to describe them are impossible to translate exactly into the other two languages: 'professionals' in English and American; *Angestellte* (employees) in German and *cadres* (management and administrative staff) in French.

Professionals are defined by their level of attainment in higher education and their pre-eminence in Anglo-Saxon nomenclatures, as a result of biologically based meritocratic theories derived from English eugenicists at the beginning of the century. These theories implicitly denounced both the former aristocracy and the supremacy of a wealthy business elite. In the United States, a key feature was the moral, civic and even religious foundations of the professions (in the

English sense of the word), and the affirmation of their importance for the nation as a whole, justified by their technical competence, but without being underpinned by any direct intervention from the state, as in France.

German *Angestellte* were a product of Bismarck's policies in the 1880s, aimed at establishing a system of social protection for all salaried workers. Manual workers (*Arbeiter*) were already well organised by the Social Democratic movement and had their own social insurance funds. Civil servants (*Beamte*) had special status and guarantees. Other salaried employees (*Angestellte*) set up their own organisations to distinguish them from the workers' movement. The German census still makes the distinction in its publications between manual workers, civil servants and 'employees', which would include the French *cadres*.

The term *cadre* has no exact equivalent in English and German. Anglo-Saxon nomenclatures distinguish between managers and executives, on the one hand, and professionals, on the other, according to whether their role is defined by their position in the hierarchy or their technical proficiency. In France these two dimensions are closely related, as was demonstrated above with reference to the civil service and the role played by the *grandes écoles* and the *corps d'ingénieurs*. In Britain and the United States, by contrast, professionals are specialists, and their position is clearly distinguished from that of management. The category of *cadres* in France is the result of political mobilisation and representation at the end of the 1930s, following the general strike in 1936 and the Matignon Agreement, instigated by the new Popular Front Government, workers' unions and the employers' federation. Middle management, engineers, technicians and supervisors had felt excluded from the negotiations. Organisations (for example pension funds) were therefore set up to meet the needs of a group whose inclusion in the INSÉÉ nomenclature of socio-occupational groupings by 1950 was taken for granted, whereas they had been excluded twenty years earlier and are still not identified in English and German classifications.

These examples demonstrate that the creation and institutional consolidation of typically national social groups can be located with some degree of precision.

The value of statistical traditions

The examples presented in this chapter show how national stereotypes, rooted in history, are often used to characterise statistical systems: British pragmatism, German legalism and French cartesianism. Similar portraits could be sketched out for other countries. In Italy, statistics have suffered from the accusation that they poorly reflect the underground economy which falls outside state jurisdiction. In the United States, the history of statistics has been determined to a large extent by the census undertaken every ten years, as required in the Constitution of 1787. It has highlighted waves of immigration, the crisis of federalism during the War of Secession, the problems of ethnic quotas in the 1920s, rising unemployment and the changing economic role of the administration with the New Deal in the 1930s. At each of these stages in the construction of the nation and the state, specific statistical techniques were developed and can still be identified in the present system.

If different countries resort to statistical arguments in social debate, each has its own labelling system grounded in national institutional traditions, which lends them credibility and authority. International comparisons of social structures, based on statistical tables illustrating the relative weight of different groups, can benefit from a comparison of nomenclatures. Yet, differences in classification systems and changes over time are frequently presented as an obstacle to research and not as phenomena that deserve to be examined in their own right. In constructing categories, useful information can be found about the underlying structures of the society itself: the status of engineers is not the same in France, Britain and Germany, as the nomenclatures make clear.

Differences between the economic and social structures of various countries do not invalidate comparisons, since they are based on conventions about the equivalence of the phenomena under observation. Even within countries all statistical analysis is dependent on conventions. The only difference is that, in the case of an established nation, they have already been recognised and codified. When a group is in the process of being constructed, as is the case today for Europe, systems of equivalence have to be created which will subsequently enable comparisons to be made. The Statistical Office of the European Communities (or Eurostat) in Luxembourg is currently engaged in developing and operating a standardised system of data collation and analysis. Although the task of the secondary analyst is made easier, it is still not unproblematic, as illustrated by Glover and other authors in their chapters.

2   Epistemological and Methodological Considerations in Secondary Analysis

Judith Glover

This chapter addresses the use of a particular methodology in cross-national research: secondary analysis of existing datasets, principally those produced by national governments. The main focus of the chapter is the consideration of technical, institutional and epistemological issues arising from secondary analysis, particularly when the method is used in cross-national comparisons. These points are illustrated by reference to different approaches to secondary analysis in cross-national research, using harmonised and non-harmonised data.

Issues in secondary analysis

Secondary analysis is a method for exploiting primary data gathered for other purposes to explore a different research issue (Hakim, 1982). Secondary analysis is, however, not just a re-working of data already analysed for a primary purpose: it has considerable potential for originality and for the testing of theoretical perspectives (Dale, 1987; Dale *et al.*, 1988, on British women's employment). Hakim (1982, p. 16) claims that it has the potential to 'break the monopolies' in social research, since government departments are no longer able to keep for themselves data gathered at considerable public expense. Secondary analysis also has considerable potential for creativity, since new variables and definitions can be derived by combining categories (Glover, 1989). It is a relatively inexpensive method and is, moreover, time-saving (Hyman, 1972; Dale, 1993). It is an exceptionally useful way of carrying out analyses of sub-populations, so that relatively small and geographically dispersed groups still retain representativeness (Arber and Ginn, 1991, on older women). Dale (1993) also raises the point that secondary analysis of large datasets is valuable in making comparisons over time. In addition, archiving of primary data for the purposes of secondary analysis means that historical data can be analysed (Hyman, 1972; see Bendikat in this volume).

A common perception is that secondary analysis is an easy option for researchers, since the primary data gathering phase of the research process is eliminated. Secondary analysts would refute this, citing the investment in time needed prior to the analysis stage in order to understand the structure of the data and the definitions used (Dale, 1993). A considerable amount of time is, furthermore, needed for examining the theoretical underpinnings of the research: there may be a tendency for research projects using secondary data to be under-theorised, since the phase of questionnaire design, which relates to a particular theoretical framework, is bypassed in secondary analysis (Dale *et al.*, 1988). Grémy (1989) also stresses the need for secondary analysts to pay particular attention to the theoretical aspects of the research questions. One danger is that technological advances in computing and data analysis distract attention from theorising the research questions (Deutsch, 1970, cited in Grémy, 1989, p. 79).

Grémy (1989) discusses the under-use of secondary analysis in social science research and concludes that the decrease in the initial optimism about the method may be due to an under-estimation of the problems. He lists three types of problems associated with secondary analysis – technical, institutional and epistemological – arguing that technical and institutional problems can be overcome more easily than epistemological ones. Technical problems cover the degree of familiarity which the researcher has with the data; the level of documentation available, including codebooks, interviewers' instructions, estimates of response rates for particular variables and the degree of representativeness achieved by the survey as a whole and by particular variables. Institutional problems include the arrangements for potential secondary analysts to gain access to data. Epistemological issues centre around the given nature of the data: the fact that the primary data were produced within a particular view of what constituted knowledge and in terms of a specific perspective. Hyman (1972), on the other hand, does not see this issue in such a problematical light:

> [The researcher] is likely to be more exhaustive in his definition of a concept, to think about it not only in his accustomed way, but in all sorts of odd ways. Vicariously he is immersed in the thought processes of others, some being products of the same milieu and period, and some far removed from him in time and place.

(Hyman, 1972, p. 24)

Hyman thus conceptualises the issue as being one of a potential slippage between concept and indicator, which presents a challenge and, perhaps, an advantage, since it forces the analyst to think carefully about theoretical frameworks. He admits, however, that secondary analysis may be particularly difficult in cross-national research. It is, he says, 'the last place for the inexperienced secondary analyst to begin his career' (Hyman, 1972, p. 291).

There is a tendency for secondary analysts to use data that have been commissioned by governments. Thus, the questions asked, and the resulting variables, are likely to be related to a specific, historically located, conception of what is politically feasible and acceptable. For example, data will be coded according to official occupation and industry classifications, either national or international. Such data, argues Grémy (1989), are likely to represent a particular universe which may be the result of a compromise between the parties involved in both the commissioning of the research and its primary analysis. Thus, the data represent a consensus around a given cultural and historical context, which the secondary analyst has to take as given.

Occupational classifications are a good example of the consensus to which Grémy refers. Classifications, such as the Standard Occupational Classification (SOC) (OPCS, 1990), which replaced the Classification of Occupations 1980 (OPCS, 1980), are the product of a series of negotiations between social actors including policy-makers, civil servants, employer organisations, trade unions and researchers. The end result represents a specific historical juncture and is a function of the views held by the parties concerned of what constitutes appropriate knowledge (Thomas and Elias, 1989).

A different epistemological perspective might have produced a different effect. If a feminist view of what counts as knowledge were prominent in the thinking of a working party set up to consider a new or revised classification, then a very different version would probably emerge. For example, the occupation of nursing might have as many sub-categories in SOC as engineering; as it is, nursing, a largely feminised occupation, merits only one occupational title, whilst engineering, an occupation where women are under-represented, has ten. The many different types of nurse have not, historically, been seen as relevant criteria in official occupational classifications. The result is that key distinctions between different nursing statuses are not analytically available and, hence, become invisible in research that is using such classifications.

Secondary analysis can also call into question a received epistemological standpoint through its potential for the derivation of new variables: for example, two or more variables can be combined to create, new categories representing different statuses within an occupation (see Glover, 1991). In the case of nursing, secondary analysis of the Labour Force Survey (LFS) allows for the creation of two categories of nurses, those with and without supervisory status, while the occupational classification contains only one category.

Increasingly, occupational classifications incorporate requirements which go beyond the boundaries of the nation-state. A specification of SOC was that its structure should be closer to that of the international classification, the International Standard Classification of Occupations (ISCO) (ILO, 1988), than were its predecessors. Thus, occupational data are now classified, not only according to a national view of what constitutes knowledge, but also according to a global view.

As these examples show, the epistemological issues arising from secondary analysis are far-reaching and may, indeed, be exacerbated in cross-national research.

Technical and institutional issues

As far as technical issues are concerned, the secondary analyst wishing to work on another country's data may have difficulty in getting hold of the documentation. Even if the necessary detail is made available, a high level of linguistic ability is required.

Institutional issues may present problems, depending on each country's attitude to allowing non-national researchers access to national data. The Consortium of European Social Science Data Archives makes available data from some EU member states, thus allowing non-national secondary analysts to use national data without charge, apart from the cost of documentation. However, no standard response is made to requests for data use. In some countries, non-national researchers need to negotiate temporary appointments in statistics agencies or research centres in order to carry out secondary analysis. In others, no distinction is made between commercial and academic researchers; both sets of users have to pay the market price for the data. In many countries, data are only available for secondary analysis in aggregated form. For research purposes, the United Kingdom has some of the most liberal data access conditions in the world. The Economic and Social Research

Council Data Archive at the University of Essex is able to provide access, after the appropriate undertakings have been given, to a wide variety of datasets to both national and non-national academic researchers wishing to carry out secondary analysis.

Access to European data clearly needs to be rationalised. According to the European Science Foundation:

> The European data base is not well integrated; large scale research is hardly co-ordinated; measurement instruments and data representation lack compatibility; data access and data protection regulations differ and even information about the availability of information is not easy to obtain. In short, the criteria for efficient organisation of data bases have hitherto been defined from a national perspective and, even within nations, there is little co-ordinated data resource management.
>
> (European Science Foundation, 1992, cited in *ESRC Data Archive Bulletin*, January, 1995, p. 2)

In the United Kingdom, an attempt has been made to rationalise European data access through the setting up of r.Cade, based at the University of Durham and the ESRC Data Archive. Its aims include helping users to find out whether data exist and where they are located, negotiating data access on behalf of users and providing data documentation. At this stage, it is too early to say what r.Cade's impact will be on facilitating European data access, but if its aims are realised, this may be a major step forward for secondary analysts and others working on cross-national projects.

Epistemological issues

For the secondary analyst seeking to carry out cross-national work, epistemological issues arise, mainly because of the difficulty for the non-national researcher of grasping the set of circumstances and ideologies within which the data were produced. If government data from another country are being analysed, it may be hard to understand the nature of the socio-political consensus which forms the backdrop to the collection of the primary data. Attitude and values data from different countries may pose even greater problems of an epistemological nature.

It is, of course, possible to argue that knowing less about the 'other' country than about one's own can be turned to advantage, since the foreign researcher engages in the classic sociological enterprise of 'making things strange', through a process of questioning what is ordinary and taken-for-granted by the indigenous researcher. Cross-national researchers thus acknowledge that their own cultural backgrounds provide the reference point for cross-national comparison. In this scenario, an in-depth knowledge of one country then affords the basis for the examination of another, less well-known, country. Yet, it needs to be acknowledged that what has been referred to elsewhere as the 'Pandora's Box of secondary analysis' (Glover, 1993) requires close contact with key informants who are indigenous to the 'other' country. This underlines the importance of close cross-national collaborative procedures.

Harmonised data

Cross-national harmonised data have been used by secondary analysts for a variety of purposes. Most analysts have used data which have been 'officially' harmonised, such as the European Labour Force Survey (ELFS) (Dale and Glover, 1989; 1990), the Luxembourg Incomes Study (LIS) (Mitchell, 1991) and harmonised administrative data (see Cheshire *et al.* in this volume). Others, such as Dex *et al.* (1993), have carried out their own harmonisation procedures: occupational titles in two national datasets, respectively relating to the employment of British and French women, were re-coded from French data into a British classification.

The harmonisation process can be illustrated by the use of common occupational classifications, such as the ISCO (ILO, 1988). The standardisation process, almost inevitably, results in a blurring of the distinctions which are fundamental to a particular country's occupational structure (Glover, 1989). To take the French classification, the Professions et catégories socioprofessionnelles (PCS) (INSÉÉ, 1983b), as an example, the distinction between private and public sector occupations and between employees and the self-employed are major distinguishing features (INSÉÉ, 1983a), emphasising the importance of social identity as a guiding structure in the occupational classification (Desrosières *et al.*, 1983, and in this volume). These distinctions are not, however, reproduced in ISCO. If they were, their relevance would no doubt be questioned by countries for whom such distinctions are perceived as less fundamental. The British occupational classification, the SOC, used for all British government surveys, does not, for example, make a systematic distinction between private and public sector workers. Instead, occupations are grouped together according to level of skill and/or experience and/or formal qualifications (OPCS, 1990, vol. 1, p. 3). Some distinctions which relate explicitly to the civil service occupational structure are found in SOC, principally because of representations from the British government's Department of Employment at the developmental stages of SOC.

As Duriez *et al.* (1991) argue, occupational classifications are the product of social, political and economic factors which are peculiar to each country. Viewed from this perspective, it is doubtful whether any classification or dataset can ever be 'harmonised'. Relating this to the question of whether cross-national research is, or should be, 'culture-free' (see Lammers and Hickson, 1979), it can be argued that an approach which sees fundamental problems in the harmonisation of occupational titles is taking a 'culture-bound' position. There are some links here with the 'societal' approach to cross-national research (Maurice, 1979; Rubery, 1988a; d'Iribarne, 1991), where the discontinuities between societies, rather than their convergence, are established. Taking this position to its logical conclusion, secondary analysis which attempts to use harmonised data in cross-national research might be seen as futile. Duriez *et al.* (1991) do not go so far as to eschew the use of harmonised data, but they make the point that researchers need to be as knowledgeable as possible about the construction and the history of national classifications. This depth of knowledge is, however, difficult to achieve in the context of harmonised data, since the detail of each national classification is invisible, unless the user has privileged access to conversion tables. It can be argued that the specificity of the historical traditions of data collection in each country means that the harmonisation of collection, coding and classification of data is never more than partially attainable (Desrosières in this volume).

In cross-national research into employment, the European Labour Force Survey (ELFS) is a commonly used source of harmonised data. Each EU member state carries out its own labour force survey, which contains around 50 variables drawn up for the ELFS. These variables use common definitions and concepts, as well as international occupation and industry classifications. A 'harmonisation' process is carried out via a working party composed of representatives of member states, who agree the questions, the definitions of key concepts and common coding practices (Eurostat, 1988). Data analysis and dissemination are the responsibility of Eurostat, whose purpose is to provide a comparative data source for a range of descriptive statistics required by the European Commission.

In cross-national work carried out on French and British women's employment (Dale and Glover, 1990), it was found that the harmonised ELFS data did not match closely different national definitions of training. A finding that French women received less on-the-job training than British women was consequently seen, after detailed scrutiny of the common codes used by each country, as the product of different definitions. The conclusion reached was that the results did not show a substantive difference, but rather reflected a definitional difference not dealt with by the harmonisation process.

Despite attempts at harmonisation, different national perceptions of a particular variable can persist. The danger is that, unlike secondary analysts, most users of published statistics will not have access to detailed information about definitions and the concepts underlying them. Nor will government departments feel obliged to cite authors' reservations about data quality if findings are put into the public domain (for example, if they are used in answer to Parliamentary Questions).

The ELFS is probably at its most useful for comparisons that require little detail. Broad patterns of difference and similarity can be established and these may be particularly helpful in the preliminary stages of a project as a basis for conceptualising a research issue. For the purposes of much secondary analysis, harmonised data are however of limited use. The secondary analyst almost always wants the greatest possible amount of detail, since this allows both for the creation of new categories or variables and some insight into the epistemological framework of the data collection. Harmonised data will always be at the level of the lowest common denominator, providing less rather than more detail; distilling information, rather than amplifying it.

On the other hand, it has been suggested that the use of harmonised data allows for several countries to be studied. Sanders (1993) calls this the 'inclusive' approach, arguing that from the point of view of theory testing, the more countries that can be analysed, the better, since theory building aims for generalisation. Nevertheless, it needs to be remembered that theory building is also concerned with specificity. Broad-brush harmonised data may allow for the identification of specificity but provide little potential for its explanation.

Non-harmonised data in cross-national research

An analysis which called for the sort of detail provided by the full national labour force datasets and their national occupational classifications is described in Glover (1991). The analyses, which used French and British national, non-harmonised labour force data, demonstrated the potential for detailed, disaggregated analysis, using large, nationally representative datasets (Sanders' 'exclusive' approach), where 'substantive illumination' about a limited number of national systems is sought, typically to throw light on policy frameworks.

The use of national datasets in cross-national research rather than harmonised data provides as much detail as possible, thereby maximising the potential for deriving variables[1]. It also allows for the customising of definitions and locating occupations in their national context; thus, functional equivalence, rather than linguistic equivalence, can be achieved. For example, seemingly equivalent occupations may have different status in different countries, in terms of the levels of responsibility and the requisite skills; differences in social constructs constitute fundamental problems for the cross-national study of occupations (Rubery, 1988). The problems are not in themselves a reason for abandoning such research; rather they need to be clearly understood, not under-estimated and explicitly discussed in research reports. Furthermore, the very act of grappling with these problems may lead to a better grasp on epistemological issues.

The use of national datasets provides maximum insight into micro-contexts. However, the more detailed the data, the greater the difficulties encountered, or perhaps the greater their visibility. The more complicated and difficult the work is, the closer the researcher may be getting to the social reality within which the data are located. Harmonised data seek to alleviate these difficulties, or at least to make them invisible. Micklewright (1993) reviewing Mitchell's (1991) study of income transfers in different welfare states, for which she used the harmonised LIS, makes the following point:

> One of my reservations about the LIS is that in putting the data on as comparable a basis as possible and in adopting common names for variables in the different data sets, cross-national comparisons are made too easy.
>
> (Micklewright, 1993, p. 99)

Micklewright's standpoint is a valuable one, since it recognises that national datasets are produced within a particular epistemological context. He implies that cross-national work which is meaningful has to address and discuss the differences between datasets in their pre-harmonised form and in terms of their historical development. Harmonised data can gloss over the difficulties, leading the researcher to underestimate the complexities of the national datasets which form the basis of harmonised data.

Towards solutions

One solution for cross-national research may be to set up a model in which common research questions are established by collaborating partners. National researchers then analyse their own data and collaborate at the level of the exploration and explanation of findings. The discussion of similarities and differences can then be located within national contexts; system-specific substantive illumination is the aim. This is the model adopted by the International Social Survey Project (see Davis and Jowell, 1989).

Quantitative data on a computer screen take on a 'single unseamed reality existing "out there"' (Stanley and Wise, 1993, p. 6), which can conceal the social processes within which data collection is embedded. Since secondary data have been collected by other agencies, and are therefore presented as given, secondary analysts have to make an effort to remind themselves of these processes. Given the appropriate technical expertise and institutional arrangements, statistical procedures can be carried out with ease on another country's quantitative data; a sensitive approach to epistemological issues is considerably more demanding.

Harmonised data have their uses for certain purposes, but need to be exploited with circumspection on the part of the researcher. On the other hand, non-harmonised national data used by a non-national researcher may pose considerable problems that relate to the need to penetrate the context within which the data were produced. The argument pursued here is that the effort needed to surmount these problems may lead to a greater understanding of this context and, thus, of the particular view of what counts for knowledge in that dataset. This process is likely to lead, perhaps through adversity, and because of it, to more insightful cross-national research.

Acknowledgements

The author would like to thank Hilary Beedham of the ESRC Data Archive at the University of Essex for information on inter-country reciprocal arrangements for data access.

Note

1. It is not the purpose of this chapter to discuss statistical problems associated with secondary analysis in cross-national research but it is worth noting that the disadvantage of using two non-harmonised datasets was that the two datasets could not be put into the same statistical model. Two models, as similar as possible, had to be constructed. This meant that whilst the interpretations of the two sets of findings could be compared, the numerical scores from each of the models could not.

3   Quantitative Comparisons of European Cities and Regions

Paul Cheshire, Ana Furtado and Stefano Magrini

The aim of this chapter is to highlight the importance of comparable data and definitions in quantitative analyses across European cities and regions, and to show how failure to adjust data appropriately can condition, even invalidate, the conclusions that are drawn.

In the first section, an attempt is made to explain why it is increasingly important, from a European perspective, to be able to make reliable comparisons between cities. The second section discusses the system of regions used by the European Union for statistical purposes and the anomalies arising from the definitions applied. Alternative, functional definitions of regions are claimed to provide a better basis for regional comparisons. The scarcity of spatial data and the lack of any coherent set of city-regions explains why so few cross-regional/city empirical studies are conducted in Europe compared to the United States. The next section of the chapter suggests potential solutions: both a stop-gap solution of how to make reasonably reliable comparisons using existing data, and a longer term solution. Finally, some of the key data are identified that are presently not generated at a European level for subnational units.

The impulse for comparative studies of cities and regions

A growing focus of recent economic literature in a broad set of fields has been cross-region/country comparisons. As the introductory chapter indicates, cross-national studies provide a potentially powerful tool for a number of purposes: discriminating between competing explanations of the ways in which aspects of the economy work; identifying the importance of the national or regional components in the changes that are occurring; and identifying explanations that are common to many countries or that are only country specific.

In a European context this scientific enterprise is even more relevant, given the long-term process of European integration, since it will become ever more necessary to achieve an efficient framework for comparative analysis of urban and regional dimensions, as manifest in the European Union Treaty's commitment to social and economic cohesion and to reducing spatial disparities (Cheshire *et al.*, 1991). Indeed, 155 billion ECU is to be spent by the structural funds for these purposes between 1993 and 1999.

A simple case illustrates the problem arising from the lack of reliable, comparable data. One of the key indicators used by the European Union to allocate funds for regional aid is per capita GDP (Commission of the European Communities, 1993a; 1994a). In the late 1980s, according to the most commonly employed indicator – NUTS (Nomenclature des Unités Territoriales Statistiques) Level 2 regions – Gröningen ranks as the richest major city, followed by Hamburg, the Ile-de-France and Greater London. Yet, it is almost certain that none of these really had the highest per capita income. For instance, Gröningen (which probably fails 'the major city test') happens to be where the Dutch account the income generated by North Sea gas, which grossly inflates the results, and the Ile-de-France approximates a widely drawn Paris, but net inward commuting inflates calculated income per resident and a substantial price differential exists between Paris and the rest of France. In fact, none of these cities is the richest, but rather one which is not even identified with any NUTS Level 2 region: Frankfurt-am-Main.

Sharpening spatial comparisons

At least two types of variation can be identified among spatial units which determine the comparability of data. The first is obvious and relates to national statistical definitions and availability. Is GDP, for example, measured in the same way in France as in the United Kingdom? The second problem is the spatial definition of the units themselves. This is a far less widely recognised problem, except by specialists. From a practical perspective, it is probably also a more important problem because, although Eurostat, OECD, and even national statistical offices, make serious efforts to standardise statistical definitions, they do not make any effort to standardise the definition of spatial units[1].

The simple question, 'Which city is bigger, London or Paris?', shows why city definitions matter. Are we to compare the City of London (population 4,230) with the City of Paris (population 2.157 million)?

Or the Greater London Council area (6.4 million) with the Ile-de-France (10.6 million)? Or the built-up areas of these two cities? Or some metropolitan region? But, a more subtle reason for a common definition concerns the phenomenon of changing locations of people and jobs, which raises a common question in urban research as to whether cities are decentralising, recentralising or declining. Again, the answer will depend on how the boundaries are drawn. If they are tightly drawn, and there is decentralisation, it will appear as population loss. Similarly, the same actual spatial redistribution of population within a different focus could appear as population recentralisation, or alternatively as population growth.

A third reason for needing comparable definitions of cities relates to patterns of residential segregation. All large cities exhibit such segregation with poor and rich neighbourhoods, ethnically specific areas, and areas of social housing. But different cities have different patterns. As a generalisation, London's poor – as with most cities in Britain or the United States – are concentrated in the centre (the 'inner city problem'); the poor of Paris, and many other French and Italian cities, are more concentrated in the large peripheral areas of social housing and other poor communities. As a result, if an observer were interested in ascertaining which city had the higher unemployment levels or the higher mean standard of living, the answer would be highly sensitive to the definition of city used.

Apart from the arguments advanced above, a case can be made for using broadly and functionally defined cities for purposes such as strategic planning, locational analysis and decision-making, and for policy implementation. If a large company is deciding where to locate a new facility and is choosing between locations, it is likely to be interested in evaluating the labour supply and costs in the metropolitan region as a whole. The same would be true for transport infrastructure or cultural and leisure facilities. If policy is implemented within small areas of cities, then the effects tend to diffuse because of labour market and transport adjustment processes. Commuting patterns adjust, and the impact of the new opportunities is quickly diffused throughout the whole metropolitan region (Cheshire, 1979; Gordon and Lamont, 1982). Even the effects of intervention in the built environment – new transport links or new housing construction – will tend to spill over from the local area because of automatic adjustment processes in densely urbanised regions.

These problems of urban definition also have implications for regional analysis in Europe. Essentially, they arise from patterns of residential segregation. As argued above, even for the commonly used NUTS Level 2 regions, regional values and residential segregation interact. London and Brussels are not only cities with many of their richer inhabitants living in their outer suburbs, but they are very decentralised cities. Rich inhabitants of 'London' live in exurban villages in Hertfordshire, Buckinghamshire, Hampshire, Kent and Surrey (further afield too); that is in at least six separate Level 2 regions. The incomes (and other indicators) of those Level 2 regions, when counted on a residential basis, are therefore distorted, compared to what they would be if they were counted on the basis of people working within them[2]. The impact of 'London' would be even greater on the indicators for the Level 2 regions of the South East, if its influence could somehow be extracted from the South East: all the employment associated with 'back' offices in Reading or Basingstoke, or the incomes generated by Heathrow and Gatwick. The same is true of Brussels. Its economic and social influence extends far beyond the boundaries of the Level 1 region of that name.

Two dimensions of income distribution need to be taken into account: a vertical, societal dimension, from the best paid (and best educated, least likely to be unemployed, healthiest) higher managers and professionals, to the least skilled and worst remunerated (also most likely to be unemployed). Because of the tendency for people to live close to other people like themselves, there is a spatial manifestation of this inequality, even though its origins are social. The result is that studies of urban deprivation using administratively defined districts as their units of analysis (such as Department of the Environment, 1983) find that the poorest 'towns' in England and Wales are some of the boroughs of London. Unsurprisingly, the same applies to some of the richest. In addition to the vertical, societal dimension to inequality, a truly spatial dimension also exists because of the substantial – for many the impossible – costs of moving from, say, Thrace to Frankfurt. This illustrates one of the greatest costs of all: that of acquiring the appropriate language to operate successfully in a prosperous, but foreign, labour market. Thus, the life opportunities of otherwise similar people, born in poor or rich regions, will be substantially different[3]. This can be thought of, in European terms, as true spatial disparities, or the purely spatial dimension of inequality. The problem arises that, because both forms of inequality have a spatial manifestation (but only in the second context is space a cause), one form cannot be distinguished from the other unless regional boundaries are appropriately drawn.

Europe's NUTS

The existing set of official regions for European policy purposes conform to no common conceptual definition of 'region' but represent a hotchpotch of historical accident, local identity and national concern – or lack of concern – for consistency or logic in defining subnational administrative units[4]. Because of the absence of systematic logic in defining Europe's official regions, official analyses of 'spatial disparities' confound truly spatial differences with differences due to social and economic stratification which, because of residential segregation, happen to have a spatial manifestation, and with the product of (changing) commuting patterns.

The current NUTS system is a three-level hierarchical classification. The European Community of the twelve was divided into 71 NUTS 1 regions. These, in turn, were split into 183 NUTS 2 regions or basic Administrative Units. Finally, NUTS 2 regions were divided up into 1,044 NUTS 3 regions.

The criteria followed in the definition of the NUTS regions are essentially political. The three hierarchical levels are designed on the basis of the pre-existing administrative divisions of the member states. The correspondence between NUTS and national administrative units is shown in Table 3.1.

One of the more bizarre consequences of this method of definition is that, because the administrative structure of the member states generally comprises only two main regional levels, it has been necessary to invent a third regional level for most countries. This additional level varies across member states – NUTS 1 for France, Italy, Greece and Spain, NUTS 2 for West Germany and the United Kingdom, NUTS 3 for Belgium, the Netherlands and Portugal – and corresponds to less important or, in some cases, even non-existent national administrative units.

In terms of economic indicators, the 1989 GDP at Purchasing Power Standard (PPS) of Level 1 regions varied from 312,846 million ECU in Nordrhein-Westfalen (Germany) to 8,191 million ECU in Nisia (Greece). Such differences increase with the level of disaggregation not only because regional economic space appears more differentiated – at high levels of aggregation differences between data calculated by workplace, or place of residence, tend to disappear and urban and rural zones are combined – but also because social groups segregate, and economic activities tend to agglomerate with higher value added economic functions concentrating in core areas. It is therefore particularly important when choosing the area of study to take into

Table 3.1. **Correspondence between NUTS Levels and national administrative divisions**

	NUTS 1		NUTS 2		NUTS 3	
B	Régions	3	Provinces	9	Arrondissements	43
DK	–	1	–	1	Amter	15
D	Länder	16	Regierüngsbezirke	40	Kreise	543
GR	Groups of development regions *	4	Development regions	13	Nomoi	51
E	Agrupacíon de comunidades autónomas	7	Comunidades autónomas	18	Provincías	52
F	Zeat	8	Régions	22	Départements	96
	+ DOM		+ DOM	4	+ DOM	4
		1				
IRL	–	1	–	1	Planning regions	9
I	Gruppi di regioni *	11	Regioni	20	Provincie	95
L	–	1	–	1	–	1
NL	Landsdelen	4	Provincies	12	COROP – Regio's	40
P	Continente	1	Comissaoes de coordinaçao regional	5	Grupos de Concelhos	30
	+ Regioes autonomas	2		2		
UK	Standard regions	11	Groups of counties *	35	Counties/ Local authority regions	65
EU		71		183		1044

* For Community purposes

consideration the aims of the analysis. For example, Goldfarb and Yezer (1987), analysing inter-regional wage differentials for the United States, used metropolitan areas arguing that such areas had the advantage of reflecting, better than states or groups of states, the economist's notion of a local labour market:

> if regional wage effects exist, these will be reflected in the wages generated in each metropolitan area in the region. Also cost of living differences, including important housing cost differentials, are based on the metropolitan area.
>
> (Goldfarb and Yezer, 1987, p. 50)

Functionally defined city-regions

The most useful definition of 'city' for comparable purposes, then, is a broadly and functionally defined city-region in the sense that boundaries are determined on the basis of economic relationships rather than history or political divisions in a uniform and comparable way. Moreover, it contains areas to which population is decentralising or from which it is recentralising. It abstracts from local patterns of residential segregation and commuting which would otherwise distort many kinds of data, and it is the most suitable area for most analytical or strategic policy purposes.

Such functional definitions have tended to follow two main models. The first one was represented by the Standard Metropolitan Statistical Areas (SMSAs), defined by the United States Bureau of the Census since 1940. SMSAs were derived from United States county-level data on the basis of a two-step procedure: firstly, a 'central city' of at least 50,000 inhabitants was identified. Secondly, contiguous counties evincing socio-economic integration with the 'central city' – at least 15 per cent of the resident workers commuting to the 'central city' – and a 'metropolitan character'[5] were added to the 'central city'.

The second model, the Daily Urban System (DUS) adopted by Berry (1973) in his analysis of the changes in the American urban system during the 1960s, was slightly different. On the one hand, the concept of DUS extended even further the emphasis placed on daily commuting. On the other hand, it overcame the strict core–hinterland distinction of SMSAs for a more complex notion of self-containment with regard to labour and housing markets.

Within Europe, Hall *et al.* (1973) and Berry (1976) made the first serious attempts to apply the concepts of SMSAs and DUS on the basis, respectively, of 1961 and 1966 British Census data. The resulting sets of Standard Metropolitan Labour Areas (SMLA) and Metropolitan Economic Labour Areas (MELA) shared a common feature that distinguished them from their American models: the cores were defined in terms of employment concentration – 20,000 jobs – rather than in terms of population[6]. This feature is also common to the system of European regions derived by Hall and Hay (1980) for 1971, and adopted by Cheshire and Hay (1989) in their analysis of urban problems in Europe. Each of these regions – termed Functional Urban Regions (FURs) – is derived from a two-step procedure. Firstly, a core is defined by identifying an urban centre with 20,000 jobs or more and, then, by adding all those contiguous surrounding areas at the lowest level of disaggregation available which have a density of 12.35 jobs per hectare or greater. Secondly, to each core are added all those contiguous administrative areas from which more workers commute to the core in question than to any other core.

Other common definitions of a city exist. In Germany, there is a legal definition of *Stadt* and, because this definition is quite consistently applied, frequently no problem is seen with it. However, largely on the initiative of Frankfurt, where the authorities saw the need for larger units for a strategic level of planning for transport, economic development and land use, a wider Rhein Neckar region has been created, the boundaries of which coincide very closely with the Frankfurt FUR as defined by Hall and Hay (1980). The French make general use of the concept of *agglomération* (broadly a built-up area). It might be thought that this would provide an internationally comparable definition of city; for some purposes, especially for physical planning, it may. Unfortunately, this is significantly less true for purposes of economic, social or policy analysis, mainly because of the different way in which land use planning systems operate but also because of varying patterns of residential segregation. In France, most urban growth is by contiguous aggregation to the existing urban fringe, so the *agglomération* covers a large and more or less consistent proportion of the population and activity of the metropolitan regions. In Britain, this form of growth is specifically precluded by a planning system which protects 'green belts' and town and village 'envelopes'. Urbanisation is deliberately forced to be discontinuous, so the metropolitan region of London, like other large British cities, contains great tracts of agricultural land and green areas; and the richest inhabitants are disproportionately concentrated in the exurban villages. In the Randstad, there is a different system again leading to four distinct and specialised, but strongly interacting, urban nodes with a large green area in the middle.

Short-term solutions

In the various studies of urban development in Europe using FURs, two main sets of solutions have been used to overcome problems of comparability; those defined by Hall and Hay (1980) and subsequently developed and exploited by other researchers; and those used by the

CURB project (van den Berg *et al.*, 1982). For various reasons, the CURB dataset was not subsequently developed and analysed.

Since data have to be gathered for the smallest units available, both the size of the task and the range of data available severely restrict what can be precisely measured at the FUR Level. In general, data are only available for the necessarily small units from censuses of population (or the equivalent registration data in countries, such as Denmark, which hold no census).

To obtain estimates of other data, such as employment, income, output and unemployment, it was essential to find ways of approximating FUR values from Eurostat NUTS data, since only Eurostat data have been adjusted to (broadly) common definitions. This was done using a simple weighting system applied to NUTS 3 data, with the weights determined by the distribution of population[7]. Using this method, it is possible to obtain data for a set of all 229 FURs in the European Community of 12 member states which had populations of 1/3 million or more in 1981. Together they accounted for 69.8 per cent of the Community's then population. The resulting data are approximate measures of consistent and appropriate conceptual definitions, rather than more or less exact measures of inappropriate and inconsistent ones.

The dataset is still, however, very restricted for urban comparative purposes; it can be and has been supplemented in an *ad hoc* way. Regional price indices also need to be standardised. Prices vary regionally – in some countries more than in others – but only national Purchasing Power Parities (standard) exchange rates are available. Any case for convergence of regional differentials should therefore be based in real terms and not in nominal terms. The point is to find an adequate deflator for regional cost of living differentials.

This is particularly relevant when dealing with wage differentials because, while regional wage differentials are usually small in nominal terms, major differences in housing costs and amenity values between regions must be included to obtain realistic comparisons of real wages. Rosen (1979) and Roback (1982) suggest that amenity differentials may be as important as the cost of goods purchased in determining the appropriate wage deflator across areas. It has been argued that:

> The empirical problem is to find an index of this compensating differential without ignoring the possibility that actual wage data reflect disequilibria as well as equilibrium compensating differentials.

> (Goldfarb and Yezer, 1987, p. 51)

In some cases, the analysis of differentials between cities or regions requires the use of micro-data (individual characteristics data for a representative sample of the city or region's inhabitants or workforce, for example[8]), as opposed to aggregate data (data for the average population of the region), in order to derive unbiased results. Empirical studies of inter-regional wage differentials (mainly in the United States), for example, have pointed to significant advantages of using micro-datasets. Whereas aggregate data only refer to inter-regional average real wage equality (because data do not adequately distinguish between workers with different characteristics), with micro-data it is possible to estimate the 'price' of both worker and job characteristics. However, studies requiring the use of micro-datasets pose a demanding task. No single harmonised micro-dataset is yet available for the case of EU regions. The only solution is to work with national micro-datasets and adjust them to make them comparable. This is a substantial task, but it is essential for some types of empirical studies (for example wage differentials) if credible results are to be obtained. The most commonly required variables for such micro-datasets in a region/city context are: income, human capital/skills, physical capital, poverty, unemployment, activity rate, environmental indicators, housing.

Reasonable data exist at a city/region level for average income (ignoring the lack of regional price indices), unemployment (but not for areas smaller than NUTS Level 3 regions or FURs), activity rates and a restricted range of environmental indicators. Virtually no systematic data are available for the others. The absence of data, such as the incidence of poverty, human capital and skills, or housing (some comparable data are available from national census sources, but there is no price information and a lack of consistent physical indicators) is particularly surprising because, in principle, the data are not too difficult to collect. Their absence means that far less is known about the spatial distribution of skills, real living standards or poverty in the European Union than, for example, the distribution of different types of livestock or cropping patterns.

Consistent definitions or perfect measures?

The evidence presented in this chapter leads inevitably to the conclusion that existing data for comparative and analytical purpose in the European Union at a subnational level are woefully inadequate. This is unfortunate for the purposes of scientific analysis.

For instance, attempts to test theories of regional economic growth or analyse patterns of urban change may lead to results which are not only spurious but spurious to an unknown extent. A much quoted study of the (supposed) convergence of regional growth rates (Barro and Sala-i-Martin, 1991) for example, because it uses data for NUTS regions, fails to account for changing commuting patterns in measuring growth rates.

From the point of view of policy analysis and implementation the inadequacy of available data injects a substantial element of the lottery into the distribution of funds, impairs accountability and nullifies policy evaluation. The structural funds of the European Union are expected to disburse some 30 billion ECU a year (Commission of the European Communities, 1993a) to help alleviate spatial disparities by the end of the 1990s, yet the data available to policy-makers do not permit discrimination between disparities caused by unmeasured commuting, residential segregation and those which really reflect differences in life opportunities because of fundamental differences in regional economies.

Given the difficulties that still exist in finding internationally comparable urban data for European countries in the different domains of economic research, a guiding principle is that, for such comparative research, it is more important to have imperfect measures of a consistent conceptual definition than a perfect measure of different or inappropriate conceptual definitions. One major problem of the existing Eurostat regional data, and national urban data, is that the underlying concepts (where they exist) are seldom, if ever, the same.

Acknowledgements

The authors would like to acknowledge the support of the Economic and Social Research Council under award number W100/26/1046. Ana Furtado is supported by PRAXIS XXI (Portuguese) studentship.

Notes

1. It is recognised that, for European comparative purposes, non-urban, rural regions are also important, but 70 per cent of the EU's population lived in city regions of more than 1/3 million inhabitants in 1981 (Cheshire and Hay, 1989). It is therefore on

the urban regions that efforts need to be concentrated, at least initially.

2. This is quite a subtle process. A region such as the GLC will have higher per capita GDP per resident; and, since net inward commuting has increased over an extended period, an inflated growth rate. GDP per capita of residents for regions with net out-commuting to London – such as Hertfordshire and Surrey – will be correspondingly reduced. The reverse would be true for calculations by workplace.

3. Though with increasing integration one might expect less difference in the current generation than in past generations.

4. The revision of boundaries currently underway in Britain will, if ever implemented, simply add further confusion. So, too, would the introduction of an official set of NUTS 4 regions which are presently used only unofficially. The French are very attached to their 36,000 communes but it is unlikely that there would be more than about 800 units in the United Kingdom to be counted as NUTS 4 regions.

5. At least 75 per cent of total employment was non-agriculture and population density was at least 150 persons per square mile.

6. These are conceptually distinct from Travel to Work Areas (TTWAs). TTWAs are defined simply on the basis of a specific degree of self-containment: for example, 80 per cent of the economically active population who live in a given area also work in the area. FURs attempt to measure the economic sphere of influence of a city (which partly depends on how close it is to other cities). Areas continue to be added to its hinterland until more economically active residents commute to some other city (excluding purely rural areas).

7. In cases where two major FURs were entirely or mainly within a single NUTS 3 region (as is the case for Portsmouth and Southampton, or Lille and Valenciennes), national data were used to disaggregate the NUTS 3 estimates. For example, the ratio of Labour Force Survey unemployment rates was assumed to be the same for national registration unemployment data between the areas most closely approximating the FURs.

8. This kind of data is usually collected through household and individual surveys carried out at a national level.

4 Lessons from a Study of Social Assistance Schemes in the OECD Countries*

Tony Eardley

The economies of European Union member states and other industrialised nations are increasingly facing similar pressures. Problems of unemployment, labour market restructuring, population ageing, and social and family change are having to be addressed in all these countries to different degrees, and there is a need for, if not necessarily common solutions, at least a shared comprehension of differing approaches to social protection. National politicians, officials, and other actors in the policy process are looking increasingly to see what can be learned from the approaches used in different countries, what works and what does not, and in what directions policy is moving.

One area of social security in which there is growing interest is social assistance, defined here as cash benefits offering a minimum level of subsistence to people in need, based on a test of resources. In many countries, the number of recipients of assistance has been increasing, mainly as a result of longer term unemployment and social changes such as growth in lone parenthood. Social insurance programmes are often poorly designed to cope with these changes. They can also produce apparent disincentives for unemployed people to return to work and, in times of economic restraint, tend to be regarded as financially burdensome. In such circumstances, shifting towards more selective or targeted provision appears an attractive proposition for many governments, a view which is reinforced by the international financial institutions in their arguments for means-

* This chapter draws on research commissioned by the UK Department of Social Security (DSS) and the Organisation for Economic Co-operation and Development (OECD). Any views expressed are those of the author and not necessarily those of the sponsoring organisations.

tested safety nets for the transitional economies of Eastern Europe (see, for example, World Bank, 1990).

Studying developments in social assistance is of interest conceptually, for two reasons. First, it provides an opportunity to explore dominant norms and values in given countries, because, more than many other areas of policy, it is concerned with behaviour: labour supply, cohabitation, family obligations and responsibilities, and so on. Secondly, assistance levels tend to become *de facto* national poverty lines, while the equivalence scales implicit in benefit rates express different countries' views of the relative needs of different family types. Thus, although assistance often represents only a small element of national social expenditures, it is here, as Leibfried (1993) has argued, that the limits of welfare states are best tested.

There are also a number of methodological challenges involved in a comparative analysis of social assistance schemes. Although pension and unemployment insurance schemes are organised and administered in different ways and have differing rules for contributions and entitlement, they are almost always nationally uniform and have structures which are relatively easy to compare. Assistance schemes, however, are far from uniform, often varying substantially from area to area within countries, and frequently operating with high degrees of officer discretion.

This chapter discusses the methods used in a large cross-national study of assistance schemes. Research interest was focused not only on the structural, legal and administrative features of these schemes, but also on the relative value of payments and on the interaction between social assistance and insurance schemes. One of the methods chosen as offering the most fruitful possibilities for such a comparison involved a technique of policy simulation using 'model families', and the chapter focuses on the advantages and disadvantages of this technique (see also Martin Evans' chapter).

Previous research on social assistance

Comparative studies of social security provision are well established, but systematic study of social assistance has been relatively under-developed, partly perhaps because of methodological difficulties. Most studies of the kind alluded to that have been undertaken have concentrated primarily on legal and structural features of assistance schemes in selected countries (see, for example, Schulte, 1989, 1993; Lødemel and Schulte, 1992). Euvrard (1989), in a review of the main minimum income schemes in the European Community for a conference on basic income, included some limited comparison of basic scale rates, while Leibfried (1993) has provided a broad overview of the range of assistance schemes in a wider study of convergence in social welfare in Europe. The European Commission's MISSOC project has begun to include basic descriptive tables on minimum income schemes for the EU member states, but they only present an outline of provision and cannot give any indication of either the spread or impact of social assistance or of the relative value of payments.

A number of important and more comprehensive studies have been mounted of groups of related countries, such as that on the Nordic countries edited by Fridberg (1993). Øverbye (1994) has also looked at the ways different European countries have combined insurance and assistance schemes. He shows how the distinction between the two can be blurred, but in ways that vary between countries for different risk groups. Stjernø (1994) has compared assistance schemes in the Nordic countries with a number of other European countries to examine how their institutional features conform to the common idea of the 'Nordic model'.

Overall, however, no previous attempts have been made to chart the provision of assistance on the scale of the study discussed here to illustrate the application of the policy simulation technique.

The aims of the social assistance study

The principal aims of the present study were to provide comparative information on the role of means-tested benefits within the social security systems of the different countries, and their legal and administrative structures and rules of eligibility; to analyse trends in expenditures and claimant numbers; to discuss policy debates and developments; and to calculate the relative value of benefits, both between countries and within countries in relation to social insurance and earnings. Initially included were the then twelve countries of the European Community, plus Norway and Sweden, together with the English-speaking group countries represented by the United States, Canada, Australia and New Zealand. The research was subsequently extended to the remaining six member countries of the OECD.

In the terms discussed in the introduction to this book, the study was cross-national, although in countries with local or regional variation the subnational context was also important. Bradshaw (1994) has suggested that most comparative studies of social policy can be located within a matrix of two dichotomies: between 'macro' and 'micro' studies and between policy 'inputs' and 'outcomes'. Within this typology, the study was essentially one of inputs, rather than outcomes, in that it was primarily the policy structures which were under scrutiny, rather than the detailed outcomes for any particular group. Such an approach is also described within another typology by Hauser (1993) as 'system-by-system'. The research included elements of both the 'micro and the 'macro', in the sense that it was concerned with drawing both practical lessons for policy-making and some conclusions about welfare state effort at the aggregate level.

Research design and methods

The core aims of the study, as is generally the case in contract research for government departments, were set by the research customers, and included a requirement to cover at least all the European countries, plus several others. Certainly there is a risk involved in attempting to cover as many as 24 countries, and some of the difficulties involved are outlined below.

Given the limited timescale (twelve months) and resources available for the study, which precluded both new empirical research within the countries and extended study visits by the researchers, the decision was made to carry out the study primarily through networks of national expert informants who would be able to comment with authority on trends and debates in their own countries. The use of expert networks also helps to circumvent problems of terminology and conceptual misunderstanding, with informants acting as interpreters of their own systems.

Because the study required both detailed descriptive material on the formal structure of social assistance schemes and commentary on their practical effectiveness, two networks of elite informants were used: one consisting of senior officials in the relevant ministries and agencies, and the other of experts recruited from universities or independent research institutes. The first group was asked to complete a *pro forma* questionnaire covering structural and legal description of their minimum income schemes, together with statements of official policy, statistical data on expenditure and claimant numbers, and summaries of recent or forthcoming changes. The independent experts provided a critical commentary, informed by research and debate in their countries, on key policy topics in social assistance. In some cases, they helped to fill gaps in the information provided by officials. Most importantly, they also completed the 'model family' income matrix to allow systematic comparison of the value of assistance payments. Respondents attended a colloquium at the mid-point of the research to comment on drafts, clarify and amend income matrix data and discuss broader policy issues.

The use of expert networks, valuable though they are, requires intensive programmatic management. Relying on the goodwill of national governmental officials can be particularly risky, especially on a topic like social assistance which is not always the responsibility of central government. Inevitably, the quality of responses from national informants varies. Research timetables also become vulnerable to delay, with projects coming to resemble desert caravans able to move only at the speed of the slowest camel. Frequent contact is required between the research team and the national informants to ensure that contributions are delivered, agreed assumptions understood and problems clarified. In this study, the income matrices in particular required a careful process of dialogue between the research team and individual informants. The model family matrix was a key methodological feature of the study and the rest of the chapter is devoted mainly to a discussion of its merits and limitations.

Simulating policy through the use of model families

The model family method was pioneered by Kamerman and Kahn (1978, 1983, 1989) in a series of international studies of comparative family policy, and was also used by Bradshaw and Piachaud (1980) in their early study of support for children in Europe. It was further elaborated in a more recent study of child support packages in fifteen countries (Bradshaw *et al.*, 1993). Information on three other countries was subsequently added and preliminary evidence on the level of social assistance in eighteen countries was presented in Bradshaw (1995). These data have also been used to investigate the structural and incentive effects of benefit policies for lone parents (Whiteford and Bradshaw, 1994), and the support given by different welfare states for married women staying at home to look after children (Shaver and Bradshaw, 1995).

Essentially, the technique involves modelling the income 'packages' notionally available to individuals or families representing a range of population groups, in a series of specified, near identical circumstances in each country. Figures derived from the matrices are entered onto spreadsheets and can be manipulated to produce a range of comparisons, including disposable income, proportion of income derived from different sources, relationships between assistance, social insurance and wage earnings, replacement ratios and many others. In theory, the amount of information that can be collected using this method is unlimited, but, in practice, the demands on both informants and analysts necessitate restricting the generation of data to a sensible level.

For the purposes of this study, the matrix included ten family types and three sets of economic circumstances (or cases). The following family types were identified: a single person aged 17, a single person aged 35, a single retired person aged 68, a couple both aged 35 (couples were assumed to be married), a retired couple both aged 68, a couple aged 35 with one pre-school child, a couple aged 35 with one school-age child (7 years), a couple with two children, aged 7 and 14, a lone parent (female, separated or divorced not widowed) with one pre-school child, a lone parent (female, separated or divorced not widowed) with one school-age child (aged 7).

Three cases were covered: social assistance, the 'worst case scenario', where people were assumed to have no entitlement to insurance-based provision and no earnings; social insurance, where people were assumed to be entitled to insurance-based pensions or unemployment benefit, on the basis of full contributions over a working life at specified national average male earnings in manufacturing; working, where specified family members were assumed to be employed at average male earnings.

The selection of family types was inevitably somewhat arbitrary. They were chosen to illustrate the range of types of families that might be dependent on social assistance benefits, and to allow comparison of the level of benefits paid to different types of claimant. Other family types could have been included, such as larger families, or people with disabilities and other special needs, but a line has to be drawn somewhere. It also has to be recognised that the extent to which the chosen family types are 'representative' of the populations varies between countries. Lone parenthood, for example, is a much more prevalent feature of some countries than others, while couples with two children of the specified age may not always be that common. The likelihood of different family types being in receipt of social assistance also varies between countries.

Estimating costs to families

The calculation of cash benefits received and tax and social security contributions payable is relatively straightforward for the national experts, given the model families' income and household circumstances. However, the estimation of other elements of the package requires the establishment of a common framework of analysis, involving detailed assumptions which are not always entirely satisfactory. Three of the more difficult elements involve health, education and housing costs.

Health costs

The baseline assumptions were that health care at the point of demand was free of charge, available to all regardless of means and of similar quality in every country. Account was then taken of variations from these assumptions. In assessing variations, a standard package of health was costed in each country. The major problems with these assumptions are first that, for those countries – including Greece, Portugal, Spain and to some extent Italy – where in theory public health services are available, but in practice the quality may be poor or the waiting lists long, families often tend to use private treatment. Secondly, in some states in the US, insurance premia required for the specified health package result in notional negative disposable incomes for some family types, a useful illustration of why so many people lack health insurance cover.

School and childcare costs

It was assumed that school education of an equivalent standard, including basic books, was available free of charge to all children of school age, that parents would have to pay for a midday meal, and that children lived near enough their school not to require school transport. Account was then taken of any charges that parents were expected to pay for education and any benefits (including the value of free or subsidised school meals) that they might receive.

A standard package was again established for each country for the costs or value of free or subsidised pre-school provision. National informants were asked to follow the most prevalent pattern of formal, full-time, pre-school provision in their country and to take account of its cost. This resulted in different types of care being costed in each country, and no account could be taken of variations in the quality of care. For comparability, pre-school costs were only taken into account in the case of the working lone parent with a pre-school age child, although this is inevitably an unrepresentative picture in some countries such as Denmark, where most married women are working and their children are attending childcare centres.

Housing costs

Housing costs are perhaps the most difficult element to resolve in comparative research. Costs vary within countries and between countries according to tenure and the size, age and location of the dwellings. In some countries, rents may be controlled for people occupying dwellings before a certain date. For owner-occupiers, loan structures and interest rates vary between countries, often according to the stage in the economic cycle, and the level of mortgage interest is affected by the stage of a purchaser's life cycle. Significant differences are found between countries in tenure distribution at different income levels. Nevertheless, housing costs cannot be ignored. In many countries, help with housing costs is a critical element in the benefit package, and even where such support does not exist, variations in housing costs mean that real income levels differ substantially before and after taking account of housing.

For this exercise, the families were assumed to be living in rented dwellings: rented from a public authority, housing co-operative or housing association, if there were common forms of tenure in the country, or from a private landlord if that was the most common tenure pattern. In those countries with high levels of owner-occupation, this assumption is less representative. However, leaving aside the difficulties of making assumptions about owner-occupiers' costs, families receiving social assistance are more likely than others in most countries to be living in rented dwellings.

National informants were asked to fix typical or representative rent levels for such dwellings in a given town in their country. Locating the families in a given commune, town or city helps to structure the comparisons where benefits vary locally, but it can be difficult in some countries to nominate a typical or 'average' location. The size of the dwellings was specified and varied with the model families. Again, this can be an artificial assumption, as families on constrained incomes will, in practice, make choices according to varying local housing markets.

Housing costs are not only a problem at the design stage of comparative projects, they are also difficult to handle at the analysis stage, particularly in a study comparing the level of social assistance payments. The problem arises because, in some countries, housing costs, or a proportion of them, are paid together with social assistance. Thus, the basic benefit takes account of some or all housing costs. In other countries, housing costs are subsidised either by a reduction in rent payable, or by a housing allowance scheme administered separately from social assistance. If comparisons are made of the level of social assistance before housing costs, then the first group of countries – those that pay the housing subsidy as part of social assistance – will appear to have higher levels than the others. Nevertheless, housing has to be included, as for many people it has a crucial impact on their disposable income. It would be wrong to compare social assistance only before housing, yet it would also be misleading in certain circumstances to compare social assistance incomes only after housing. The answer may be to present the results in most circumstances both before and after housing costs, but also to bear in mind that results are inevitably affected by the assumptions made.

Strengths and weaknesses of the model families method

The powerful advantage of the policy simulation approach is that it maximises the possibility of comparing like with like, which is one of the perennial difficulties in comparative research. When combined with detailed descriptive data on national systems collected by national informants, it allows for a large number of countries to be included in the analysis, without researchers having to start from scratch in understanding and interpreting the operation of social systems and policies.

As stated earlier, the kinds of analysis possible through the model families approach are extensive. In relation to social assistance, the study was able to compare the relative value of assistance payments for the range of family types and to break down the benefit package into its separate components. Thus, the importance of child payments, housing or health costs, or other special payments in particular countries can be demonstrated. Analysis also reveals the implicit equivalence scales within different payment structures and shows the relationship between assistance benefits and insurance pensions, unemployment insurance and earnings (Eardley *et al.*, 1996).

As well as its obvious strengths, this technique clearly also has a number of limitations which should be highlighted, not least as a means towards greater refinement. First, this method inevitably produces a description of the way a system should work rather than how it necessarily does. For example, the study implicitly assumes that all those eligible for means-tested benefits are claiming them, despite the fact that take-up of these benefits is known to be far from complete in some countries. It is possible to address this difficulty at the analysis stage by excluding such benefits, or even by building in some assumptions on take-up. But because of the complexity of the interactions within the different systems this is not always a safe or easy solution. The data on which to ground these assumptions are also often missing. A similar problem arises from special factors in some countries which create distortions in the comparison, of which health care costs in the United States are a good example. Other behavioural effects of policy are also inevitably missing from the analysis. For example, the high cost of formal childcare in some countries means that, in practice, many working lone parents find other informal solutions. In modelling their net incomes, it may, therefore, be unrealistic to take full childcare costs into account. These are limitations which make it necessary always to emphasise that it is the structural features of tax/benefit systems which are being compared, not the outcomes for actual families. Concentrating on the formal arrangements and the intended impact of the policies being evaluated can, however, be as valid as examining the actual impact.

Secondly, looking at families at one point in time obscures the more complex life-cycle effects of tax/benefit systems. In particular, while employees' social security contributions are taken into account as reducing disposable income, there is no way of modelling the future benefits which accrue from them. In so far as higher contributions may bring better benefits (which is not always the case), this may distort the picture for some countries from a longer term perspective, especially in relation to retirement pensions. However, by counting benefits received at the time, some account is taken of the distributive effect of contributions previously paid by the family in question and by other contributors.

Thirdly, the more assumptions that are made about the circumstances of model families, the less representative those families are of actual populations. This problem is the inevitable cost of achieving comparability. It has to be accepted that the model families in the study are most unlikely to exist in all their characteristics in any country. They are also all 'nuclear' families. The complexity of attempting to model the policy framework for the presence of other adults in the household, or for other wider family and household obligations, arguably outweighs the possible advantages. Specifying that all couples are married also means that differences in the treatment of cohabiting couples cannot be analysed. These model families are thus not representative, but illustrative. They illustrate a range of experience and, being comparable, they enable us to demonstrate and compare the tax/benefit 'environment' implicitly created for families in a variety of circumstances in a number of countries. Ideally, other families and other aspects of the benefit systems would have been included. However, with three categories of benefit, nine family types, two adult ages, three children's ages and a variety of different benefit systems in each country, the matrix was already large and complex.

Fourthly, difficulties arise from the assumptions made about social insurance benefits and earnings. For example, basing insurance entitlements on an assumption of full contributions at a permanent level of average male earnings is obviously a simplification of real experience in many countries. Pension entitlements have often changed a number of times in the last 40 or so years, and do not reflect the real earnings trajectory of most workers. Also, in order to be able to calculate the value of special support going to lone parents, compared to couples with children or single people without children (although specified to be mothers), they were assumed to have been receiving average male earnings. Clearly, this would often be unrealistic, but it was necessary in order to avoid confusing the structural effects of tax/benefit policies with wage differentials by sex.

Up-to-date earnings figures are not available for all countries and have to be estimated by indexing earlier data, which also probably builds in some inaccuracies. In considering the net disposable incomes of working families, the researcher is not starting from a level playing field, because average gross male earnings differ between countries. Earnings in Greece and Portugal, for example, are between a third and half of those in the United States and Canada after taking account of differences in purchasing power. Among the remaining countries, earnings are remarkably similar, with three exceptions: Finland, Sweden and France. Partly, this is a function of Purchasing Power Parities (PPP), but it relates mainly to the level of the 'social wage' in those countries. Employers' social insurance contributions in these cases are all particularly high in relation to wages. It is likely that workers are effectively foregoing higher earnings for the benefits – often in the future – of a generous social wage. High social security contributions can thus be seen as a form of deferred wage. By contrast, earnings are higher in Canada and the United States, for example, partly because employers are not required to contribute so much to the social wage. If this were the explanation for differences, then, as Whiteford (1995) has argued, when comparing the earnings levels of workers between countries, it might be more appropriate to include employers' social security contributions as part of earnings.

Fifthly, it needs to be emphasised that the matrix figures for countries with local assistance schemes often have to be viewed differently from those with national scale rates, such as Australia and the United Kingdom, or where regional variations are slight, such as Germany. In countries like Switzerland, Norway and Italy, in particular, the amount of benefit paid to particular families depends not only on their individual circumstances, but also on the discretion of social workers operating within local guidelines. For these countries, the figures given are the best estimates of the national experts, but they apply only to the specified municipality and cannot necessarily be seen as representative of the country as a whole.

Finally, comparison of benefit levels uses OECD PPPs, which are generally more satisfactory than exchange rates in that they take account of differences in the price of a common basket of goods and services in each country and are less subject to the sharp fluctuations that can occur in exchange rates. The relationship between exchange rates and PPPs tends to vary between countries. PPPs do have their limitations, however. Their primary use is for aggregate national data, rather than at a micro level, as applied to benefit rates or individual household income and expenditure. Using them for the comparison of disposable income after benefits and charges may introduce an element of double counting, as variations in some of these costs are already taken into account in the calculation of PPPs. They were thought to be the most useful way of comparing monetary values across the countries in the study, but they need to be taken as indicators of relative benefit levels rather than exact measures.

Although these methodological constraints might appear formidable, they should not deter researchers from exploiting the considerable opportunities offered by the methods described here. Not least, they have the advantage of providing flexibility in the permutations that can be inserted in the models being constructed.

Part Two : Qualitative Methods

Clare Ungerson

The chapters in this section indicate and advocate exciting innovations in comparative methodology and argue for qualitative methods rather than, or as well as, quantitative methods. However, to speak of 'qualitative methods' as though that phrase has one understood meaning within comparative analysis is misleading. Each of the chapters follows a different methodological path. Spicker, by rejecting the broad brush of modelling in regime analysis, argues for more, and multidimensional evaluative criteria in cross-national work. Jobert uses 'maps' of research traditions and literature – a kind of cross-national sociology of knowledge – in order to understand the differences between nations with reference to the relationship between training and employment. Schunk uses 'maps' to understand the service delivery systems of two cities in two countries and, then, uses model hypothetical cases to reveal cross-national differences. Chamberlayne and King set out an elaborate stepped analytical technique to approach qualitative data culled from small sample interviews.

Notwithstanding these major differences in approach, the chapters have a number of features in common. First, all the authors are reluctant to accept the validity of broad-brush comparisons that use aggregate data collected on a national basis. For example, they all suggest that profound difficulties arise in constructing single, comparable meanings from data generated within different structures and cultures. Regime analysis based on modelling is driven to rely on the quantitative data most easily available in the form of aggregate expenditures and transfer payments. In consequence, it loses both a sense of welfare states as service deliverers and also fails to indicate fully how the everyday lives of citizens are affected by the structure and objectives of 'their' welfare state. Second, the use of qualitative methods, particularly of the kind described by Chamberlayne and King, and by Schunk, reflects trends in social research methodology over the past twenty years which have revalued ethnographic and 'grounded theory' approaches to social knowledge. Third, the chapters reflect a general desire to use research to understand how private lives are affected by, and interact with, public issues and policies. Thus, the chapters have in common their commitment to the detail rather than the broad brush of analysis – a form of social science pointillism – and to a whole story which includes how private lives relate to structure.

The authors also highlight some of the problems with qualitative work, which may be equally applicable in quantitative research. Language emerges as an important issue in two senses of the word. First, there is the difficulty, as Jobert points out, of fully understanding the meanings of terms which, within a particular national context, have a cultural loading. This makes direct comparison daunting. Jobert uses the examples of the words 'work' and 'education'; other examples spring to mind, such as the term 'care' (Ungerson, 1990).

The second problem with language, which is unique to qualitative work, and which two of the chapters implicitly recognise as a difficulty, arises from the corruption of data by translation. Chamberlayne and King, and also Schunk stress the fact that their interview data were collected either by native speakers or by researchers with very considerable language skills. Hence problems of translation, at least at the data collection and analysis stages, were minimised. However, very good language skills are in short supply in the social science world; it is also very unusual to find people able to deal qualitatively with work in more than two languages. Hence, qualitative comparisons may have to be restricted to those carried out between nations that share a language, or to no more than two countries that do not. But analysis may be the least of the problems associated with language. A further problem arises out of the language of publication. Where qualitative methods, leading to grounded theory, are used, the loss of meaning and nuance arising from the translation of direct quotation can be an insuperable difficulty. Publication will lock the culturally loaded meanings of interview material from many languages into a single language which can only provide a very partial key. While no immediate answer can be given to this problem, one possible solution is to use multilingual teams of researchers who are involved throughout the research process, including the writing-up stage. This, in turn, means that qualitative methods in comparative research demand generous and long-term funding.

It is the nature of qualitative work, particularly that based on interview material, that it is confined to small localities. A further issue raised by the chapters, and referred to explicitly by Schunk, is the question as to how far qualitative methods, which are intended to unwrap national differences, actually unwrap community, local and regional specificities. To be certain that the differences found between, for example, two cities in two nations arise out of cross-national differences in structures, it is therefore necessary to amass a wealth of detail about the national structures themselves, and assess how far they allow for locally specific characteristics to develop. In an important sense, then, a detailed national context is needed, based on broad-brush categorisation and almost certainly on quantitative methods to 'place' qualitative data. Once again, this has a message for funders: just as qualitative work can have greater validity than quantitative work, so qualitative work has to be set within a context of quantitative data.

However, these problems of language, and of small locality research that draws conclusions at a national level, while real, can nevertheless be dealt with in analysis that points out the difficulties. Qualitative methods in comparative research are in their infancy; all the chapters demonstrate an understanding of the difficulties involved, but they also offer some valuable insights into the solutions to them and provide a foretaste of some fascinating research results.

5 Normative Comparisons of Social Security Systems

Paul Spicker

Normative analysis in comparative social policy serves two main purposes. The first is descriptive; it is used to identify similarities and differences between countries or systems. Arguing that a system is 'residual' or 'institutional' is saying something about its characteristics, the intentions of policy-makers, and its resemblance to other systems with similar characteristics. This kind of classification can in turn be related to empirical data. The proposition that liberal regimes spend less on unemployed people than corporatist ones, for example, is empirically testable (unless of course the definitions have been drawn in such a way as to make the statement tautologous).

The second purpose is evaluative; normative analysis is used to say which policies are relatively good, and which are relatively bad, by some criterion. 'Residual' and 'institutional' welfare are not simply descriptions; they imply an attribution of intention, and a judgement about commitment to welfare. Comparative studies are often driven by the desire to influence specific policies; the current growth of studies in European social policy is concerned with arguments for social policies both within member states and at a European level. Comparative social policy, like any other social policy, is not based in a neutral, value-free social science; it has important practical applications, and the kinds of analysis which are undertaken are directly framed in terms of the moral perceptions of the people who make them.

Examining systems

Much recent comparative work is based on the identification of the broad characteristics of systems. Describing social policy in terms of a 'system' depends on certain assumptions about the relationship of its parts. Systems are not simply collections of different policies; the constituent elements are inter-related. This does not mean that they all have to work in conjunction with each other; tensions and conflicts may arise. What it does mean is that there is something about the way in which the parts are related which makes it possible to talk sensibly about the system as a whole. There are three main stages in analysing a system: identifying its elements, examining the relationships between them and, finally, within them. This way of thinking through issues is usually called a 'systems approach', though sometimes it is more grandly referred to as 'systems theory'. Explaining social policy in these terms is simply a useful way of describing what is happening, while breaking down information into manageable chunks.

Systems in social policy can be identified in several ways: for example, the organisational context (state, commercial, mutualist or voluntary sectors), the focus of activity (health, personal social services, social security), or the mode of production (professional, bureaucratic, managerial). A social security system is most usually taken to consist of the range of benefits that are available. It might be broken down into different systems for elderly people, family benefits, unemployment and so forth (for example Korpi and Palme, 1994); alternatively, it might be seen as being composed of different types of benefit, including insurance-based benefits, means-testing, non-contributory benefits and so on (Spicker, 1993).

The main purpose of describing systems is to classify the constituent parts in terms which facilitate subsequent analysis. The terms used are generally conventional. Social security can be identified with health care in a classification of systems based on social insurance, with tax reliefs in systems based on income maintenance or redistribution, and with discretionary social assistance in an analysis focusing on the relief of poverty. In the context of normative analysis, the important relationships between the elements of the system are normative ones; there is an implicit assumption of inter-related purposes. An 'institutional' system, then, is informed centrally by the principle that personal needs are the responsibility of society; a system based on 'citizenship' offers rights to everyone as a member of that society. However, the conventional nature of the classifications means that terms which are apparently descriptive might also be associated with a normative content. So, 'pluralist' systems are not just taken to be systems in which diverse means of provision occur, but are associated with an intention or preference for diversity; 'corporatist' systems are not just systems in which the state co-ordinates the activities of different sectors, but those in which welfare is taken to be subordinate to the wider aims of the state and the economy.

It is important to recognise that the methods that people use to analyse a problem can change the way that they think about the material. Sociologists have become suspicious of systems approaches, because they have learned to be cautious about assuming connections between complex social phenomena. These problems are not quite so acute in the discussion of many social policy systems, which are designed and directed in a way that societies cannot be, but there is still a risk of imposing an artificial order in theory that does not reflect the situation in practice. One of the reasons why the French system, for example, is so difficult to classify – it appears in the literature as institutional, corporatist, residual and 'rudimentary' – is that it has evolved gradually in a complex, patchwork development. Systems approaches shift the emphasis in analysis from specific issues to the context in which policies are set, and focus attention on the inter-relationships between the issues. This is often valuable, but it can also be misleading, and the exercise has to be undertaken with care.

Two common pitfalls deserve particular attention. The first is to assume that systems must have some identifiable global characteristics; the test of a system lies in the inter-connections, not the characteristics of each element. All social security systems, in practice, are mixed, and classifications which are appropriate to some part of a national system do not necessarily apply to others. Korpi and Palme (1994) have made an initial assessment of family benefits, pensions and unemployment insurance in several countries. Though some countries do have similar policies across the range of benefits – France, Italy and Germany are consistently described as 'corporatist' – others do not: the United States mixes basic security and targeted programmes, while Switzerland mixes basic security for pensions, voluntary subsidisation for sickness benefits and encompassing provision for unemployment. The closer the detail in which systems are examined, the less tenable are generalisations made at the level of the whole system (Bolderson and Mabbett, 1995).

The second common error is to seek to identify systems in terms of particular characteristics, rather than the relationships between them. Countries that have a big health or social security budget are not necessarily like others that have the same kind of budget; countries that have insurance-based systems are not necessarily like others that also have insurance-based systems. According to Przeworski and Teune (1970, p. 45): 'Systems differ not when the frequency of particular characteristics differ, but when the patterns of the relationships among variables differ.' Similarities and differences are identified by considering a constellation of factors, not issues in isolation. Esping-Andersen (1990) seems to fall into this trap in his consideration of 'decommodification'. This refers to the degree to which welfare provision is treated as a social right rather than as a marketable commodity. Because the Australian system is largely based on means-tested provision, he classifies Australia as a 'liberal' state. But Castles (1994) argues that what matters, in his view, is coverage in practice, not the form of the benefits; the coverage of the Australian system is extensive. Cass and Freeland (1994) make the case, further, that the use of means-testing has a different impact in Australia than in other systems; they suggest that Australia should be seen as radically redistributive. The point is not simply a question about the indicators which Esping-Andersen has used; the problem is that his attention has focused on a particular characteristic, rather than the inter-relationship between that characteristic and other features of the system. In a liberal system, there should be an identifiable relationship between low decommodification, limited coverage and limited redistribution, and in Australia there is not.

Normative models

The description and evaluation of systems is most commonly undertaken in comparative work through the construction of normative models. There are three main approaches. The first classifies welfare on a spectrum from least developed to most developed welfare systems. The classic example is Wilensky and Lebeaux's (1958) basic distinction between 'residual' and 'institutional' models of welfare, developed in many later works including those of Titmuss (1974). Mishra (1981) refers to 'residual', 'institutional' and 'socialist' models of society, with socialism representing the most developed provision of welfare. Leibfried (1992), considering European welfare states, identifies the Scandinavian welfare states, mainly represented by Sweden, Norway, Denmark and Finland, as those where welfare is most highly developed; the 'Bismarck' countries, Germany and Austria, which in his view offer 'institutional' welfare; the Anglo-Saxon countries, which include the United Kingdom, United States, Australia, and New Zealand, which he sees as 'residual'; and the 'Latin Rim', covering Spain, Portugal, Greece, Italy and perhaps France, where welfare is 'rudimentary'.

The second basic approach is to classify welfare systems according to their distinctive approaches to welfare. Models of 'industrial-achievement/performance' and 'institutional-redistributive' welfare, as represented by Titmuss (1974), refer not to different stages of development but to alternative principles on which welfare may be delivered. Esping-Andersen's classification of capitalist welfare systems as 'liberal', 'corporatist' and 'social democratic' can be seen as a movement from least to most developed patterns of welfare, but it also mirrors the models of Titmuss: the corporatist model is not an intermediate stage between liberalism and social democracy, but a different kind of provision from either.

The third approach is to use a functional or organisational classification of services as a guide to the normative position with which a system is identified. In French writing, the classification which is most often referred to is a distinction between 'Bismarckian' and 'Beveridgean' systems. This is sometimes presented as a functional division between different organisational arrangements (see for example Lenoir, 1994, p. 22) but equally is identified with different normative approaches. Bismarck stands for a system of insurance geared to occupational status, Beveridge for universal protection:

> History shapes law and institutions appropriate to each nation, but which always refer to one of two logics: social insurance based on solidarity between members of professional groups, or national social security founded on solidarity between citizens.
>
> (Translated by the author from Majnoni d'Intignano, 1993, p. 23)

Van Parijs (1994) identifies the Bismarck model with 'insurance' – mutually pooled risks in order to protect income – while Beveridge is associated with 'solidarity', understood as generalised coverage of risks at a minimum level through redistributive processes, and Thomas Paine is taken as the exemplar of a system based on 'equity', social justice and universal benefits. Ultimately, this is not dissimilar in its effect to the classification of 'corporatist', 'institutional' and 'citizenship' models mentioned above, but the distinctions have been arrived at in a different way.

The problems with models

The countries which are being studied rarely seem to coincide with the general outlines defined in the way described here. This might be taken as an indication that the models have not been adequately defined, or that the information on which the classification is based is in some way defective; both may, of course, be true. But there is reason to suppose that the practice of modelling itself is doomed to failure.

The objections which might be made to systems approaches can also be made to this kind of modelling. But there are further problems, some of which are based in the weakness of the normative categories which are being applied.

First, the criteria adopted are often vague. 'Institutional' welfare is commonly used to describe any system of welfare that is extensive; 'corporatism' can be applied to any country in which the state does not possess a substantial monopoly of the production of welfare, a situation which holds generally, for example in relation to pensions provision (van Gunsteren and Rein, 1984).

Second, different countries understand their welfare systems differently, and this leads them to put a different construction on their successes and failures. The system in the United Kingdom has been largely predicated on the principle of providing universal basic benefits at a low level – the 'Beveridge' principle – which means that classification of benefits as 'liberal' or 'residual' on the basis of their limited adequacy seems perverse. The main aims of social security in France have not been the relief of poverty, but supporting families and the avoidance of 'exclusion'; so it seems strange to judge the success or failure of certain policies on the basis of their impact of poverty.

Third, even within ideological classifications, there are often further shades of opinion. The United States seems, to many outside observers, the nearest we have to a model of individualised, residual welfare. That is clearly not the view of the radical conservatives of the Republican party, who commonly represent the federal government's commitment to welfare as a model of extravagance and misplaced generosity (see Karger, 1991). The problem is that the use of broad-based ideological classifications may fail to provide insights into the impact of ideology in particular contexts.

Fourth, from the point of view of normative classification, the models are much too elaborate. Models like Mishra's or Esping-Andersen's are composites, and composites are always vulnerable to the complaint that part of the model applies while other parts do not. They incorporate systems of discrete values, rather than simple normative criteria. The inter-relationships which may seem evident from certain perspectives – like residual welfare with liberalism, or citizenship and institutional welfare – are undermined when they are examined in comparative perspective, because the process of definition of ideological blocs is different in different countries.

Fifth, the kinds of generalisation used in modelling are often too broad for the purpose of evaluation. The models generally refer to overall systems. When the focus shifts to subsystems, the normative classifications are much less helpful. Particular problems also come from trying to interpret empirical data normatively.

The sixth problem is that normative distinctions are not necessarily identified with clear differences in the approach to policy. Nothing in the distinction of 'residual' and 'institutional' policy, for example, tells us whether or not social work should be attached to social assistance; whether insurance is preferable to non-contributory benefits; whether benefits should be earnings related or flat rate; or whether services should be provided by the state or independent mutualities. In other words, there is no real basis within the 'institutional' or 'residual' models on which to distinguish Beveridge from Bismarck. Conversely, neither Beveridge nor Bismarck gives a clear indication about the extent to which responsibility is individual or solidaristic, the degree of redistribution which is appropriate or the extent to which discretionary elements might be incorporated in the benefits system.

Seventh, the categories are static, while policy-making is dynamic. Israel is currently moving away from a collectivist ethos towards a more individualistic one (Doron, 1985); France is shifting towards comprehensive provision; Britain is becoming increasingly pluralistic.

These objections are important, but they do not mean that modelling serves no purpose. It is often necessary to make generalisations, because there may be no basis for a comparison otherwise; models provide a useful shorthand for discussing different types of system. The central problem with most current models is more basic; they just do not work very well as descriptions of what is going on. The United States is much too corporate and communitarian for a bastion of liberal capitalism; the Swedish system is too heavily geared to occupational status to be a true model of social-democratic citizenship; and the United Kingdom is not residual, institutional/redistributive or corporate, but something with the characteristics of all three (Spicker 1993). Effectively, the exercise of modelling depends on the use of a range of ideal types, which are most useful for description when they are counterpoised against each other, rather than standing alone in their own right.

Using normative criteria

The examination of specific normative criteria has several advantages over modelling. In the first place, it assumes much less about inter-relationships than modelling does. Institutional welfare does not have to be redistributive; work-merit does not have to be corporatist. Examining each criterion separately permits more dimensions of a problem, and more combinations of factors, to be taken into account. The analysis in *Poverty and Social Security* (Spicker, 1993, chapter 9) is based on five dichotomies: residual versus institutional, individualistic versus solidaristic, labour force participation versus citizenship, basic needs versus social protection, and pluralistic versus comprehensive systems. This material could be presented in terms of two ideal models, each with five characteristics. By contrast, keeping the raw material in terms of five dichotomies offers 32 combinations (2^5).

This approach substantially meets two of the objections above: that models are too elaborate, and that they are too broad to use for evaluating subsystems. At the same time, as a way of describing systems, it is also vulnerable to one of the pitfalls referred to earlier. If inter-relationships between issues are crucial to understanding a system, breaking down the issues into constituent criteria may sometimes be inappropriate.

Another set of objections to models relate to the vagueness of the terms used. Although specific normative criteria may still be ill-defined, they are capable of much more precise definition than the kinds of terms used in modelling. The effect of over-defining a model is often to destroy its power to describe or explain; the more precise the definition, the less generally it can be applied. By contrast, normative criteria can be selected which offer specific predictions about the shape of services, or tests against which services can be measured. This does not avoid all the difficulties, but it does mean that far fewer problems arise in relation to the use of specific normative criteria than general models.

Similarly, normative criteria can be used in specific contexts as the basis for evaluation. In an attempt to compare Britain and France in general terms, it is important to understand that the British system has often been directed at the relief of poverty, while the French system has focused instead on family policy (Baker, 1986), which does not, however, preclude the possibility of examining which system provides benefits at a more adequate level. Equally, because no attempt is made to use a single criterion as a description of everything about a system, some of the problems of relating the criteria to the empirical data disappear, while the special problem of coping with changes over time becomes much less daunting.

These points answer most of the objections made to the process of modelling: those which are concerned with the problems of generalising across models, and those which relate to the weakness of the normative categories (the vagueness of the criteria, and the use of inappropriate generalisations). The problem of lack of sensitivity to important dimensions may remain, but at least the application of a specific criterion does not claim to identify the dominant characteristics of a system.

Two general reservations should be noted. First, the terms which are used in normative criteria are often contested concepts. The effect of imposing meanings on specific principles can be arbitrary: people do not necessarily mean the same thing when they think of 'citizenship' or 'equality', and there is no necessary reason why the evaluation implicit in the criteria being used should be accepted. Second, the criteria can be difficult to operationalise. The appropriateness of different measures depends on the theoretical links between norms and practice; the figures produced are generally indicators, rather than a clear and unequivocal test of any proposition. The empirical material cannot be separated neatly into distinct normative groups; the division into alternative categories is done on a relative basis. This means that the selection of the group of countries can be crucial in determining the relative position of particular countries; the United Kingdom looks very different when compared with European countries than it does in classifications which include the United States or Australia. These reservations are basic to any normative analysis, and they are probably unavoidable.

The limitations of normative examination

Several problems remain in relating normative examinations to data about different systems. The description of activity in different welfare states is often taken to imply something about the normative content of policy, which assumes that the structure and operation of services is a direct indication of their normative character. This may be true, but there is a risk that outcomes might also be taken as indications of intention. A discrepancy often arises between policy, implementation and effect (for example, because other social factors have intervened). If the normative content of a policy is not necessarily reflected in practice, the argument that practice can be taken as evidence of normative intention is defective.

Although normative analysis can be used for description or evaluation, some kinds of empirical data lend themselves to normative description more effectively than others. Ideology is couched in normative terms; so, often, is policy. The structure or operation of services, by contrast, are not necessarily described appropriately in normative terms, and substantial problems have arisen from the consideration of certain aspects of the process of provision (notably means-testing) as if they were good indicators of normative intention. The same is true of discussion of outcomes, which cannot be taken as evidence of intention. Conversely, normative terms provide useful criteria for evaluation of the provision of welfare and its impact, but do not help much with evaluation of ideology or policy, because they do not develop an understanding of ideology or policy on their own terms. The danger is that an attempt to examine every part of a system normatively can lead to an uncomfortable mixture of description and evaluation, which can obscure as much as it reveals.

Policies in other countries often attract attention because of their ideological motivation. Examples include workfare (Ogborn, 1988; Walker, 1991), child support (Collins, 1992), and the French idea of *insertion*, which has exercised some influence in the European Community (Economic and Social Consultative Assembly, 1989, p. 18; Masprone, 1989, p. 13). Examination of the ideological intentions may explain something about the relative attraction of particular ideas. However, nothing in the kind of information contained in a normative analysis can identify whether such a policy is applicable in another social context; that calls for a different kind of comparison, and a different method.

6   Comparing Education, Training and Employment in Germany, the United Kingdom and Italy

*Annette Jobert**

This chapter focuses on the methodological issues which arise in international comparisons of education and training systems in different socio-economic contexts and looks at the relationship between training opportunities, labour markets and employment. Particular attention is paid to the access of young people to labour markets, education and training (systems, policies, practices). It examines the ways in which these issues have been debated and analysed in three countries from an economic and sociological perspective. Particular attention is paid to the analysis of the conflicts between two conceptions of skills: those based on individual knowledge and those based on job requirements.

Research aims and approaches

The first aim of the study was to extend to other European countries work already carried out in France in the mid-1980s, taking account of major changes that had been occurring during the preceding years, in particular, the growing problems of employment, and unemployment and, within this context, the role assigned to education and training as instruments capable of offering responses. The study was also prompted by the increasing pressure from European institutions to develop comparative research in the field. From the outset, it was clear that a number of obstacles would have to be overcome, such as preconceived ideas contained in the use of nomenclatures, national classification systems (age categories for example) and the social categories specific to each country, the use of

---

*   The comparative study described in this chapter was conducted by three researchers: Annette Jobert, Catherine Marry and Lucie Tanguy of the Centre National de la Recherche Scientifique. The findings from the study have been published in Jobert *et al.* (1995).

concepts such as qualification, competence, skill, transition, which differ in meaning from country to country.

Another difficulty facing researchers in this area is how to take account of the effect of different cultural and intellectual traditions. Comparative analysis in this field is far from being a new departure. In the area of work, employment and training, the number of studies grew rapidly during the 1980s, but very few authors, at least in France, attempted a critical appraisal of the methods being used. Among the comparative studies that were undertaken, the social analysis developed by the Laboratoire d'Économie et de Sociologie du Travail (LEST) in Aix-en-Provence has provided a useful framework for researchers (Maurice, 1979; Maurice *et al.*, 1986). It stresses the features and patterns that are specific to each country, or what the researchers call the 'societal effect'. However, the limitations of this type of analysis became apparent to the authors of the present study when they began comparing intermediate levels of qualifications and skills with reference to the German and the British educational systems. Because the approach focuses on differences at national level, it tends to obscure internal diversity. The criticism also applies in comparisons of employment, since differentiation by gender, generation and region is specific to each country.

Intellectual mapping

The intention here is not to provide a comparative analysis of the research fields as such, but to present the conceptual and methodological tools needed for comparisons. This involves describing the contours of the research field in a given country; identifying the main areas of research; and reflecting on the categories and nomenclatures used. The approach requires an understanding of historical realities and also the intellectual traditions which are inherent in any community. An attempt is made here, for each country studied, to characterise the employment and labour market situations, vocational training and educational systems, economic and sociological traditions. Attention is paid to the way research is organised, the main research centres and their links with the universities, sources of funding, and what in France is called the 'social demand', emanating from trade union organisations and public administration, and with reference to the main developments over the past 15 to 20 years.

In doing so, an attempt has been made to establish a kind of 'intellectual map' for each of the three countries which gives a condensed image of research in the field. This part of the work is based on documentary sources and interviews with key informants (researchers, academics, programme leaders), who were selected in the three countries because they were able to report on the history of a particular area of research and were known by the scientific community to have played an active role in the construction of research parameters. They were asked to identify and describe the main areas of research (covering research questions, methods and patterns) in their national context. In each case, five main areas of research were selected, concentrating on the theoretical approach and topics which best characterised that country. Whereas similar approaches were found for educational sociology or labour markets, this did not apply for other areas. For example, transition studies are more numerous in the United Kingdom and Germany (even if the notion has a different meaning from one country to another), pedagogic research on vocational thinking is specific to Germany (*Berufspädagogik*), and regional approaches were most characteristic of Italy.

The area being covered and the aims of the research were very broad: to identify the relationship between phenomena in the fields of work, its techniques and organisation, the definition of qualifications and the transmission of knowledge, and the institutions providing education and training, at a point at which they were undergoing major change. It was therefore necessary to use multidisciplinary approaches. Every discipline has its own tools for analysing a particular aspect of reality but it does not have the capacity to cover other disciplines. Hence the value of bringing to bear a number of different approaches in the study of a particular object, making it possible to avoid linear explanations of the relationship between education and training and to illuminate the processes enabling its construction as well as the links between the two fields.

Tools and concepts

The field of research is hampered by its inchoate development: the central concepts in the study – education and work — are subject to constant change precisely because the purpose is to conduct an analysis of the relationships between two spheres of social activity. Why, one might ask, were these concepts used rather than training and employment, which are more often referred to in social debate? The concepts of education and training are sometimes used interchangeably or in competition with one another. The shift can be explained by the extension of training opportunities to waged workers and by the success of the principle of the dual system (school/enterprise), which most European societies are trying to introduce. The progression which can be observed from the concept of education towards that of training takes a variety of forms. The opposition between sociology of employment and sociology of work found in France is not, however, stressed to the same extent in other countries. Although, as elsewhere, in France schools occupy a central position within society, their responsibility for transferring knowledge and values is increasingly being challenged. In France, the concept of *education* is often used to refer narrowly to schooling. The term 'education' has a far broader meaning in the United Kingdom, where the school as an institution does not have the same importance in society for all social groups. The expression used in the United Kingdom 'participation in education' has not therefore been translated as *scolarité* (schooling). Instead, a broader term, that of *études* (studies) is used.

Another relevant conceptual issue is that the category of 'young people' is not the same in each country. In Italy, it is a broad category covering the age group 15 to 29. This has to be located in relation to public policy for integrating young people into the workforce and with reference to the characteristics of unemployment statistics which show particularly high levels for this group. It can also be explained by the fact that more young people are continuing to live with their parents until a much later age. In Britain, by contrast, the age group described as 'young people' refers to 16 to 18-year olds.

The concepts of work and employment have also been called into question. Levels of unemployment, the lengthening of the transitionary phase between school and work, the wide range of employment statuses, and the trend towards less secure forms of employment are all contributing to the reinforcement of employment as a social construct and are making it a more important factor in determining working arrangements and social stratification. Some researchers dispute the primacy being given to the concept of employment and, instead, consider that work (not only paid work but also domestic work and voluntary unpaid social work) is central to an understanding of social relationships.

Even if employment is nowadays at the centre of social and political concerns, the choice of the term 'work' implies that work remains a central reference point in societies. All analysis requires appropriate conceptual tools and the use of indicators that are not necessarily those referred to in public debate to support ideological viewpoints. The measurement of unemployment provides a good example of the problems encountered in international comparisons. At the time of the research, in public debate it was, for example, being claimed that unemployment among young people aged 15 to 24 was 4.5 per cent in Germany, compared with 19 per cent in France. These figures can be criticised on several counts: firstly, for adopting this age category, as in many societies almost all young people of 15 are still in education. In France 80 per cent of young people of 18 are in full-time education and 64 per cent at the age of 19. It would be more appropriate to consider young people between 20 and 29; then the differences are not so marked. Secondly, in Germany, young people in the dual system – some 1.5 million – are included in the working population. In France, vocational training takes place mainly within the educational system. It would therefore be more appropriate to examine the links between four factors for each age group: education in its different forms (school-based or otherwise), activity (also in different forms), unemployment and inactivity.

The marked differences noted in unemployment rates for men and women also need to be examined with care. The United Kingdom was the only country in the European Community where unemployment rates were lower for women than for men in the early 1990s. However, when unemployment rates are considered in relation to part-time work, which represented 43 per cent of female employment at that time, the labour market position of women was found to be less secure than that of men, since part-time work applies to a range of different working hours, which are sometimes below the number of hours covered by social insurance.

These examples show how the object of research is constructed differently from one country to another, how dangerous it is to make international comparisons using indicators in isolation and how necessary it is to situate them in relation to their socio-economic contexts, as argued by Hantrais and Letablier (1996).

National research issues

The relationship between education and work is also conceptualised differently from one country to another depending on the way in which the two are perceived and analysed at a given point in time.

The same problems, such as economic recession or increasing youth unemployment give rise to different debates and issues and, therefore, to different research problematics. The debates and issues are linked to the national context, the history of vocational training institutions and the development of social representations and practices. For example, factors like the place given to schools in a particular society, the forms and degrees of state intervention, or demography play an important role, making it necessary to track research themes over a period of nearly 20 years, and maybe more. This allows us to emphasise continuities, shifts and breaks within research traditions.

In the United Kingdom, traditionally the majority of young people have left school at the age of 16 at the end of compulsory schooling, to follow training or enter employment directly. Until the early 1980s, this early school-leaving age could be explained by the interest in apprenticeships as a sought-after form of training and by the high salaries offered to young people. Little value was placed on schooling and further education. The rapid decline in apprenticeships and the growing level of unemployment among young people have made it necessary for them to undertake training to improve their qualifications, resulting in later labour market entry. This change has not automatically been translated into an extension of the length of schooling in a country where labour market experience continues to be highly valued. The situation explains why studies have focused on the transition from school to work and on policy supporting it, particularly for young people in the 16 to 18 age groups who were the target group for policies being promoted in the late 1980s and early 1990s.

In Germany, the main issues raised in the debate about the relationship between education and work have to be understood by referring to the German system of education and training, particularly the emphasis given to the dual system which young people move into when they leave primary school and which continues to be the main form of occupational socialisation for the young in Germany. It should not be forgotten that, even if this dual system is widespread and highly valued (and is extending into higher education), the most prestigious route remains high school and university, which is attracting more and more young people, calling the dual system into question. When these changes in the educational system and in vocational training are combined with the problems resulting from reunification (particularly the high level of unemployment in the *Länder* of the former German Democratic

Republic and the restructuring of education, training and research institutions), they provide a backcloth for the main issues being debated in German society and in the research community. They have involved introducing new approaches and concepts for examining the operation of the dual system and its future, which has been a major topic for analysis in German research.

Whereas interest in Britain is focused on the transition from school to work for the 16 to 18 age group, who have traditionally left school at a younger age than in the other countries being studied, in Germany emphasis is on a much broader concept of transition, which is applied to both activities and education, as shown by longitudinal studies of young people. It involves the blurring of the frontiers between the status of being at school and belonging to the working population in the dual system. Another explanation may be the low level of unemployment among young people.

In Italy, two phenomena are worth noting: firstly, 90 per cent of young people continue in education after the compulsory school-leaving age of 14 in both the North and the South of the country; secondly, major regional disparities are found between the North and the South, both in economic and social terms, as illustrated by differences in the level of unemployment (with unemployment rates three times higher in the South, at 20 per cent compared to 7 per cent in the North in 1992). In addition, the disparity between men and women is particularly marked. For many years, the relationship between education and unemployment has been a major problem area. In the 1970s, the main issue was the high level of unemployment among well-qualified people. Interest has since shifted to training issues within the regional context. Questions are being raised about the implications of a highly decentralised system of vocational training on the role of the state as well as on training provided for waged workers faced by organisational and technological change.

Education and training in context

From a comparative perspective, the subject has raised a number of issues: male–female differences, long-term exclusion from the labour market, the importance of training within employment policy, which varies from one national context to another, and also the importance of evaluation of education, training and employment policies. But two topics appear to be of lesser importance: continuing education and the place of young people in the division of labour.

This research shows once more the difficulties of international comparisons. Its aim was to underline the diversity of situations and of possible interpretations, both within countries and between them. Comparative research has made it possible to provide an account of the issues being examined at a given point in time in each country and of the way in which they are developing. In doing so, it has shown that the relationship between training and education, on the one hand, and work and employment, on the other, has been established through a long chain of mediating processes which require further unravelling.

Acknowledgements

The research was supported by the French Ministry of Higher Education and Research, the CNRS and ESRC, and European institutions (Task Force and CEDEFOP).

7 Constructing Models of the Welfare Mix: Care Options of Frail Elders

Michaela Schunk

Over the past few years, elder care has stood at the forefront of welfare policy reforms. It has led to the restating of central questions about the development of welfare states, such as the meaning and extent of 'social citizenship' and the responsiveness of welfare provision to emerging social problems. Some authors, looking at changes in the provision of care services for frail elder people, claim to have found evidence of a convergent transformation across all welfare states towards greater exclusion, less regulation and residualised public welfare provision (Baldock and Evers, 1991).

Yet, a closer look at national welfare systems reveals considerable variations between countries both in the nature and workings of the 'social state' and in the organisation of welfare provision. Despite similar socio-demographic pressures and political demands, recent health and social care reforms exhibit surprisingly different outcomes regarding care provisions for frail elders. This draws attention towards different starting points and the complexity of institutional and organisational welfare state arrangements embedded in national histories and cultures.

A comparative qualitative study of health and social care of frail elders in Britain and Germany offers the opportunity to assess and evaluate the effects of two contrasting welfare systems on the position of frail elders and their carers in relation to the nature, range and quality of care provisions. Britain and Germany differ not only in the type of health system, but also with regard to levels and types of care services and substantially different 'mixes' of welfare providing sectors. The concept of 'welfare mix' entails some conception of the interplay and interdependence among the different welfare producing sectors and can be used to characterise different types of welfare states and welfare traditions. Particular attention has been drawn to the role of the 'third' or voluntary sector in some welfare systems, not only as service provider but also as 'negotiator of the extent of the welfare state' (Room and 6, 1994).

In Britain, the postwar state expanded its role in the provision of welfare, whereas the 'dual welfare structure' of statutory and independent agencies has long characterised welfare policy in Germany (Tennstedt, cited in Lorenz, 1994). However the recent community care reforms in Britain have induced considerable changes, such as the purchaser/provider split and increasing involvement of the third sector in service delivery, whereas care reforms in Germany have been built on prevailing institutional structures of the welfare system (Walker, 1993; Alber, 1994). Although there might be a superficial appearance of convergence between Britain and Germany, it is argued in this chapter that any broad comparison of welfare responses in different countries must be sustained by detailed micro-analysis of finance, access and delivery of care services to people with particular needs in particular places.

This chapter presents one approach to comparing welfare systems which recognises the substantially different 'mixes' of welfare providing sectors, with the aim of contributing to the understanding of determinants of 'welfare outcomes' for the individual. The importance of bringing the need transformation process into the comparative analysis of welfare states is increasingly recognised (Doyal and Gough, 1991, chapter 11; Sen, 1993). While several recent, large-scale cross-national studies on elder care have made a useful addition to the quantitative information available, more detailed knowledge is needed on the patterns and workings of the welfare mix to enable exploration of the context and determinants of welfare outcomes in different countries.

In the first section of the chapter, recent cross-national research into elder care is reviewed. The remainder of the chapter provides an example of a study which emphasises 'local welfare mixes' as a conceptual framework for analysing elder care from a comparative perspective. A small-scale qualitative study is used to exploit the capacity of case-oriented comparative methodology in gaining access to complex data structures and to enable each case to be viewed as a combination of characteristics, as a configuration (Ragin, 1987). By confining the scope of the comparison to two countries, it is possible to provide a detailed account of the distinctive features in each of them. Since the study was undertaken by a researcher of German origin based at a British university, personal experience, language skills and contextual knowledge could be drawn on from living and studying in both countries. Inevitably, cultural and language barriers remain. These are treated as necessary elements of the cross-national research process and are recognised and discussed in the study.

Recent cross-national research into elder care

'Care for frail elder people' has recently been the subject of much cross-national social policy research in Europe. The most comprehensive study encompasses not only health and social care of frail elder people but also a detailed comparison of social and economic conditions of old age, based on twelve EU country reports produced by national teams of experts, for the European Observatory on Older People (Walker *et al.*, 1993). The European Foundation for the Improvement of Living and Working Conditions has published a report on family care of dependent older people in the EU member states, similarly based on information from national reports (Jani-Le Bris, 1993). Drawing on the detailed background material which has been created by these research projects, several British researchers have compiled monographs on various aspects of elder care across Europe (Hugman, 1994; McGlone and Cronin, 1994; Tester, 1996).

An earlier generation of cross-national studies of elder care consists of compilations of country reports, written by national experts. These are complemented by a thematic introduction and/or a subsequent comparative analysis. Thus, the emergence of 'new' health and social care arrangements of older people is portrayed in fourteen country studies, including some East European countries (Evers and Svetlik, 1991). Another study focuses on home care policies and provision for older people in eight countries (Jamieson, 1991b). A number of secondary publications have arisen out of these studies, illustrating particular service developments in various countries (Kraan *et al.*, 1991; Evers *et al.*, 1993) and providing more compact comparisons of three or four countries (Jamieson, 1991a; Baldock and Evers, 1992; Alber, 1995).

Simultaneously, the comparative social policy literature experienced a fast expansion as government departments in several countries commissioned cross-national studies into funding arrangements of long-term care and benefit schemes for care-dependants and carers in the wake of national reforms (see, for example, Evers *et al.*, 1992; Gabanyi *et al.*, 1992; Glendinning and McLaughlin, 1993). These reports – relying on expert informants in each country – document and compare the situation in a number of EU member states and are produced by teams of national researchers, usually working within tight budgets and schedules.

Finally, international organisations such as the International Social Security Association (ISSA) and the OECD have organised expert conferences on elder care (ISSA, 1990; OECD, 1994a). The resulting collections of edited papers consider several aspects of the subject area, mostly drawing on the experience of one country at a time. Some authors have endeavoured to analyse trends across several countries. In addition, the OECD frequently undertakes comparative inquiries into health systems, a policy field with great relevance to the issue of elder care and with a long history of comparative analysis.

Altogether, these studies provide a vivid national picture of elder care policies and provisions, often against the background of dense descriptions of the overall welfare system in its basic principles and institutions. The comparative analysis very often draws closely on the country specific evaluations from the national experts, thereby providing culturally sensitive information, but lacking meaningful meta-standards for comparison.

Moreover, the national approach, which is also very common for studies of social security systems, has severe limitations. All national policies and legislation work through regional and local offices, where discretionary decision-making processes are to be found (Cornwell, 1992). Thus, national and regional or local levels must be matched in order to provide insights into the actual performance of a system, even though some countries rightly claim a higher degree of uniformity of their social security system than others.

The matching process is even more indispensable in the case of elder care, where service provision plays a significant role apart from monetary transfer schemes (Alber, 1995; Anttonen and Sipilä, 1995). Not only does the availability of data vary greatly between and within countries, but also patterns of service provision may critically differ between regions and localities within countries. Overall, empirical knowledge on services and their availability, quality and costs is very limited. Even when national experts have been able to produce data, they are extremely difficult to compare because the classifications and categories used in different countries are closely tied into respective health and welfare structures. Nevertheless, most studies treat any data on service provision levels at its face value and rank countries accordingly.

Despite this array of research, little is known about the relative effects of different levels of service supply on actual welfare outcomes for the individual. Thus, although there is some understanding of different arrangements of care provision and recent policy changes in several countries, implications for the position of the individual frail elder person in relation to health and social care services and benefits have yet to be examined.

A framework for the comparative analysis of elder care

The two-country study described below attempts to do two things: firstly, to chart welfare mix patterns in one locality in each country and, secondly, to construct 'care options' in order to compare and evaluate the responsiveness of care regimes to the needs of frail elders and their carers. In this chapter, it is argued that care options offer a view on availability, access, quality and costs of care provisions from the user perspective, which is by definition a context-bound perspective. National policy provides no more than a context of probabilities for local welfare mixes.

Localities clearly are interconnected with national patterns of provision, regulation and finance of care services embedded in wider institutional arrangements, policy programmes and social welfare cultures. From a comparative perspective, these national patterns can be called 'care regimes' (Chamberlayne, 1993; Ostner, 1994). They differ considerably between Britain and Germany, for example in relation to the role of voluntary sector welfare organisations in shaping the provider mix, the codification of social rights and the mechanisms of resource allocation. The notion of 'care regimes' is used here as a descriptive concept necessary to structure the comparative study of the welfare mix and its effects on elder care. The purpose is not to arrive at an explanation of similarities and differences in care regimes or to analyse origins and objectives of welfare policy-making in the two countries.

In the following sections, the methodological approach used to map welfare mix patterns and to construct care options of frail elders based upon them are outlined. Data collection and analysis are briefly described, and reference is made to some of the difficulties encountered. Finally, overall benefits and drawbacks of the approach are discussed, together with a brief indication of the results and prospects for future research.

Mapping the welfare mix

Care options for individuals are constrained by the particular welfare mix environment of one locality. It is here that entitlements and rights, but also expectations and choices, are transformed into care arrangements. Therefore, care options must be understood in relation to the local welfare mix. Two urban localities were selected for the fieldwork study, representing these 'welfare mixes': Manchester in England and Nürnberg in Germany. Both cities are similar in size and in the proportion of elder population, and they offer a wide spectrum of health and social care provisions for frail elders.

A two-stage design was employed in both cities. The first stage produced a comprehensive overview of welfare mix patterns by constructing a service provision map, charting the range of services, availability, staff levels, access and costs across the local geography. In the second stage, service provider and delivery characteristics were explored, such as position, ethos and organisation of service providers as well as overall co-ordination and planning of services. An analysis of national service developments, provider structures, regulation and funding arrangements complement and contextualise the local case studies.

The data collection used a combination of sources: analysis of primary documents, participant observation and interviews. The document analysis included all available information on services and service providers of elder care, ranging from institutional care to home-care services, from medical provisions to support services for carers. Directories and lists of service providers were one major source, followed by reports and surveys of service levels and usage where available. Statutes and regulations of agencies and service providers, as well as assessment and documentation forms, provided insights into the organisation of services. Strategy documents and records of meetings on elder care planning together with information on budgets and grants were collected to understand the workings of the local welfare mixes.

The availability of material varied considerably between Manchester and Nürnberg. Different data sources serve different purposes in respective national and local administrative contexts. One of the aims of the study was to expose those differences, but they were a factor limiting the scope of the study. For example, whereas lists of institutional homes in Nürnberg included their prices, they were not available in Manchester. Health and welfare organisations within each city varied greatly in the extent to which accurate data on staff were available. It became clear that, unless considerable attention is paid to differences in service structures as well as national and regional characteristics, the cross-national comparability of aggregate data on service output is severely limited and generalisations can be extremely misleading.

Participant observation and semi-structured interviews were carried out to complement and build on the information obtained from written material. These included visits to services of all types of providers, shadowing of front-line staff, observation of assessment procedures and visits to local events and meetings such as road shows and open days. Interviews were conducted with managers of welfare organisations, front-line service staff, public and para-public agency staff and people involved in planning and co-ordinating services. The interviews were semi-structured and included questions on organisational culture, position within the local welfare mix, users' profiles, new developments and current problems.

A sampling frame for interview partners and services to be visited was drawn up for each city, based on knowledge of local structures. It included a minimum of one visit for each type of service covering the full range of services available. Secondly, a minimum of one visit to all types of provider agencies, in cases where the same kind of service was provided by different agencies. In addition to health and social care providers, all public and para-public agencies dealing with claims from frail elders were visited, including all bodies involved in local elder care service planning. The main difficulty was to account for the selection of services and observed activities. For example, it was not possible in Nürnberg to observe assessment situations, because they are regarded as relatively formal events which fall under strict data protection laws. Another example, which applied to both Nürnberg and Manchester, was the reluctance of commercial service providers to share information about users, costs and access routes.

Carrying out the research involved contact with the spectrum of local actors and access to a large amount of information, as indicated above. Strategies had to be developed to maintain a neutral position when information was influenced by local politics (Back and Solomos, 1993). The context of interviews in Manchester was more politicised and included political statements by interviewees, whereas this was not the case in Nürnberg.

Care options

In order to illustrate not only how welfare systems operate but also to study welfare outcomes, the technique of 'model families' has been employed in recent studies on social security (Bradshaw *et al.*, 1993; Eardley *et al.*, 1996). It is also called a 'policy simulation approach' (see Eardley's and Evans' chapters in this volume). The method draws upon effects at the individual/household level, so that 'determinants of the primary distribution and . . . the operation and interaction of taxes and benefits' (Bradshaw *et al.*, 1993, pp. 4–5) can be understood in some detail. Furthermore, circumstances and characteristics of the 'model cases' can be varied and accumulated, so that the interaction between a wide range of variables and variable clusters and the welfare system can be simulated.

The value of the model case approach is that it provides, in a way which no other approach can do, a picture of the range of services potentially available to individuals with particular needs. It thus approximates 'real life' situations in the specificity of a particular locality and at the same time makes them accessible for cross-national comparison. For the application of this method to a comparison of care options of frail elders, a wider framework is required than in previous studies which focused on social security systems.

Three emerging differences were identified. The most obvious is that 'care' cannot be viewed solely from a monetary perspective. Availability and access to services frequently play a much more important role when researching elder care than in the field of social security, or even family policy. Professional judgements about 'need' and appropriate service provision are important in determining access to services. Social assistance benefits may also be contingent upon professional judgements about a certain degree of disability. Different mechanisms of entitlements to cash benefits and benefits in kind must be identified.

Types of care include health as well as social care, but 'non-task aspects of care', such as service culture and acceptability of the service and its providers to the person, must also be taken into consideration. Furthermore, some formal elder care services include support services for carers. Hence, one must look at the divide between 'formal' and 'informal' care. Professionalisation of care-giving is a predominant feature of the formal sphere, whereas the 'informal sphere' ranges, with much differentiation, from family care to grey labour markets (Leira, 1993). Private contracting exists in both the private and public sphere. Monetary exchanges also take place between generations/kin: recent research in Britain has shown, that family care quite frequently includes money transactions (Baldock and Ungerson, 1994).

Thirdly, health and social care needs and individual circumstances change over time and lead to new care arrangements. It is crucial therefore to look at 'pathways' through the welfare mix. Unlike the 'model' studies in the social security area, which conceptualise matrices of fixed characteristics, elder care studies must capture the transitions and key points of decision-making over time.

In this study, care options were operationalised as pathways through a particular welfare mix environment of one locality. The typology of 'model cases' was constructed along the health and social care needs of frail elders. The first case considered an older person who had a stroke and needed rehabilitative treatment. The second case looked at a person with Alzheimer's disease. Progressive stages of severity of impairments were traced. Clearly, these profiles are not representative of all elders with health/social care needs. However, both diseases lead to a wide range of different health and social care needs and exemplify two of the most common chronic diseases of old age (Görres, 1992). Alongside the key illnesses, reference was made to a wider range of medical and social needs, although these conditions did not feature prominently in the model cases. Welfare provisions for dying elders and support services for carers were considered separately.

To exemplify the heterogeneity of individuals with similar medical/social needs, variables were selected to denote the main assumptions under which the two 'model cases' were analysed: these were age, gender, race, wealth/income, education and family type. Within each variable, a small number of scenarios were distinguished, such as the three following for the variable 'family type': no informal carer; informal care for some domestic tasks and advocacy; informal care for all domestic tasks, advocacy and (in the case of spouse care) personal care. In addition, differences in care options are identified according to the area of each city where the person is living.

One difficulty with the method of 'model cases' was in deciding how much detail to include. On the one hand, it is desirable to take account of many social and cultural variations when specifying the impact of the set variables, such as education, or even to take on additional variables which influence the pathways through services in one or both cities; for example, differences in communal attachments or cultural expectations and standards. On the other hand, this inevitably overloads the model cases and factually limits the capacity of the comparison.

The data collection for constructing the model cases very much resembled the strategy for mapping the local welfare mixes. Available documents were collected, including user information about services, assessment forms and criteria for service allocation, as well as formal regulations on user entitlements for benefits and services. Interviews with front-line service staff and administrative staff in public and para-public agencies again provided information on user's entitlements, but this time within the framework of 'street-level' decision-making rules and effective availability and access to services. Of particular relevance were the influence and interest of service providers in organising service packages, common routes of referrals between services and perceived gaps of either entitlements or service provision, or both. Time and resource constraints did not allow interviews to be conducted with elder persons themselves.

The main focus for the subsequent analysis and evaluation of care options and welfare outcome between Manchester and Nürnberg was the extent to which any disabled person of a certain age, health, gender, race, income, education and social network/informal support could use formal care services according to their own choices. The importance of control and decision-making on the part of the care-dependent person has been highlighted by a number of authors in relation to the debate around the disabling notion of 'dependency' (Dalley, 1988; Oliver, 1989).

Reflections on the method

Taking the welfare mix as the starting point of the analysis, it is possible to compare service provision maps of Manchester and Nürnberg in some detail and, instructively, to place them in relation to the national context. Quantifying service levels and provision may perhaps be an obvious thing to do in studying and comparing the mixed economy of care, yet it requires considerable attention to the distinct types of provision, finance and regulatory structures in each country. It is in the nature of social inquiry that all information collected will of necessity remain incomplete.

In comparing the effects of welfare systems for (groups of) frail elders, this research refined and applied the method of constructing model cases to study health and social care. By following pathways of care options of elder stroke patients and elders with psychogeriatric illnesses, characteristics of elder persons and care needs were measured against service usage patterns within particular welfare mixes. These care options can be analysed with regard to the responsiveness of care regimes in providing equality of welfare outcomes for groups of frail elders differing in health status, age, gender, race, socio-economic status and family type.

The argument behind the choice of criteria and the construction of model cases for the comparison of welfare systems is that the individual is the transformer of welfare resources into welfare outcomes. Resources, expectations and competences of the individual, which are crucial for the processes of welfare transformation, are linked to experiences with a particular welfare system embedded in broader cultural settings and social structures. Thus, the analysis of organisational forms of the welfare mix in their effects on individual welfare cannot be separated from a detailed and contextual description of particular welfare systems.

The findings of the study provide some insights into the actual operation of social entitlements within the framework of complex welfare mix patterns and social welfare cultures. If welfare outcomes are to be examined over a wider range of situations, it will be necessary to increase the knowledge of different forms of need satisfiers and requirements of need satisfaction in relation to other social, political and cultural contexts.

8 Biographical Approaches in Comparative Work: the 'Cultures of Care' Project

Prue Chamberlayne and Annette King

In recent decades, European social policy thinking has shifted away from a narrow focus on state provisions and interventions to perspectives of partnership and facilitation within a context of 'welfare mix', and more emphasis on supporting and strengthening informal social infrastructures (Evers and Nowotny, 1987; Rosanvallon, 1988; Abrahamson, 1991). In the words of Maheu (1995, p. 240), the state now 'tends to define its role differently in the management of the social sector'. This has major implications for comparative social policy research, which has thus far been in large part quantitative. One reason for this has been that league tables on social expenditure patterns and inequalities became incorporated into the arsenal of political legitimacy in postwar West European democracies. But charting and understanding the dynamics of the neglected informal sphere and the associated gender and intergenerational relations in different societies demands more use of qualitative methods. While such methods have developed strongly at the national level, especially among feminists and networks analysts, and while there has been considerable theoretical and secondary work on family and gender issues (Björnberg, 1991; Lewis, 1992; Offen, 1992; O'Connor, 1993), very little primary, cross-national, qualitative research has been conducted into the dynamics of the informal sector.

Efforts to democratise welfare through consumer politics, the enhancement of user voice and power, and parallel attention in theoretical work to the exploration of agency as well as structure in welfare, similarly call for new directions in research. Touraine (1992) contrasts the 'individual', who is related to the logic of the economic or political system, with the 'subject', who is an actor with the capacity to 'oppose cultural and political domination, to be involved and to transform his or her own material or social environment'

(Touraine, 1992, p. 65, quoted in Hamel, 1995, p. 245). Understanding 'the subject' and relations between the personal and the social in welfare also requires a turn to qualitative methods, and their development for comparative purposes.

In its task of extending comparative analysis of social policy to the informal sphere and of exploring inter-relations between the personal and the social in caring situations, the Cultures of Care project adopted biographical interpretative methods. The first stage of the project, which is used to illustrate the method, comprised a comparison of caring situations and carer strategies in East and West Germany[1]. This chapter begins by placing the project's method of research within the broader field of narrative methods. This is followed by discussion of the focus, design and management of the study, with examples from the German material.

Biographical methods

Within the rich and diverse field of narrative methods, it is useful to distinguish life-history, discourse analysis and biographical interpretative methods, and to discuss their respective strengths for social policy.

Life-history and reminiscence methods have great value in uncovering hidden histories, both collective and individual, and can be used to great effect for purposes of empowerment and identity. Such methods literally 'give voice' to the dispossessed, and have inspired such projects as Survivors Speak Out, Age Exchange, and the Gloucester Project[2] (Bornat, 1994). In recent years, oral history has been greatly influenced by post-structuralist or discourse analysis. In this approach, the collective structuring of accounts rather than the individual person is the focus of attention, as in the study of 'myth' in everyday life (Tonkin, 1990; Thomson, 1994). Indeed, for post-structuralists 'the author is dead', 'our mouths are filled with the words of others' and the 'self' is a fiction. For Lyotard, 'the paradigm of language has replaced the paradigm of consciousness' (Benhabib, 1990, p. 112).

In contrast to life-history methods which aim to empower and celebrate the individual, discourse methods virtually downplay, even deny, individual human agency as having explanatory power for the analysis of human action. Indeed, such approaches might seem of doubtful use in social policy, since there is no 'reality', there are no 'life events', only fictions, performances, characters. But attention to the text as a collective construct has also stimulated a focus on the role of the interviewer/interpreter, a perspective on biography as auto/biography, and attention to power relations in interview settings. Thus, discourse and conversation analysis has produced valuable insights into power relations in social policy situations, such as interviews between professionals and clients (Bornat and Middleton, 1994). Indeed, ethnographic methods, and discourse and conversation analysis are widely used in medical, mental health and social work research (Kohler Riessman, 1994).

Freeman's *Rewriting the Self* (1993), which draws much on the work of Ricoeur, tries to rescue the self, or at least the 'sense of self', while holding on to post-structuralist insights into the self as narrative fiction. Much memory work also maintains a sense of individual experience and consciousness, even while examining how these are filtered through public memory. Thomson's *Anzac Memories: Living with the Legend* (1994) is a fine example of this. Passerini's renowned work on 'mythobiography' in *Fascism in Popular Memory* (1987), while tracing collective representations in individual accounts also has the purpose of bringing myth to consciousness. However, this kind of narrative work tends to explore specific cultural contexts in particular national settings; there have been few attempts to use such methods comparatively.

In contrast with either life-history or discourse analysis methods, biographical interpretative methods are rooted in German phenomenology and hermeneutics, which foreground meaning and intentionality. Not that the study of meaning necessarily invokes the individual self, given the distinction between phenomenological and structural hermeneutics. For, whereas phenomenological hermeneutics, as in the work of Ricoeur and Gadamer, privileges the interpretation of intentionality of the individual self, structural hermeneutics, as in the work of Levi-Strauss, is concerned with the reading of objective structures in human behaviour, in the manner already discussed in relation to post-structuralism (Erben, 1993). In her account of developments within German qualitative research, Gerhardt (1988) contrasts sociology of language and biographical approaches.

In biographical interpretative methods, however, individual meanings deriving from individual biographies do stand at the centre of analysis. A major advantage of this approach for the Cultures of Care project has been its facility to relate the personal to the social, and to probe unconscious, latent meanings. For, by this means, the study has been able not just to present carers' accounts of their situation, but to make an interpretation of underlying personal meanings and family dynamics. Conscious and unconscious personal meanings and family dynamics bear a double significance, for while they are highly specific to individual caring situations and carer strategies, they are also cultural artefacts, arising from particular social and cultural contexts. An important issue for comparative social policy, and for cross-national training in the social professions, is to define cultural differences at the micro-level, and to evaluate the extent to which such differences result from the welfare systems to which they are linked.

The method is also essentially a Gestalt approach in which the significance of the single event or part of a life can only be understood in relation to the whole, and the whole in relation to parts. In this perspective, biographical narration itself is conceptualised as a process of linking experiences thematically and temporally into a biographically relevant pattern. In the interview narrative, a vast amount of past experience is organised into a selective, meaningful whole, in a structure which has an objective quality outside the subjective intentions of the narrator. Reconstructing the organising patterns or 'rules' which underlie the narration, and placing the individual life and narration into the context of social constraints and options is the task of the analysis. For this reason, the method is also referred to as one of 'case reconstruction'. In contrast to more intuitive methods, this approach attempts to control the procedure of analysis through a formalised process in which each step in the process of interpretation is made explicit.

Despite its psychological insights, case reconstruction remains an essentially sociological exercise. The starting point is that biography stands at the crossroads of the personal and the social, and interpretations of actions and meanings constantly refer to the social context, with which the researchers must have familiarity. In the Cultures of Care project, the interpretation of individual cases involved constant reference to the social contexts of East and West Germany and of particular social milieux. Yet it was at the stage of comparing cases that 'system effects' sprang clearly into view. The term 'system effects' signifies that key structuring elements from the 'public world' ranged beyond the impact of the formal welfare system as such. East German informal social networks, for example, which were a pervasive vehicle for social engagement and mediation, had formed in response to, or as an 'effect of', the system, rather than as intended policy.

Case reconstruction procedures

The individual case reconstruction proceeds by means of the analytic steps suggested by Rosenthal (1993). She has developed this procedure from three sources, all of which have wide currency in West Germany: the narrative interview method of Schütze; the objective hermeneutic textual analysis of Oevermann; and the thematic field analysis of Fischer-Rosenthal (Rosenthal and Bar-On, 1992). There are several steps in the procedure: sequential analysis of the biographical data, or 'lived' life story, where life events are picked out of the text and either re-ordered chronologically or charted in the form of a genogram of family relations; sequential analysis of the textual structure of the first interview, of the 'narrated' life story. This stage examines the temporal and thematic ordering of the account, the modes of discourse, and the patterns of interaction between interviewer and interviewee, and makes detailed analysis of key text segments which are of particular salience to the interpretation of the text.

Each analytical step is conducted in a sequential process of hypothesis building. This is based on the premise of selectivity of social action, which regards any social action as a choice among others. By using the procedure of 'abduction' developed by Sanders Pierce, units of data (a biographical item, a theme in the narration) are investigated for their potential biographical or textual meanings. Progressing sequentially, more global structural hypotheses about the case are formulated, gradually leading to a more overall theory about the person's biographical pattern or the structure of narration. Then, through the systematic comparison of the lived and narrated life stories, and the testing of this theory through detailed analysis of the text passage, the case is reconstructed. Thus, a 'theory' about the case is formulated, which may be tested and developed through other contrasting cases.

The individual case reconstruction explicitly and systematically demonstrates its analytical procedures. However, this does not exhaust the issue of objectivity, to which Oevermann, who coined the term 'objective hermeneutics', lays great claim. He uses the term in two ways. Firstly, the task of the researcher is to be 'objective', retaining analytical distance from the material and considering the potential for different interpretations in the text. By alienating him/herself from any prior knowledge of the particular case in question and openly considering what next action could have been taken by an abstracted possible actor, the significance of the action that has been taken is thrown into relief. This objectivity is maximised by a collaborative group procedure, at the beginning but also at other key junctures in the interpretation. Secondly, objectivity also refers to the 'objective structures of meaning' in social phenomena. For uncovering the 'textuality of the social event' and its latent meanings is to reconstruct the 'structural rules' of meaning which underlie social action. In her version of this method, Rosenthal has been concerned to place more emphasis on self-understanding and self-reflection, whereas Oevermann and his followers, even more than himself, are accused of treating the individual in a socially deterministic manner, emphasising the 'rules' of social interaction which lead to particular and overly rational choices (Denzin, 1989, p. 58; Schneider, 1994, p. 177).

The group of three (or more) interpreters in which the Cultures of Care project to a large extent worked, brought different biographical experiences, and therefore outlook and attitudes, to the case material, which influenced the range of interpretations offered in the analytical process. Group procedures guard against the 'narrowing' of the horizon of potential meanings discovered in the text, but the interpretation is also an interactive process, between the interpreters and the text. Empathy with the research subjects also contributes to the research process itself, whether it be in the development of possible trajectories in a particular case, or in the distilling of key characteristics of the case from a set of structural hypotheses or general theories, or in the making of comparisons between cases. As Freeman argues, life-history inquiry needs attunedness to the 'poetic figuration of life itself' and exercise of the 'hermeneutic imagination' (Freeman, 1993, p. 231). We regard the researchers' subjective engagement as a vital resource in the research process.

Making comparisons

Among those who use biographical interpretative methods, there are two ways of generalising from case studies. Rosenthal's own method is to present one particular case, in its complexity, as a 'type' from which to extrapolate social theory. This has three advantages: it avoids the invocation of grand narratives, retains the individuality of the case while highlighting its key dynamic, and elucidates the process of analysis and interpretation (Rosenthal and Bar-On, 1992; Rosenthal, 1993). A quite different method is to abstract from the cases a 'structural type' or typology, as has been the practice of Schütze (1992). From interviews with men who had been young soldiers in the Nazi period, he identified a 'collective German trajectory', which had three main characteristics: the sublimation of memories through new social energy, a scapegoating of 'them', and a repressive 'we'. He claims that even those not fully committed to Nazism tended to be caught in this dynamic. Likewise Roos (1987), in a study of the new middle class in Finland, developed a three-fold typology of the enduring inner world of bitterness, resentment and submission arising from early relationships with authoritarian, peasant fathers[3].

In the Cultures of Care project, the concern was to find a conceptual framework based on themes emerging from the interviews, which would highlight generational, class and gender differences as well as East-West comparisons. The process brought to bear specialised prior knowledge of the German situation, particular theoretical perspectives, and a particular distillation of key features of caring situations emerging from the case reconstructions, inevitably involving subjectivity. The process developed around a number of key themes, all of which seemed to illuminate inter-relationships between public and private spheres, and the personal and the social in the two societies. These themes were: control in caring situations, mobilising resources inside and outside the home and coming to terms with disability. The next step, working from these themes, was to abstract a matrix of principal features of informal caring in East and West Germany. Key dimensions in the matrix were forms of informal support, relationships with the public world and services, and biographical continuity or change. The clusterings which appeared within this matrix were designated as 'traditional' and 'modern' modes of caring, and highlighted distinct East-West dynamics in caring situations. For, whereas 'system effects' in East Germany propelled the carers in our study out of the home into greater negotiation with the social world, the West German 'subsidiarity culture' pulled carers into the home, possibly into extreme isolation and a situation of impending crisis. Countervailing circumstances, and particularly the 'holding onto' or development of alternative identities and social repertoires, enabled some West German carers to resist or transcend these pressures. This conceptual framework provides a reference point for further comparative analysis of the informal sphere and contributes to debates concerning the modernisation of the private sphere (Balbo, 1987; Born and Krüger, 1993).

Research management issues

Biographical methods are intensive, requiring group working, a relatively lengthy time allowance for the analytical stage, language fluency, and considerable knowledge of the relevant social context. In the case of the Cultures of Care project, lengthy stays and frequent visits allowed familiarisation with local sociological and social policy literature, which became a crucial resource at the analytical and comparative stage.

The project operated with a flexible team structure and a rather special balance of insiderism and outsiderism. The two core team members, who worked together throughout the project, had specialist knowledge of East and West Germany respectively. One was a native of West Germany, the other was British, had graduated in German and was a specialist in East and West German social policy. Each conducted interviews with a range of key informants and welfare officials in one of the cities, located, recruited and trained local interviewers (mainly through academic contacts), conducted some interviews with carers themselves, and supervised the local interviewers in other cases. The transcripts of the interviews were corrected and sequentialised by the interviewers responsible[4]. The local interviewers were also involved in some initial analysis of interview texts at a joint workshop, which was itself an interesting East-West encounter.

The fact that the East German interviews were conducted either by an English researcher with evident knowledge of and interest in the GDR, or by local interviewers for 'a lady in London', but not by West German interviewers, was important in getting the research accepted in the context of 1992–93. The value of the team approach at the interviewing stage, with the range of views which it brought to the study, continued at the stage of analysis and interpretation. Three research staff were involved in this work, and much of the analysis was conducted in open workshops.

The work of comparing and theorising the cases required a conceptual framework which would incorporate and illuminate the themes which had emerged from the case reconstructions. This was provided by locally specific literature, including work on the contradictory relations between public and private spheres in East and West Germany (Chamberlayne, 1994, 1995); supplemented by German debates concerning modernisation, which had been a major sociological theme in West Germany in the 1980s. Indeed, the grounding of much of the wider literature on public/private relations in liberalism meant it could not address social relations in either corporatist or state socialist societies. One issue raised by the project is whether qualitative research of necessity demands knowledge of the local literature. The argument that the exploration of welfare subjects' cultural meanings will best be mediated to outsiders through sociological work of that society, assuming that relevant work exists, is rather persuasive. Whether necessary or fortuitous, however, such a procedure has the advantage of mediating social scientific work of one society to another, and therefore of widening accessibility.

Overall the organisation of this project resembles the 'safari' approach, in which a team undertakes a study in one setting and moves on to another. The research in the East and West German cities was carried out simultaneously, with close co-ordination by the project leader. The subsequent 'move on' to the British study, 'brings back' the new perspectives learned on safari, perhaps generating a fresh view of caring in Britain.

There is no reason to assume that biographical methods necessitate the safari approach, though they would always require intensive co-operation and understanding of cultural meanings. In fact, biographical and life-story methods are used quite extensively in social policy research on the European continent.

Research and policy

A reorientation of social policy to the strengthening of informal social infrastructures, which is given considerable emphasis in EU policy, requires a great expansion of research, probably of a qualitative kind, and equal opportunities policy demands careful attention to gender relations in the private sphere. Comparisons between welfare systems must be extended to include their underlying foundations in informal structures and cultures.

The Cultures of Care project has made an initial substantive and methodological contribution to this broad task. Its biographical interpretative methods demonstrate a research instrument which makes accessible inner, somewhat hidden, dynamics in caring situations, and has the capacity to explore the interaction between personal and social factors in welfare. Its findings have applications for further comparative work on the informal sphere, for policy development and for professional practice.

By highlighting the distinction between socio-structural and personal dynamics in welfare situations, the method points to the need for different types and levels of intervention strategy. It identifies both the barriers to and potential for personal change in different welfare systems and opens a new field of cross-national study which compares the impact of welfare systems on human action. The Cultures of Care project thus offers an example of how qualitative methods can restore the study of human agency to social policy, in cross-national as well as national work, and of how research can be brought closer to policy-making and to the devising of intervention strategies.

Acknowledgements

The Cultures of Care project was funded by the ESRC (R000 3920), 1992–94. The second stage of the project, the comparison with London, was funded by the University of East London.

Notes

1. The terms 'East' and 'West' Germany recognise the two parts of Germany as distinct societies, with 40 years of counterposed welfare systems and social policy values, based respectively on subsidiarity and state socialism. 'East Germany' denotes the GDR regime and the specific conditions of Eastern Germany following unification, and the term 'West Germany' denotes the whole of Germany since 1990.

2. Survivors Speak Out is a self-help movement for survivors of mental health systems; Age Exchange does reminiscence work with groups of elderly people, and with a wide range of groups in institutions; the Gloucester Project (Gearing and Coleman, 1995) pioneered the notion of life-history work by professionals in the assessment of client needs and choices. See also *Oral History*, in particular the special issue on 'Health and Welfare' (1995).

3. For a discussion of theorising from case studies, see Platt (1992). A broad discussion of 'trajectory' as a biographical social process is given in Riemann and Schütze (1991).

4. Sequentialisation involves setting out the structure of the text in terms of the order of themes, the mode of discourse and turn-taking, with a brief notation of content.

Part Three : Accessing Information

Robert Anderson

Work on the front-line to access data that are adequate for international comparisons requires clarity of focus, imagination, perseverance and flexibility, as well as technical skills. The authors of the chapters in this section draw on a wide range of experience to illuminate a variety of strategies and methods. Rainbird gives a broad overview of the process whereby researchers can establish a comparative cross-national study, while the other authors consider more specifically the development of approaches to access attitudes (Soydan), historical processes (Bendikat) and the operation of social security systems (Evans).

The process involves identifying and gaining access to the relevant sources of information – individuals, workplaces, libraries, government departments – in order to collect appropriate data systematically. As illustrated by the chapters, the agreement of 'gatekeepers' to make information available may be enhanced by generating support from 'significant others', such as employers' or workers' representative organisations, politicians or government officials.

Rainbird points out that negotiations for awarding access may need to be nurtured. In some cases, it may be necessary continually to reinforce this concession, for example by routinely reporting on progress. Without substantial investment of time initially to provide assurances about confidentiality, respect for the rights of respondents and security of data storage, the success of such research may be in jeopardy. In cross-national studies, the maintenance of access to specific equivalent cases and situations may be especially critical as the researchers aim to ensure that, in all countries, they are examining similar phenomena. It goes without saying that gatekeepers to information should receive an explanation of the goal of the research and be told specifically why an international comparative dimension is needed.

Evans' study of national social security systems illustrates clearly the alternative approaches to dealing with a societal issue even in countries with rather similar economic and social situations; particular approaches are not inevitable but arise because of cultural traditions, social history and specific forms of organisation or decision-making. It is instructive to learn that systems in another country can operate without features that are viewed as essential in one's own. The systematic revelation of these differences through cross-national research is a means, as Rainbird and others point out, of questioning national assumptions and the framework of policy debates.

As a means of promoting better access to basic data, the European Union has encouraged the establishment of transnational networks of researchers to undertake studies, each in their own country, which puts a premium on the development of team-working. Rainbird emphasises that the key research questions must be worked through and resolved collectively by team members to ensure relevance and functional equivalence in different national contexts. Obviously, in discussing access to information, a common understanding is a pre-requisite for researchers to be able to study the same question. This issue of clearly specifying the research question is perhaps somewhat less explicit in these chapters than the parallel concern about the clarity of concepts and the difficulty of measuring them in the same way in different contexts.

Soydan's chapter is primarily concerned with the question of developing methods to access information from individual respondents, in this case about their attitudes. He points to common problems with the method of self-report about beliefs and attitudes, such as a bias towards socially desirable responses and the concern that interviewees are not able to make certain judgements about their own behaviour or, indeed, that their attitudes are formed only at the time when the question is asked. As a solution, he proposes the 'vignettes' approach, consisting of a concrete detailed description of a hypothetical social situation.

Importantly, the vignettes are intended to approximate situations in which 'real-life decision-making' takes place, and the follow-up questions are designed around these key decisions. This exposes the respondents to the risk of revealing the sort of discrimination which is part of their everyday life but which may be only vaguely articulated in direct questions about attitudes. Soydan's research shows that social workers in different cultural settings found the vignettes meaningful, although their interpretations were quite varied and needed to be integrated in the researcher's typology or theoretical framework. As with other cross-cultural research, data analysis demands cultural sensitivity and knowledge of differences between the contextual circumstances within units of comparison: differences which may reflect national characteristics, but which may also be due to more local factors such as degree of urbanisation or racial diversity. In his analysis of the strengths and weaknesses of the vignette technique in cross-cultural studies, the author makes the important point that such a promising approach merits more systematic assessment of the method.

Drawing upon experience of several multinational research endeavours, Rainbird highlights issues concerning collegial communication and exchange of ideas and information needed to ensure that data refer to the same phenomena, and to generate relevant research questions, as well as a common understanding of the framework for data collection and analysis. She emphasises the requirement for mutual comprehension of the social realities in the different countries together with awareness of the contexts of different policy debates and theoretical perspectives. The effectiveness of this dialogue is evidently not only a question of linguistic skills but of understanding the categories used to describe and analyse institutions in another cultural context. The process of developing a common research agenda will involve clarifying concepts and focusing upon agreed operational definitions. This demands not only time and resources but also flexibility and an openness to negotiation among the research team members.

Each of the papers identifies a number of pre-requisites for accessing information, including the necessity of working with well-defined concepts. In short, a theoretical framework should inform the identification of key dimensions and the specification of the data required. Bendikat underlines the importance of defining precisely the units of research, which in her case are municipalities. She emphasises the vital need to control variance among units of comparison and argues the case for a well-defined, or narrow-gauge, focus as a basis for comparative studies. Differences between units of analysis – for example capital cities fulfilling a similar role in different countries – obviously must be reviewed in the light of the specific patterns of urbanisation in each country and in relation to the different socio-political and institutional contexts.

The complexity of the phenomena and processes under study argues for approaches which draw upon a range of methods, both qualitative and quantitative. In the case of historical analysis, limitations on the availability of source material encourage the adoption of a plurality of methods; but contemporary case studies, too, should enhance the validity of their assessments by employing several methods to address the same issue and to put the results into the relevant context. The researcher in cross-national urban history needs to document the economic, social and political scene and to analyse events and administrative processes in relation to their context; but the researcher may also need to examine the everyday urban experience of social groups and individuals. Bendikat considers some of the practical limitations but also the opportunities to use historical data sources such as periodicals, newspapers, letters, diaries and the minutes of debates.

National data, even when well-defined and measured, may hardly be amenable for use in comparative research. Evans considers data from the social security systems in Britain, France and Germany, and illustrates how their different conceptual histories and current policy frameworks inhibit cross-national comparisons. Even with considerable knowledge of the national systems and understanding of the data, innovative and significant effort was required to develop a model that could reduce the complexity sufficiently for highly aggregated comparative analysis. The author emphasises that even an imaginative and sophisticated methodological strategy to generate comparable data must be complemented by analysis of contextual differences to interpret results.

As all the authors point out, cross-national research amplifies the conceptual and methodological problems of definition, classification, methods and data source experienced in national and comparative research in general.

9 Negotiating a Research Agenda for Comparisons of Vocational Training

Helen Rainbird

Conducting a research project always involves a process of negotiation. In the early stages, obtaining funding may require negotiation and compromise as the researcher's initial idea for a project is adapted to the funding agency's criteria for awarding finance. If more than one researcher participates in the application, then the project may undergo a series of redraftings before it is finally presented as a concrete proposal. As a result of internal or peer review, the funding body may require some changes in the methodology and focus of the project. For field researchers, the question of access involves a process of negotiation with potential interview subjects and gatekeepers, extending to a consideration of both entry and exit strategies, as well as the establishment of an exchange between the researcher and research subjects. This may demand assurances about the accuracy and confidentiality of findings, respect for the anonymity of respondents and the exchanges established in the interview process itself, and various forms of feedback to those who have contributed to the project. The final stage may be the negotiation with publishers or with the editors of journals, who themselves rely on peer review. Conducting and publishing research, then, always involve negotiation and compromise, whether it be in the way that new empirical and theoretical research contributes to the existing body of knowledge and is recognised by subject specialists in the field, or in arriving at the norms of good practice for conducting fieldwork.

In this chapter, the focus is comparative international study and the ways in which researchers can conduct research and access relevant sources of information and expertise. In this instance, the processes of negotiation outlined above are overlain by a series of other issues concerning how different national realities are addressed through research methodology. Although a single researcher conducting comparative study confronts these issues, they are present particularly where different national teams work together. The research methodology has to take account of distinctive national institutions, the articulation of different policy debates and perceptions of significant issues, and the reference points of distinct intellectual traditions. These multiple differences pose particular challenges to researchers. In participant observation, it is common to draw the distinction between insider and outsider accounts of the reality under study. In other words, the tension between the actors' perceptions of their own culture and practices and the observer's supposedly more objective perspective. In cross-national research, there may be any number of equally valid 'outsider accounts' which need to be reconciled through a process of exploration and interpretation. The process can be extremely fruitful in so far as it requires researchers to question what they normally take for granted about their own culture and institutions (Hyman, 1994). Nevertheless, it has to be emphasised that it can be a conflictual process which requires a disposition to seek sometimes unconventional solutions where radically different approaches are proposed.

The field of vocational education and training (VET) is one in which there are a number of impulses for the development of comparative international study. In so far as VET is closely linked in the public policy debate to economic competitiveness and labour market policies to combat unemployment, it is seen as contributing to the success or failure of national economies (see, for example, Commission of the European Communities, 1994b; House of Commons Trade and Industry Committee, 1994). Although it may be conducted in the context of a national policy agenda, a significant tradition of cross-national study has been established, for example through the 'societal approach' developed by the Laboratoire d'Économie et de Sociologie du Travail at Aix-en-Provence (Maurice et al., 1986) and the comparative work on education, training and productivity conducted by the National Institute of Economic and Social Research in London (Prais, 1990). Although adopting different theoretical frameworks, both these groups have conducted research examining the relationship between national VET systems and the deployment of skills in the workplace. Another major impulse for comparative international research in this field derives from the creation of the

Single European Market and the development of European institutions and policy. The European Centre for the Development of Vocational Training (CEDEFOP), established by the decision of the Council of Ministers in 1975, has the task 'of assisting the Commission in order to promote at Community level the development of vocational training and continuing training' (CEDEFOP, 1994, cover page). This body has been responsible for documenting national training systems and commissioning European research in the field of VET. In addition, CEDEFOP has been responsible for conducting a comparison of vocational qualifications in the member states, which is intended to contribute to the Treaty of Rome's objective of the free movement of labour. Finally, in so far as vocational training constitutes an element of the social dialogue between the interest groups of labour and capital at European level (Heidemann *et al.*, 1994), there is also a sense in which this field (and the demand for information about it) is itself contributing to the development of European policy and institutions.

The concept of the negotiation of a research agenda implies, firstly, the involvement of a number of parties with different positions and perspectives. Secondly, it assumes a process of dialogue to develop a common approach to problem-solving as well as agreement on substantive topics. Thirdly, it presupposes the establishment of a means of communication and a common understanding of key issues. In this chapter, the experience of working on a number of different comparative European projects on vocational training will serve as an exemplar[1]. The projects have drawn on a number of methodologies and varying degrees of fieldwork. They range from the participation of five national teams to just a single researcher. In all cases, data were collected from different national contexts, and sources of national expertise were developed and mobilised.

The chapter is divided into four sections: the issues facing individuals carrying out cross-national research; the problems confronting teams working in a cross-national context; and questions concerning the development of a common language and definitions as a precondition for more effective joint work.

Conducting cross-national research on an individual basis

There are many similarities between conducting comparative research on an individual basis and the ethnographic tradition of social anthropology. The main difference lies in the fact that the comparative element has always been implicit in studies of other cultures rather than explicit. Both involve immersion in another culture, although cross-national European research usually takes place in the context of collaborative institutional arrangements rather than an isolated fieldwork situation. It is this institutional context, established through academic networks and exchanges, which contributes to determining the orientation and induction to field research.

Where comparative research is conducted by an individual or a single national team, the research project may be defined independently or by the funding agency in consultation with the researcher. Since one of the realities to be studied may be unfamiliar, institutional links in the country which forms the comparator are important in providing a source of collegiate advice. Although library and bibliographic searches are a valuable tool in conducting any research, colleagues play a major role in providing a guide to the literature and to public policy and academic debates, thereby creating a succinct framework for understanding the key research issues. Colleagues also constitute a guide to the main institutions under study and can contribute to the researchers' understanding and interpretation of the 'other' reality. In this respect, academic peers are both key informants and gatekeepers. There is no direct negotiation in this instance, although colleagues might have strongly held views on how the research should be approached and which organisations should be included in the fieldwork. The researcher will, of course, have views on the significant elements for comparison, based on knowledge of the national context of origin, but it would be foolhardy not to take account of the views and advice of colleagues. In this respect, dialogue between peers contributes to the process of familiarisation with the other reality, the exploration of significant research questions and the key institutional actors in the field.

As with participant observation more generally, the field researcher has to become acquainted with the unfamiliar (Burgess, 1984). In studying any policy field, it is important to be aware that institutions may not be directly replicated from one country to another so, to a certain extent, the principle of functional equivalence becomes significant, even if it is found in surprising forms. An appreciation of the categories of language used to describe and analyse institutions contributes to the understanding of the other cultural context and may even be illuminative of social relationships. The concept of the 'three pillars' of Belgian society is an example of this. Vilrokx and Van Leemput (1992) define the three pillars as institutionalised socio-cultural, economic and political mechanisms for the defence of specific interests. Each ideological pillar provides a comprehensive package of services for its members, and all important societal functions and needs may be met within it. The pillar has three essential characteristics: it forms a framework for socio-cultural, economic and political exchanges; it defines the frontiers of competitive, but not antagonistic, power domains; and it provides formal and informal control mechanisms which regulate exchanges within and between pillars, sustaining the legitimacy and stability of the system. The structure is crossed by three cleavages: between capital and labour, Catholics and non-Catholics, and the Walloon (French-speaking) and Flemish (Dutch-speaking) communities, each with their own institutional arrangements.

(Vilrokx and Van Leemput, 1992, pp. 361–2)

It is therefore no surprise that, in Belgium, the trade unions, along with employers and other voluntary associations, have a major role in training and employment policies.

This contrasts with the situation in Britain, where the field of vocational training and employment policy-making has been characterised as having been transformed from a tripartite to a neo-liberal regime (King, 1993). Here, trade union interests are excluded from authoritative decision-making in both fields, and the Conservative government has delegated policy responsibilities to employer-dominated local institutions in the form of the Training and Enterprise Councils/Local Enterprise Companies. In Belgium, 'les groupes à risques' (groups at risk or those disadvantaged in the labour market, primarily the unemployed) are recognised as a category in collective bargaining, and there is widespread policy concern about unemployment. In contrast, in Britain the Conservative government has succeeded in changing the terms of the policy debate on vocational training and labour market policy to such an extent that, between 1979 and 1988, unemployment as an issue was transformed, even though as a pervasive structural problem little had changed. Moreover, the Trades Union Congress presence on the Manpower Services Commission was dispensed with in 1988 without major opposition (Moore and Richardson, 1989). In this policy domain, it is also important to be aware of *faux amis*. For example, in Britain, 'partnership' refers to public sector/private sector partnerships or education/industry partnerships and is not to be confused with the Belgian notion of partnership, which concerns concerted actions by 'the social actors': trade unions, employers and voluntary associations.

Working in international teams

Where an individual or a single country research team engage in comparative research, much can be gained from consultation with overseas colleagues, even if their role is only advisory. The project may be weakened by a failure to heed advice, but it does not require the researcher to make fundamental changes to the research focus and methodology. This is not the case with team-working, where different teams are actively involved, each with their own perspectives on the research focus and methodology.

The advantages of team-working are enormous: it mobilises sources of expertise and experience and brings fresh perspectives to research problems. However, it can also pose problems of co-ordination and negotiation, as each team brings its own perceptions on the research problem, its concerns with particular national policy debates and academic traditions (both in terms of theoretical debates and methods of conducting research). This is particularly a problem where the objective of the research is to go beyond a description of institutions and to examine how they operate in practice. Each team, therefore, has to attempt to understand the social realities that the other teams are studying and how they locate their concerns within particular theoretical and policy debates. In this context, there may be a direct confrontation between ethnocentric assumptions and the team's need to develop flexible ways of meeting these challenges. A certain amount of intellectual investment is required in exploring preoccupations and developing shared understandings. The experience of working on a project on union policies towards the training of workers with a low level of qualifications, co-ordinated by the Institut de Recherches Économiques et Sociales (IRES), Paris, illustrates some of these points[2].

The project was financed by the French Ministère de la Recherche and developed a policy concern about workers with a low level of qualification, who were seen as being particularly vulnerable to unemployment. The objective was to investigate the role of trade unions in this policy area. It is important to point out that, because the focus of the research derived from the French national policy debate, a definitional problem existed from the outset. 'Les bas niveaux de qualification' is not a statistical category which can be readily transferred from one country to another. In fact, each national team defined the research problem differently: the Belgians translated the term as 'les groupes à risques' (as mentioned above); the Italians interpreted it as the problem of implementing the 1993 agreement on vocational training between the Confindustria and the union confederations, although they also stressed the regional dimension of low levels of educational attainment in the south of Italy. The British contribution focused on the restricted scope for trade unions to influence policy in a deregulated training system and labour market, in a country with a relatively high proportion of workers possessing a low level of qualification. In contrast, the German contribution identified the problem of skilled workers employed as unskilled production workers on assembly lines. These different definitions derived in part from the lack of clarity in the category to be addressed, but also reflected different national contexts and concerns. However, a more fundamental definitional problem was at stake: was the project concerned with workers with a low level of qualification (relating to the characteristics of individual workers) or unskilled workers whose structural position in the organisation of production meant that they were particularly disadvantaged? Although the two are clearly linked (and in some countries the link is more apparent through the formal role of qualifications in determining wage rates), it was agreed that it was, in fact, the structural characteristics which were of interest. In other words, the category in question was that of unskilled workers rather than workers with a low level of qualification, although the two overlap. Despite the apparent difficulties outlined at this stage in the project, the presentation of the different national contexts was important in establishing an understanding of different national realities among the teams and, thus, constituted a basis for developing a common methodology.

The first phase of the project raised definitional problems in the focus of the research; the fieldwork phase involved specifying the actors and levels at which interviews should be conducted. Although the objective was to examine union policies towards workers vulnerable to unemployment, the term 'union' covers many different realities: its principles of organisation; the degree of centralisation; the level, depth and extension of negotiation; its representative status (whether recognised in law); and the extent to which the unemployed retain their membership. Moreover, unions are represented on training and labour market institutions and at different levels in each country (national, sectoral, regional and at the workplace), which may involve co-determination, consultation or information only. Since the emphasis was on practice, it seemed logical to choose the workplace as the primary site for fieldwork and then to permit each team to trace back the higher levels of representation which were significant in influencing workplace practices. This meant each team could take account of the levels that were perceived as important in each country, while allowing the workplace level to serve as a point of reference. Even so, this high degree of autonomy was not without its problems; for example, several countries have separate systems of employee and trade union representation, and questions of comparability are not resolved.

Similar issues arise where questionnaire methods are proposed. In a feasibility study for a survey of collective bargaining on continuing vocational training[3], similar definitional problems arose both in terms of research focus and the questions of the level at which interviews should be conducted. The initial proposal by the Italian co-ordinators, CESOS, was for a survey based on collective agreements, which, in Italy, may run for hundreds of pages. Whereas Italy may have collective agreements on training at many different levels, in Germany co-determination at enterprise level is not subject to formal agreement but is part of social dialogue on a day-to-day basis. In France, the works council is formally consulted on the company training plan, and it has a duty to negotiate at company and sectoral level (though there is no requirement to negotiate in good faith and to reach agreement). In Britain, it is rare to find agreements on training *per se*, though training may be discussed by committees whose primary purpose is not training. Some companies, for example Rover, may have a training committee but no formal, written agreement on its constitution and remit. In this context, a survey of written agreements was not feasible. Given the range of national institutional systems, it was impossible to develop a single survey instrument, but instead one which could be adapted to different legal and collective bargaining systems. For example, it makes no sense to ask about the legal requirements for training and consultation, if they are the same for all companies in one country. Similarly, there is no point in asking questions about levels of bargaining which do not exist. Questions also arise concerning whether the appropriate level for such a questionnaire is the company or the establishment (which will vary according to organisational structures and competences as well as the predominance of particular types of company in each national economy), and who should be asked to complete the questionnaire, given the fact that managers and union representatives will have different perceptions of the significance of agreements and training practices.

The two experiences examined in this section indicate some of the problems that have to be confronted in this policy field by teams attempting to conduct cross-national research. In seeking to develop a joint approach, it is necessary to invest time and intellectual effort in establishing common understandings of the different elements which are significant in each country. What may appear as an eccentric demand on the research agenda of one team may be quite valid, but equally it has to be incorporated into a framework which is appropriate for all the parties. In this respect, it may be useful to distinguish between the substance of what is under negotiation, and the ways in which national teams, working together, find mechanisms for reaching agreement.

Developing a common language for conducting cross-national research

As these examples show, for researchers to conduct cross-national research, a common language needs to be developed for describing institutional systems. The work conducted by CEDEFOP on vocational training systems provides a basis for understanding institutional frameworks in Europe. In the field of industrial relations, a number of textbooks have been published on Europe (for example, Baglioni and Crouch, 1990; Ferner and Hyman, 1992; Crouch, 1993; Hyman and Ferner, 1994), and the European glossaries of industrial relations, published by the European Foundation for the Improvement of Living and Working Conditions (Dublin Foundation), explain terms in their institutional context and, thus, serve as a useful reference. However, there are additional problems affecting communication between social scientists which relate to their understanding of the conceptual language of different societal and intellectual traditions. For example, in the field of vocational training, terms such as 'skill', 'qualification' and 'apprenticeship' derive from distinctive historical traditions and do not necessarily have equivalence from one country to another. Social scientists also work in the context of different national traditions: here a project to map the main currents of research in the field of education and work in Britain, Germany and Italy has had the objective of promoting communication between researchers at European level (Jobert *et al.*, 1995).

Beyond the development of these aids to communication, researchers must also seek innovative solutions to communication problems among themselves. The 'crossed interview technique' developed by Dufour and Hege (1993) involves researchers from multinational teams participating in fieldwork interviews in a number of the countries studied. It requires a high level of linguistic competence on the part of the researchers and provides individuals with the direct experience of the comparators in the study. Not only does it contribute to the establishment of a common understanding of the range of institutional variations and team building, but it is also a fruitful mechanism for raising new research questions. However, these types of solutions are expensive as, indeed, is any research contemplated on a European level. It is worth emphasising that most funding which is available is for co-ordination and pump-priming rather than for primary research.

Advantages and disadvantages of team-working

This chapter has drawn on the experience of a number of cross-national research projects in the field of vocational education and training. Given the range and complexity of different institutional systems as well as theoretical and policy debates, the field poses many challenges for cross-national research. It is important that particular methods of formulating research questions, derived from one national source, or from a dominant model, are not imposed on the research agenda. Therefore, it has been argued that cross-national research must be viewed as a negotiating process if the research agenda is to be appropriate to the different national realities and capable of developing a meaningful synthesis. This involves working towards a common understanding and the disposition to seek innovative solutions for resolving different perspectives. Team-working is a productive way of mobilising national resources and expertise, but it is more challenging and potentially more conflictual than situations where a single team or one researcher works on a cross-national study. Given the resourcing issues surrounding cross-national comparison, it is clear that team-working is likely to emerge as the predominant method for cross-national research. As a consequence, there is some urgency for social scientists to create frameworks for communication among themselves, to broaden their perceptions of their research agenda and to prepare to negotiate with their colleagues.

Notes

1. The project on union policies towards the training of workers with a low level of qualification was co-ordinated by the Institut de Recherches Économiques et Sociales (IRES), Paris, and was funded initially by the French Ministère de la Recherche. It involved five national teams: French, Belgian, British, German and Italian. The fieldwork phase was financed by the European Union's Poverty 3 Programme. The project comparing employment regeneration and training programmes in the Birmingham and Brussels regions was financed by the Région Bruxelloise and was conducted by the author, with the institutional support of the Centre d'Économie et de Sociologie Régionales, at the Institut de Sociologie, Université Libre de Bruxelles.

2. See *La Revue de l'IRES*, 1993, no. 13, Autumn, for the national contributions to this project.

3. The project examining collective bargaining on continuing training was co-ordinated by the Centro di Studi Economici e Sociali (CESOS) in Rome. It involved British, French, German and Italian researchers and was funded by the European Union's FORCE programme.

10 Using the Vignette Method in Cross-Cultural Comparisons

Haluk Soydan

This chapter presents a cross-cultural study of the delivery of personal social services in the United Kingdom and Sweden. The aim is to discuss some of the main problems which arise in using the vignette technique in cross-cultural comparative social work research. Although the technique is often exploited in the United Kingdom and in other English-speaking countries, it is not well known in Scandinavian social research, and it has rarely been employed in cross-cultural comparative social research.

The chapter begins with a discussion of some of the main premises underlying the use of the technique in cross-cultural comparative studies. Then follows an example of the vignettes applied in the research. Finally, outcomes are examined in terms of the value of applying the technique in data collection and analysis.

The vignette technique and cross-cultural comparison

One of the classic problems in cross-cultural comparative social science is the incommensurability of concepts. Osgood, father of the semantic differential, raised the questions: 'When is the same really the same? When is the same really different? When is different really the same? When is different really different?' (Osgood *et al.*, 1957). His rationale was that social reality has a specific meaning and relevance for the human beings who are members of the same social reality. Ontological questions with related methodological implications have been raised by many classical social scientists, including Weber and Schutz.

What is meant by 'the same reality'? A basic assumption in our study is that we are living in a globalised world where actual experiences, lifestyles and social circumstances are becoming more alike, while, even if they remain different, the knowledge of foreign experiences and lifestyles are becoming more accessible. We live in a world of cultural complexity, constituted by cultural flows within and between 'small-scale societies' and global meaning systems, or 'contemporary worlds of meaning', as Hannerz (1992, p. 43) puts it. Hannerz emphasises four major frameworks for a comprehensive understanding of contemporary cultural flows: lifestyle, market, state and movements in culture (organisations for the transformation of meaning). They all contribute to the globalisation of meaning systems. Globalisation of the social world has important implications for comparative research models: similarities between units of comparison become more accentuated, and increasing similarities between these units of comparison makes the search for 'uniqueness among uniformities' (Sztompka, 1990, p. 53) more interesting in comparative studies.

The traditional techniques of survey research in the social sciences mainly involve questionnaires and interviews. They are used for the study of human attitudes and behaviour in various social settings. Access to different forms of social action is variable. Some attitudes and behavioural patterns are less accessible and less assessable than others. The main concern of the researcher who is trying to measure interpersonal attitudes, judgements, beliefs and feelings is to avoid influencing the objects of the study in the process of describing them. Traditional techniques are mainly based on self-reports and are subject to bias due to social desirability, reactive arrangements, the Hawthorne effect, demand characteristics, and the possibility that interviewees are not able to make certain judgements concerning their own behaviour when they are approached directly (Burstin *et al.*, 1980, p. 148).

A number of methodological approaches can be used to alleviate some of the problems; among them is the 'vignette' technique. Vignettes are 'short stories about hypothetical characters in specified circumstances, to whose situation the interviewee is invited to respond' (Finch, 1987, p. 105). For Alexander and Becker (1978, p. 94), 'vignettes are short descriptions of a person or a social situation which contain precise references to what are thought to be the most important factors in the decision-making or judgement-making processes of respondents'.

Vignettes consist of stimuli that are interpreted as concrete and detailed descriptions of social situations and circumstances. Vignettes present real-life contexts which give the respondents a feeling that meanings are social and situational. They are, therefore, less likely to express beliefs and values in abstract contexts than traditional techniques. Accordingly, their capacity to approximate real-life decision-making situations is extensive. Since the stimulus is held constant over a heterogeneous group of respondents, the research instrument secures uniformity which is a prerequisite for its reliability. In the context of labour relations, Alexander and Becker (1978) summarise the main advantages of the technique as follows:

> First, the respondent is not as likely to consciously bias his report in the direction of impression-management (social approval of the interviewer) as he is when being asked directly about how he would handle two different types of employees. Secondly, most people are not particularly insightful about the factors that enter their own judgment-making process. This is especially true for factors that are highly correlated in the real world, such as, employee's age and length of service. Finally, the systematic variation of characteristics in the vignette allows for a rather precise estimate of the effects of changes in *combinations* of variables as well as individual variables on corresponding changes in respondent attitude or judgment.
>
> (Alexander and Becker, 1978, p. 95)

The advantages and disadvantages of different structures are discussed in the literature, in terms of the number of vignettes, the key variables incorporated and the prompts and follow-up questions (Alexander and Becker, 1978; Burstin *et al.*, 1980; Stillion *et al.*, 1984; Thompson and West, 1984; Finch, 1987).

So far, the experience of using vignette technique in social research emanates from single-culture studies. The work described in this chapter involved applying the technique across two cultures, with a view to comparing social aspects of different cultural settings.

A case study of the vignette technique

In our comparative study of personal social services in Sweden and the United Kingdom, the aim was to examine the different options social workers choose when they are looking for material to help them understand the client's real social situation.

The research is based on the assumption that the nature of the welfare system plays a decisive part in determining the orientation, scope and character of daily social work practice. Legislation, organisational structure and education are three central elements which together create what might be called the culture or the symbolic environment within which social work is practised. This culture shapes the values, attitudes, thinking and working methods of 'street-level' social workers.

In order to discover as much as possible about the different structures of social work and its various contents, cases were constructed that would encourage a comprehensive and fruitful discussion while leaving room for a number of options and choices.

The vignettes used in this research embrace fictional but plausible stories. They describe a social problem that social workers will recognise and can identify in their daily work. They are constructed in such a way that they progress over time. The vignette is presented in three stages, as shown in Table 10.1, each stage involving a complex array of factors, but providing a wealth of information. The presentation of each stage is followed up by a number of questions that probe the respondent's understanding of the vignette's content. The vignette is based on the theme of child abuse. Alcoholism and drug abuse were introduced as additional themes.

The vignettes were filled in by social workers in the child and family care sector. Social workers were visited either at their offices or

---

Table 10.1 Sample social work vignette

Stage 1
The district nurse calls the social service agency to tell them about Eric Andersen. S/he has been told by a patient there is a small boy in the locality, aged about four, whose parents seemingly fail to look after him properly. Eric is allowed to be out late in the evenings. Sometimes his parents seem to leave him alone at home when they go shopping. The parents are a young couple, just over 20.

Stage 2
Some months later the agency receives a call about the same family. A neighbour of Mr and Mrs Andersen has called the manager of the agency saying that she often hears a small boy screaming in one of the houses. The other day she saw the father hit the boy hard. The boy had broken a window when he was playing football with some older boys. The father got very upset, shouted and hit the boy. It was not the first time she was the witness of the father being hard on the boy.

Stage 3
Six months later, the health officer found several bruises on the boy's back and some burn marks on his cheek and arm on the last visit. The parents say he often falls over and bruises himself because he is a very active boy. He got the burn marks colliding with a cigarette.

When the health officer visited, s/he found that Eric had lost weight over the past six months. The mother said that the boy had a poor appetite and often had infections.

---

invited to central offices in groups of five to ten and were asked to complete the vignettes.

The social worker was asked to address questions such as: 'What is your reaction? What kind of additional information do you need?' and 'What are you going to do now?'. Other questions were raised about the professional background of the respondents. Individual variables such as age and gender were also recorded.

Different types of analytical procedures were used in this project. One approach using qualitative analysis is demonstrated in Soydan (1995). The empirical data are examined to discover meaningful patterns by comparing assessments and decisions of social workers in the respective countries. The empirical material is analysed by applying a number of theoretical concepts.

The vignette presenting the child abuse case was analysed using a quantitative research model. Background variables such as age and gender were taken into account as well as the respondents' assessment of the social status of social work as a profession. The social workers' reactions were also recorded in follow-up questions.

The analysis shows clear differences between English and Swedish social workers in handling an identical case. One palpable difference is that the majority of the Swedish respondents perceived the case as a problem at a very early stage of the vignette. Furthermore, Swedish social workers accepted the information as reliable in the early phase of the vignette, while English social workers were less willing to take the story at face value. Swedish social workers focused on the family as the principal client, while English social workers focused on the boy. The Swedish social workers were more likely to take the boy into custody. The statistical analysis (using SPSS) could not confirm that the differences between the Swedish and English social workers' assessments and decisions could be explained in terms of social workers' age, gender and professional experience.

The vignettes covered three different themes with some variations in the content of the case. For instance, the vignette used as an example in this chapter was presented in two versions: the first version was about indigenous Swedish and British families, while a second version referred to an immigrant family, the Habibs, in the respective countries. Thus, in this specific case we have the possibility of comparing social work practice in two different cultural settings with reference to the same case but with different ethnic/cultural family backgrounds[1].

The value of the vignette technique

A number of conclusions can be drawn from the research, and they are summarised here (reported in detail in Soydan and Stål, 1994; Soydan, 1995).

Cross-cultural comparability

A basic problem to resolve in this type of a research is the question of incommensurability. Correctly constructed vignettes can handle the problem successfully, at least in societal settings with some common denominators. The vignettes must be representative of the phenomena they intend to describe, and they must be realistic. This is important if the risk of misunderstanding the case is to be avoided. It is worth preparing the vignette carefully. Since vignettes are concrete, living and often compelling stories, they develop a special character. They are a good instrument for identifying and describing trans-societal meanings. The content of vignettes are seen by the respondents as concrete and representative of meaning systems in a particular country. In general, social workers found them meaningful.

Soydan (1995) has generated a typology utilising empirical data to reveal two distinct variables: social workers' cultural sensitivity and their concern about the reliability of information presented. By focusing on the interaction between these two variables, specific types of social workers' attitudes were identified. A set of concepts were developed to characterise attitudes. The concepts that refer to social workers' attitudes towards clients are ethnocentric, culturally relativistic, bureaucratic minded and client oriented. The data demonstrated that social workers in different countries may make different assessments when they are confronted with information about an immigrant family. Social workers in Leicester immediately thought that the information might be false or malicious simply because the family were immigrants, while the Örebro respondents considered the information to be accurate. The data are interpreted in terms of ethnocentric, bureaucratically minded social workers in Örebro, and culturally relativistic, client-oriented social workers in Leicester. This study is an example of how the vignette method generates cross-national data that are comparable and permit a fruitful exchange between empirical findings and theoretical assessments. Different national (cultural) settings can, thus, be assessed and compared in terms of the chosen unit of study.

Comprehensiveness and flexibility

The vignette technique may be used as an instrument in quantitative as well as qualitative research. In the research project described here, the vignettes integrated qualitative and quantitative elements. Some of the questions were formulated in such a way that quantification and processing by statistical programmes were possible.

Reliability

Qualitative research methods are often criticised for their unreliability. This certainly pertains when compared to quantitative research methods, even if some of the criticism can be countered by paradigmatic arguments (Denzin and Lincoln, 1994, pp. 10–11; Gibbon and Lincoln, 1994). The low degree of reliability in qualitative research is due, it is argued, to the low degree of standardisation of questions. The vignette method used in this study achieved an adequate degree of reliability as the vignette stories are not only concrete, vivid and focused but also standardised. However, further studies are needed to establish the general reliability of the method.

Timescale

A considerable problem in using the technique is the time required to respond to the vignettes. This depends on a number of factors, such as the setting where the vignette forms are completed and the time that respondents took to answer all questions. The amount of time spent by most of the respondents filling in the vignette forms varies. In the study reported here, about an hour was needed to respond to one vignette; more than two vignettes creates pressure on respondents. Most respondents managed two hours' work with vignettes.

Data collection

The research project demonstrated that data collection through vignettes has to be administered personally by the research staff. This means that the respondents must be invited to a data collection session during which the research project can be presented; instructions must be given on how to handle the vignettes, and on how to distribute and collect them.

Richness of the data

The vignette technique easily generates a tremendous amount of data with relative ease. Since the vignettes are constructed in a progressive and developing manner, the intrinsic dynamism of the story stimulates the respondents to be reflexive, analytic and expressive. Each vignette yields vivid responses. However, precautions are needed to control the proliferation of data when using the vignette technique.

Evaluation

Cross-cultural social work research gives rise to a number of problems of data collection and interpretation, including the traditional problem of incommensurability of concepts. The basic premise that the social world is becoming more and more globalised leads researchers to seek uniqueness amidst uniformity. In such a context, the vignette technique is an adequate instrument of data collection for the purpose of comparing the delivery of personal social services. It avoids some of the shortcomings of other data collection methods and offers tangible scenarios to which all the respondents can be exposed. Analysis of vignette data demonstrates the usefulness of structuring the data in terms of a model which reveals both uniformity and uniqueness in the social units compared.

In sum, since the vignettes present hypothetical but concrete and realistic descriptions of real life situations that are recognised and can be assessed by respondents of different cultures, the research instrument can be applied cross-culturally. Since vignettes can describe situations that develop over a period of time, social processes can be monitored from a cross-cultural comparative perspective. A particular strength of the method in this context is that processes can be studied in both qualitative and quantitative terms. The vignettes can be constructed in such a way that not only attitudes, norms, and assessments, but also the actions of the respondents are documented and can be analysed with reference to their cultural settings. This endeavour requires the co-operation of national research teams with cross-cultural understanding and administrative capacity. Interpretation of data demands cultural sensitivity and a sound knowledge of national circumstances and literature.

Acknowledgements

The research project was funded by the Swedish Council for Social Research and was conducted by Rolf Stål and the author; Elinor Brunnberg worked as research assistant. The British data were collected with the assistance of the Centre for Research in Social Policy, Loughborough University, and Leicestershire Social Services.

Note

1. In total, 247 vignettes were collected, 165 in Örebro, Sweden and 82 in the United Kingdom (73 in Leicester, and 9 in the rural areas of Bangor, Wales).

11 Qualitative Historical Research on Municipal Policies

Elfi Bendikat

The marked increase in research on cities in various academic disciplines since the 1960s can be explained by the growth in urban problems and by the acceptance of urbanisation as one of the most important processes in the development of modern society since the mid-nineteenth century. A connection can also be made between the stage of urbanisation and the development of urban research as a discipline (Engeli and Matzerath, 1989).

Refining the focus of study

This expanding productivity does not apply to cross-national urban historical research. On the contrary, examination of the international bibliography on urban studies for the nineteenth and twentieth century in the periodical *Informationen zur Modernen Stadtgeschichte* reveals three trends in cross-national urban historical research: an extremely small number of such studies compared with an increase in social history (Saldern, 1991; Matthes, 1992; Kaelbe, 1993); a concentration on West European and transatlantic metropoles and capitals; and, in the field of urban problems, a focus on infrastructure, architecture and urban planning. In sum, there is a general deficit in cross-national urban historical research, as well as a reduced spatial focus and urban problematic. Yet, the state of research runs counter to the increase in city-partnerships and European as well as international organisations requiring comparative approaches in order to strengthen international understanding and co-operation. How can this backlog be explained? A well-considered answer to this question requires specialised research which has yet to be undertaken. Nevertheless, some hypotheses can be suggested.

Only at first sight does the city as a politico-socio-geographical entity seem to offer more relative homogeneity than a nation or any other area, particularly in the case of the agglomerations which were developing in Western Europe by the end of the nineteenth century. Modern megalopoles like Randstad in the Netherlands or the Ruhr area in Germany give rise to problems of definition because of their high complexity: the geographical unit of research needs to be very precisely defined.

The focus on metropoles and capitals in Western Europe and the United States highlights three conceptual issues. Firstly, capitals have traditionally been studied from a national perspective, that is as part of national history and as municipalities whose self-government was restricted by national legislation. Paris and Berlin serve as examples. Capitals have never lost their strong national bias, and the concentration of research on them indicates that this approach is still influenced by the concept of the nation, which in the 1960s served as an impetus for cross-national research in the social sciences.

Seemingly, the metropoles and capitals display similarities in their classification. They have common comparative parameters such as their political and cultural symbolic role. Metropoles are agencies and prototypes of 'modernity' at national and international level. Being multifunctional centres, they are targets of admiration and criticism from the so-called 'province'. In the case of Paris and Berlin, the result was strong curbs on self-government. Metropoles have to cope with a wide range of social problems forcing their municipal governments to search for rational solutions for intervention. Similar parameters can be deduced from their particular demographic growth and geographical expansion, which transform them into large urban systems, in some cases reaching the status of city-states. Common parameters are also found in similar urban infrastructural problems, indicating the strong attraction of similarities as a basis for comparative studies.

A third explanation for the deficits in cross-national urban historical research derives from the specificity of the approach, which is not a comparison between nations or national aggregates but a comparison of one urban phenomenon in at least two socio-political contexts with distinct and separate institutions. Differences should not, therefore, be defined as predetermined by national systems. Such an approach requires knowledge of the specific development of urbanisation at national level, a sensitivity to different cultural impacts and a readiness to accept that familiar concepts might be inappropriate and that unexpected results may be obtained (Matthes, 1992). In contrast to narrative history, a readiness to deal with complex issues in a reflective, conceptual and methodological way is fundamental. Consequently, the cross-national perspective increases the conceptual and methodological problems already experienced in comparative research in general.

Methodological approaches

With regard to research strategies, modern comparative analysis has been able to take advantage of a large increase in the quantity and quality of data, the development of innumerable research techniques and the proliferation of many new interpretative models and theories. However, the methodological issues facing contemporary analysts still cluster around three methods: the quantitative, the qualitative and a mixed approach. This means that the methodological issues have changed much less than data and theories. Quantitative analysis has mainly been used by social scientists. Its strength lies in the ability to aggregate information on a large number of different units for macro-studies. Its weakness arises from the fact that many research objectives can only be managed in a limited way at best. These limitations principally derive from the failure to locate information within its context and from correlations which remain unexplained if they cannot be linked to an empirical basis and interpreted in a qualitative way.

In contrast to quantitative empirical macro-studies, qualitative research often produces unexpected results. It offers the advantage of correlating theoretical assumptions and empirical material in a tighter way than can be done when using standardised statistical methods. A further strength lies in its contribution to the description of social dimensions of urban life, for which statistical methods are no substitute. Quantitative methods often reduce the complexity of the empirical field of research and unravel complex structures. In order to make valid inferences, however, this approach has to be more open to methodological challenges than it has been traditionally. The qualitative method uses *verbatim* sources in a heuristic way and is more context oriented. The mixed approach is more pluralistic and fragmented, but it combines the advantages and disadvantages of both methodological approaches while restricting the number of research units.

The American social scientists, King *et al.* (1994, p. 229) aroused considerable controversy by arguing in a positivist way that, both in principle and in practice, the same problems of inference exist in quantitative and qualitative research. They reached this conclusion by considering the qualitative approach as an importer of quantitative methods. But after having processed the data, qualitative researchers interpret the information in their own way: assessment of the two methods should, therefore, be kept separate. Historians often approve of a plurality of methods, and this may not be a weakness. It might rather prove to be a strength in terms of operationalisation. Moreover, this form of flexibility stems from the fact that historians are bound to their sources.

Regardless of the choice of strategies, when using the comparative method researchers encounter problems of comparability (Lijphart, 1971; Ragin, 1987; Collier, 1991). The classification of the urban unit reduces the variation of inherent phenomena and converts the operative variables into parametric constants. Since urban units often have several characteristics, classification is always an act of selection and reduction which reflects the theoretical preferences of the analyst. The problem of comparability also arises in connection with the need for a systematic collection of the same information across research units.

The issue of comparability involves the choice between similar and dissimilar units. Since urban units are seldom subject to the same level of development, diachronic comparisons will be the rule rather than the exception. The qualitative approach also confronts the researcher with the problem of the numbers of units to be compared. From the perspective of a context-orientated historian and from that of a qualitative comparative researcher, numbers should be kept small. The strength of a limited number of cases lies in the control over the frame of comparison. Thus, the strategy of advancing by pairs is attractive. The problem of reduction also applies to the choice of the common urban problem to be analysed. Studies of public transport or water supply might serve as an example. Moreover, one of the advantages of the in-depth case study method is that, given the dearth of contextual information on many cities, it provides a large amount of information and description. A reduced frame of reference is also indicated by pragmatic considerations, as required by the research project.

Research sources

In the past, urban research concentrated on five subjects: administration, technical infrastructure, socio-political processes, economic and geographic factors. This can be explained by the existence of a number of relevant sources of a multifunctional quality. For research on administration and social politics, in particular, municipal reports are available, as well as administrative correspondence, publications for jubilees, memoirs, surveys by various organisations and biographies of mayors or politicians who have entered national politics. As a rule, the central municipal archives of big cities are well organised and, through publication of handbooks, sources for research are easily accessible (see, for example, Landesarchiv Berlin und Arbeitsgemeinschaft Berliner Archivare, 1992; Wetzel, 1992). Yet, research on capitals has to include national archives which stock correspondence with ministerial agencies as well as district collections.

A further rich source are periodicals. Until the era of national socialism, Germany offered a vast range of periodicals on municipal subjects such as housing, technical infrastructure, education, public health and administration. For example, the *Handwörterbuch der Kommunalwissenschaften*, published in 1924, listed 54 periodicals on municipal subjects (although incomplete). The same applies to France and Britain where periodicals on municipal subjects have also flourished since the beginning of the century. This evidences a strong need for information at all professional levels, and especially by municipal officials. The growth of big cities, as well as the process of bureaucratisation, induced the municipalities to adopt administrative standards already practised at state level. In order to reach these standards, the officials had to subject themselves to a lengthy phase of instruction. Although a number of cities founded technical schools for officials at the turn of the century, further education by individual instruction remained a priority. In the case of research undertaken on the role of interest groups in local politics, the contemporary periodicals and pamphlets recount how they contribute to the shaping of local politics by setting up a catalogue of demands for reform. Due to the priority of housing in local politics, related publications by interest groups are abundant in the case of Western metropoles. Access to this category of sources may be easier where materials are centralised as in the French Bibliothèque Nationale in Paris, which stocks most local French periodicals, whereas in Germany the researcher will have to cope with the problem of regional dispersion.

A source, which has been under-rated with respect to its complex information on urban matters, is newspapers. The capitals, as a rule, have not only been their place of origin and expansion – such as London after the abolition of censorship in 1695 – urban metropolitanism also shapes the character of the press. New York, London, Paris or Berlin offer a considerable variety of high quality papers which intercommunicate in their reports and commentaries.

Moreover, they have a large local news section providing vital contextual information. While London, with respect to quality papers such as *The Daily Chronicle, The Standard* and *The Times,* and Paris with *Le Figaro, L'Humanité, Le Monde, Le Rappel* and *Le Temps* have offered a politically highly differentiated press landscape and display a strong continuity of names, Berlin, due to its political history, offers less variety of conservative press as well as strong discontinuities of publication. Until the National-Socialist era, liberal papers like *Berliner Tageblatt* and *Vossische Zeitung* and the socialist paper *Sozialdemokrat* were highly informative about diverse aspects of urban life. Whereas the liberals displayed considerable interest in technical infrastructure, the socialists concentrated on housing, public health and education. Supplements on urban issues have existed in Berlin since the beginning of this century. After press reorganisation in the aftermath of the Second World War, *Der Tagesspiegel* and *Berliner Morgenpost* survived as leading newspapers in West Berlin. In Paris, the press landscape remained highly monopolised by quality papers of national reputation. On the other hand, due to their district administration, London and Berlin offer, in addition, a number of district newspapers which were, however, often ephemeral. As a matter of course, the information given by this source should not be taken unproblematically as reality, since newspapers are agencies of interpretation. In the case of urban news, the researcher has to consider that the local section often serves as the training ground for young journalists. As a consequence, the articles offer more information than commentary.

Studies of everyday urban life – the agency element in history, or the experience of actors and the question of collective memory – are not so readily accessible. By the end of the 1960s, American historians and social scientists put research on everyday experiences, using quantitative methods and social scientific concepts, on the agenda of the so-called 'New Urban History' (Dyos, 1976). The theoretical response in Britain, France and Germany was positive since it allowed a shift of focus away from the material environment to concerns such as deducing the discontent or content of the urban population. If the quality of urban life is analysed from the perspective of the agent, then personal data sources are needed. Unfortunately, sources for analysing the agency element in urban history are rare. Diaries are a key source of information about private emotional matters, but in most cases they are not intended for reading by other parties.

Nonetheless, there are four sets of sources available for qualitative research on the urban agent and everyday life. The vast range of media, especially print, local news and readers' letters, are a rich source for information and commentary. Their disadvantage is the time-consuming character of the research they entail. Pragmatically, investigation has to be restricted to periods of high activity in public life, such as local elections. In this case, the last three months before an election may be the most informative. The end of the year is also an opportunity for enlightening retrospective articles and comments. A cross-national comparison of urban public culture would, for example, reveal that Paris, in contrast to Berlin, has always had a very active and critical public opinion on the whole city, despite a strong *quartier* orientation in private life. Londoners, however, living in Europe's largest agglomeration and, due to the system of local taxation, have shown a much stronger district orientation in public and private life. Thus, they manifest many similarities with the district orientation of Berliners, which in the case of the German capital is, however, partly due to its late administrative unification in 1923 and the traditionally decentralised administrative organisation of the agglomeration.

A rich source of not only factual information but also of the personal experience of social groups and individuals is the minutes of the proceedings of municipal representative bodies. Before the 1960s, these materials were rich in detail and illustrative. With the upsurge of the modern mass media and the popularisation of the argumentative style, discussions have become more vague and phrasal.

Pleas, petitions and complaints to the municipality contain a variety of information. They are often written in informal language and have a personal flavour. Yet, they can be highly tendentious or one-sided.

Last but not least, audio-visual material offers a vast stock for consultation. Not only documentary films on urban life but also the fictional genre provide insights into the everyday life of a city and urban problems. Although subjectivity, individuality and visuality are their characteristics, they transmit vivid details of a socio-political and economic urban reality.

Current research strategies

The method of oral history can also be an attractive option and has been employed in the United States and especially by the British History-Workshop Movement for Research on the History of the

Working Class, on immigration, unemployment, and in Germany for research on the National-Socialist era. Here, the researcher uses interviews with participants in historical processes. The History-Workshop Movement did not, as traditionally was the case, solicit representatives of elites to obtain commentary on changes at the politico-economic level. Rather, it aimed at enquiring into the personal experience of everyday life. The methodology is interdisciplinary since it draws on techniques developed in anthropology, sociology and industrial relations. It requires a sound analysis of the socio-linguistic, interactionist and cognitive levels of the interview process (Grele, 1975). The persons selected for the interview should be respected for their conception of the past and for the fact that the past, in their memory, is often a torrent of events without a structure (Norman, 1968). Account should also be taken of the possibility that the interviewee might invent stories or might be tempted into self-promotion and euphemistic accounts. These problems cannot be ignored. Nonetheless, it must be conceded that, besides concrete events and dates, there is also wide scope for corroborative interpretation of the truth. What counts in the first instance is what the contemporaries consider to be objective reality.

A renaissance of national perspectives?

This brief overview of possible qualitative research strategies in cross-national urban history does not give much idea of its content. The subdiscipline of urbanisation is difficult to isolate methodologically from industrial, social or political history. Moreover, specific methods of research can be difficult to identify. Urbanisation is a complex topic and, due to the influence of social sciences, the methods applied in historical research are modern. Compared to other subdisciplines, researchers must be interdisciplinary, but they are recruited from traditional disciplines which may not be used to co-operating. This means that, regardless of their mutual research interests, their strategies and models of explanation differ in accordance with scientific traditions. Moreover, the practice of 'cohabitation' between historians and social scientists, which in the 1980s gave rise to a large number of cross-national comparative studies, is presently waning. More confident in the merits of their own discipline, historians are raising anew the question of historical specificity as the traditional bone of contention. Thus, they stress the specific features and individual characteristics of urban developments, a perspective which can be counterproductive to cross-national comparative research.

12 Exploring Statistics and National Rules on Social Security

Martin Evans

This chapter analyses the research methods used to study means-tested minima in Great Britain, France and Germany. A quantitative approach was adopted, and the chapter examines the problems of accessing comparable data. An underlying objective of the project was to compare social assistance systems and their links to social security, taxation and work in neighbouring European countries. Three major themes are discussed: firstly, the absence of a shared conceptual framework which could facilitate cross-national policy analysis, since provisions are substantially context-bound in each national policy environment; secondly, the problem of consistency and comparability of data produced by systems based in very different policy contexts; and thirdly, the technical and methodological problem of producing a comparative model which can analyse incentive structures. Two major questions were addressed: What are the differences in the populations of claimants who rely on means-tested social minima, and how can they be accounted for? How do the different national systems assist or deter claimants in exiting from dependency on means-tested minima and in entering the labour market?

The importance of the research topic for the British debate can be demonstrated by the dominance in current British policy of the growing necessity to target social security to the poorest, and the problem of ensuring that incentives to work or to save are maintained.

Policy context and conceptual frameworks

The means-tested transfer policies which make up each country's social minima are defined as schemes which provide a state-funded transfer for basic daily living costs (excluding specific costs such as housing), which are paid on the basis of a test of income or other means.

The task in comparative studies is made more problematic because such schemes are a reflection of the wider policy context in which they operate. Social minima are often designed as a 'safety net', subsidiary to more universal provisions of social insurance, family policy, employment policy, health and education and so forth.

Much contemporary comparative research has examined broad characteristics of 'models' of welfare. Typologies of welfare regimes based on common characteristics do not concur in their classification of Great Britain, France and Germany (Wilensky and Lebeaux, 1958; Mishra, 1981; Esping-Andersen, 1990; Leibfried, 1993; Korpi and Palme, 1994), as Spicker argues in his chapter. More recent comparative studies of means-tested assistance have investigated provisions, rules and aims (Lødemel and Schulte, 1992; CERC, 1994a, 1994b; Bradshaw, 1995). The original focus of the present research was the relationship between social minima and other provisions, which makes it very dependent on context.

In recent years, Britain has reprioritised the aim of poverty relief through social minima within an increasingly residual social security policy, whereas France and Germany differ in remaining more firmly wedded to the principles of social insurance. National preferences diverge in other ways, too. What is seen as a residual safety net in one country may be a significant part of the whole system of social transfers in another. The growth of means-testing may be an intended consequence of moving towards more income-related provision, a symptom of failure of social insurance to adapt to new needs or to gaps in contributory provision, or a positive commitment to provide a comprehensive underlying minimum income guarantee. These reasons are not exhaustive or mutually exclusive.

In short, research on means-tested social minima must be undertaken with the divergent national policy contexts firmly on the agenda. It is not enough to dissect the data, rules and outcomes of means-tested minima. Context, if not all, is essential.

Contextual equivalence

In Britain, social insurance has been made less generous, returning to flat-rate benefits at or about the same level as assistance. This means that use of means-tested minima has grown, especially in response to higher unemployment. In Germany and France, this is not the case, and contributory social insurance still plays a significant part in unemployment policy. Indeed, in Germany social insurance was extended in 1995 by introducing a new contingency of long-term nursing care to alleviate pressures from the frail elderly on *Sozialhilfe* (German means-tested minima). When family allowances and tax systems in France and Germany, and French nursery provision are added to social insurance, the context becomes very important in determining what part of the population is at risk of falling into means-tested provision, and the extent of those risks.

Employment policy is also crucial in understanding the role of means-tested minima. Minimum wages, state subsidies, active employment measures and differentially structured labour markets all affect the risks of becoming unemployed and, subsequently, re-employed.

In addition, institutional differences in the organisation of means-tested minima must be taken into account. Germany's constitutional basis for welfare makes the system far more legalistic than in France and Britain. The division of responsibilities for means-tested provision among many agents in France, and between federal social insurance and regional or local *Sozialhilfe* in Germany, makes for far more complex funding arrangements and gives incentives for policy agents to transfer responsibility between regimes by measures to stimulate recipients' re-qualification for social insurance, which would be a rather pointless exercise in Britain.

The identification and modelling of incentive structures was a major theme of the research in Britain, but was not relevant for France and Germany. Reducing unemployment, ensuring economic growth, and increasing economic opportunities for individuals are common aims, but they are approached using very different policy mixes. In Britain, supply-side measures are dominant: increasing the stringency of job search requirements for the unemployed; increasing the financial pressure on the unemployed by reducing the relative value of benefit to earnings; and increasing the financial incentives to enter into work (especially part-time and low-paid work). In France, on the other hand, the emphasis has been more on combating social exclusion and re-insertion into social, community and economic activities.

From a methodological point of view, it is clear that the concerns of domestic policy (work incentives, and poverty and unemployment traps) do not travel well. A researcher seeking to describe and analyse such problems and the populations they affect must be sensitive to the varying underlying policy priorities. Since the role played by means-tested social minima reflects different policy aims at the macro-level, any conclusions obtained from quantitative results must be placed in a policy context. And, since underlying policy contexts are so different, there are limits to the comparative consistency of any results. The following discussion therefore emphasises the importance of context and comparability.

Comparing claimant populations: problems of consistency and comparability

Department of Social Security claimants can be counted at a single point of time, for instance by a sample of total caseload (for example *Income Support Statistics: Annual Enquiry*, DSS, 1994b), or cumulatively at the end of an accounting period. Additionally, the count can be of households, claimants, or of the whole population who benefit. Each system will define its claimant population in different ways. It is important to establish how national statistics are derived or what is being reported as a claimant total. For instance, MISSOC (1993, table XII) reports the number receiving *Sozialhilfe* HLU (the federal means-tested social minimum) in Germany in 1990 as 2.89 million and provides a figure of 4.82 million for Income Support in the UK. Even if they were fully consistent with each other, the bare figures tell us nothing about the comparative level of dependency.

A consistent and comparable claimant count is the total number of individuals who rely on benefits (claimants and their dependants) expressed as a percentage of the total population. Table 12.1 shows such totals and the comparative difference in incidence of means-tested social minima in each country. Great Britain has 16 per cent of its total population relying on Income Support and a further 3 per cent on Family Credit. This is double the proportion in France and four to five times the proportion in Germany.

The differences in policy also underlie administrative data produced by each country. For instance, the test of being unemployed in all three countries is based on similar principles but is open to wide variations in practice. Hence, while internationally comparable unemployment rates are available from the OECD and ILO, these do not strictly correspond to the way in which each system identifies its unemployed as claimants of benefits. For instance, HLU claimants in Germany can identify themselves as unemployed if they cite this as the primary reason for claiming. In Britain, the test is one of registration for benefit. The French system is different again: claimants of the unemployment assistance schemes, *allocation solidarité spécifique* (ASS) and *allocation d'insertion* (AI), must be registered unemployed, while the number of unemployed *revenu*

Table 12.1   Population dependent on means-tested social minima in Great Britain, France and Germany in 1993

	Great Britain		France	Germany (1992)
	Income Support	Family Credit	All schemes	HLU+ *Arbeitslosen- hilfe*
Claimants + dependants (millions)	8.8	1.8	5.5	3.3*
% of all individuals	16.0	3.2	9.9	4.1

*   Estimated number relying on *Arbeitslosenhilfe* at 950,000, based on 529,000 claimants.

Source: Author's calculations and CERC (1994a, 1994b).

Table 12.2   Proportion of the unemployed reliant on means-tested minima in Great Britain, France and Germany

	Great Britain (1993)	France (1993)	Germany (1992)
Total unemployed (000s)	2763	2911	1808
% unemployment	10.2	11.5	5.8
Proportion of unemployed relying on means-tested provision			
% on contributory benefit	18	70	46
% of specialised unemployment assistance	–	14	23
% on non-specific social minima	81	12–14	23–25

Notes: Specialised unemployment assistance is ASS and AI in France and *Arbeitslosenhilfe* in Germany; non-specific social minima are Income Support in Great Britain, RMI in France and *Sozialhilfe* HLU in Germany.

Sources: Bruer (1994); CERC (1994a), table IV–8; CERC (1994b), table 3; OECD (1994c); DSS (1995), table 7.

minimum d'insertion (RMI) claimants can only be estimated according to their contract of insertion, family status or other indicators. Counting unemployed claimants, then, involves a mixed quality of data. However, fairly robust estimates can be made from official administrative data which can allow for double counting and other problems. These are shown in Table 12.2 which divides a comparable unemployment count, using OECD Labour Force Statistics, into proportions receiving contributory and means-tested benefits.

Comparing incentive structures: the problems of model building

The importance given to the issue of incentives in Britain is not internationally shared. Although concern is expressed about replacement rates during unemployment, there is also a priority that those on means-tested benefits should have an incentive to work. But these concerns are not so central to French and German policy-making and evaluation. Their systems are still strongly bound by the contributory principle, which rewards those with a long or regular working history (an incentive of a different kind). The accrued contributory rights of current workers are a strong political force. Thus, what is of central importance to Britain is of secondary or tertiary importance to France and Germany, because their emphasis is on other ways of delivering social transfers.

That is not to say that incentive measures do not influence policy in France and Germany. In France, for example, contributory unemployment benefit is reduced every four months in order to maintain incentives, and the *allocation de parent isolé* (API), the means-tested benefit for single parents, is only paid for a maximum of one year. In Germany, the operation of *Sozialhilfe* at the local level complements commitments to provide public or community work for recipients – *Hilfe zur Arbeit* – which, in turn, will re-establish a social insurance record and lift them out of dependence on it.

There are also rules in the benefit system which try to offset the 100 per cent reduction of benefit as income rises, to ensure incentives to work. However, these rules are viewed as necessary but marginal adaptations rather than the key to ensuring that dependence on benefits is mitigated.

Building comparative models

One strategy for exploring incentive structures is the method of 'hypothetical families', enabling calculation of the levels of social security benefits (means-tested and non-means-tested), income tax, housing allowances, and social security contributions that would accumulate for different ranges of income (see also Eardley's contribution in this collection). The original idea in the project reported here was to recreate tax benefit tables (as in DSS, 1994a) for all three countries.

The complexity of the different systems, together with the need to take into account a mass of contextual information, means individual calculation of each potential family type is very labour intensive and does not easily allow results to be displayed graphically. Computerised calculation is, therefore, essential to establish a range of family types and circumstances. British computer programmes have been produced to calculate benefits and taxes in this way, for instance TAXBEN by Atkinson and Sutherland[1]. For the three-country comparison, a model was produced using a layered Lotus123 spreadsheet.

This format was chosen because it required no learning of programming language; it enabled each part of the calculation to be transparent (each stage in the computation of tax and benefits can be seen on screen, making fault-finding easier), it can easily be taught to others familiar with this mainstream software and is easily amended. The main disadvantage of using a spreadsheet is that it restricts programming ability to those imposed by the spreadsheet conventions.

The huge volume of rules which determine eligibility for benefits, liability for taxation and social security contributions constitutes a significant research task in itself. Once the rules have been clarified and translated into spreadsheet formulae, a number of underlying problems remain to be solved to ensure that the income profiles and the resulting analysis of incentives are consistent and comparable. Firstly, they concern the temporal criteria for benefit calculation. The basis of the British system is the contemporary weekly calculation of entitlement to benefits. Only Family Credit is provided for six months, irrespective of changes in income during the period of entitlement. However, the domination of a contemporary weekly time horizon is not shared in France and Germany. A monthly calculation and payment basis is far more common, and the previous year's annual income is often used. Changing benefits for each weekly change in income makes for a great amount of administrative friction and must in itself affect incentives to report one-off sources of income.

Secondly, the way in which tax and benefits treat family composition differs between countries. 'Children' over the age of nineteen continue to accrue benefit or tax allowances for their parent(s) in France and Germany. The income of 'children' will also affect tax and benefit calculation. Entitlement to *Sozialhilfe* in Germany is individual: for example a family of two parents and two children can total four claimants.

Thirdly, the issue of context is important. A comparable hypothetical family may exist in the imagination, but to enable a comparison to be made they must also exist in a realistic policy environment. This means that rent data must be derived from actual representative rents in each country and not from calculated monetary equivalents. Rates of pay are also a problem. Research is needed to determine relevant rates of pay open to those on means-tested social minima in each country. An example of wage rates used is the 'McDonald's pay rate', which is based on the hourly rate obtainable from unskilled work in the fast-food chain in London, Paris and Frankfurt.

To summarise the results briefly, a comparison of gross income, net income after tax, social security contributions and housing costs for a single person aged 30 receiving the lowest level of means-tested social minima shows that France and Germany provide greater encouragement to enter into work while entitlement to social minima continues.

The effect of taxes and social security contributions is reflected in the net income received. Social security contributions are payable on all earnings in France and, hence, payable on earnings whilst claiming RMI. This leads to a divergence between net and gross income which does not occur for claimants in Germany and Britain.

The model represents an empirical situation in which a potential worker can decide to work an additional hour every week over a succession of weeks. There are very few jobs which are that flexible, especially for employees of fairly low status. Secondly, in the model the outcomes of social security and tax rules are computed. However, in some systems these rules are more fixed than in others. In Britain, the rules are fixed and there is little discretion. In Germany, on the other hand, the rules are more flexible and a 'typical' or common variant is plotted. Lastly, different time horizons underlie the calculations. For example, income tax in France is not payable until the following financial year; as a consequence, the immediate incentives to work are greater.

Therefore, it is misleading to talk of extensive or limited poverty traps on such a superficial analysis. Even with all the caveats appended to these calculations, the context in which they operate must be taken into account. Different schemes work in varying policy contexts alongside non-means-tested provision. Analysing the incentive structures is only one element of a much larger comparative task.

Reconciling context and content

Domestic policy concerns about the role and effects of means-tested social minima arise out of wider issues about the aims of state transfers and the respective roles of social insurance, contingency-related transfers and social assistance. In comparative research on means-tested social minima, it is essential to address differences in the policy context of other countries. Different emphases on non-means-tested provision are obviously reflected in divergent concerns about poverty traps and work incentives. This does not, however, mean that there is no basis for consistent comparative research. It does mean that the researcher has to be aware that there are conflicts and constraints in making quantitative assessments of the performance of means-tested social minima.

The issue of context is essential, but research in this area must not be distracted from its specific focus into a more general study of income maintenance. The issues of consistency and comparability are equally important and can be addressed through a variety of statistical and heuristic devices to calculate claimant populations or estimate work incentives among countries. However, these devices are not 100 per cent solutions, they involve choices in method and presentation, and these should be made transparent. Neither do such devices overcome the problem of context, and results must be accompanied by sufficient commentary to ensure that the reader is aware of this. Lastly, the issue of complexity: quantitative comparative research on means-tested social minima requires knowledge of a plethora of rules and exceptions across the whole range of national state transfer and taxation systems. Choosing hypothetical families provides a way to cut through this complexity to show the effects of the systems on similarly composed households in each country. However, for each hypothetical example an almost infinite number of exceptions can be identified.

This form of comparative research, therefore, necessitates an essential accommodation of methods and constraints. The difficulties of context, consistency, comparability and complexity provide an opportunity for a methodological response which is robust and clear, but which, above all, recognises and accepts its own limits and makes these transparent.

Acknowledgement

The research referred to in this paper was funded by the Joseph Rowntree Foundation.

Note

1. This programme was written at the London School of Economics to produce tax benefit models for hypothetical families as part of research under the ESRC-funded Taxation, Incentives and Distribution of Income Programme undertaken at STICERD.

Part Four : Evaluation

Robert   Walker

All four chapters in this section address the difficulties of undertaking comparative research, and three of them grapple with the problems, often bureaucratic in origin, of carrying out studies on behalf of the European Commission.

Several common threads can be identified that concern the feasibility of comparative evaluative research. Unless real account is taken of the lessons presented in the chapters, it may not even be worth attempting such evaluative work, at least not under the aegis of the European Commission.

Simonin seeks to evaluate the contribution of the European observatories and networks on social policy and to ascertain whether they are adequately equipped to evaluate policy. Some observatories and networks have limited briefs to describe policies and policy development; others have sought to provide an informed judgement of the value of such policies. However, the networks and observatories seem woefully under-resourced and ill-structured to assume the latter role.

The crucial difficulties revolve around specification of policy objectives and negotiating common evaluative criteria. The objectives of ostensibly similar polices vary from country to country and, indeed, from one period of history to another. Moreover, radically different policies can share similar goals. A central dilemma in cross-national policy evaluation is whether the performance of policies should be matched against the national (or local) objectives that spawned them or against some standardised checklist that may ignore local imperatives and conditions. At present the issue is frequently fudged if, indeed, it is recognised at all.

A second conundrum relates to evaluative criteria. These require common definitions and compatible measurements that are often unavailable. Their absence is sometimes imposed by divergent policy objectives that deny the possibility of common modes of measurement. But more often the lack of compatibility results from under-resourcing – research workers simply do not have time properly to address the issue – and from poor management structures that obfuscate clear lines of direction and accountability.

The cost of effective evaluation is high, far beyond the meagre resources available to today's networks and observatories. The lack of funding may reflect both on-going debates about the competence of the European Commission to evaluate national policies and the understandable reluctance of national governments to see the outcome of their policies compared in any form of league table. But administrative structures and management also conspire against worthwhile outcomes. Observatories are frequently required to report on the basis of fragmentary information, provided and interpreted by national informants, which is then synthesised again by co-ordinators, who necessarily lack detailed knowledge about national and local conditions. Lines of authority are often confused and the competing objectives of research teams, that may not ever have worked together before, frequently remain unresolved.

Against this bleak scenario, must be set positive achievements and great potential. Networks and observatories have an important role to play in constructing a social space: a recognition that the European Union has a social dimension, irrespective of the extent to which it is made explicit. By helping to define terms, sifting information and clarifying comparisons, they precipitate and facilitate public debate that can enhance political accountability and counter the democratic deficit that many European institutions share. Simonin is right to emphasise the importance of observatories and networks being transparent. They must strive for quality and set targets that reflect the best that social science can offer, rather than working to the principle of the lowest common denominator, which sometimes comes from the need to engage investigators from a range of countries irrespective of skills and experience. Observatories and networks should encourage self-criticism, confront the critiques offered by the wider policy research community and be open to the value of methodological and cultural triangulation.

Although Duffy's chapter recounts the evaluation of Poverty 3, a policy initiative launched under the aegis of the European Commission, her account serves as a definitive case study of many of the deficiencies that Simonin identifies. The ambitious and ambiguous objectives and minuscule budget of Poverty 3 created enormous difficulties for all involved. The aims were to promote experiments among the twelve member states to change the lives of the poor and those at risk of becoming poor, to stimulate debate on poverty and social exclusion and to evaluate the 'partnership' delivery mechanism in promoting social change. However, despite the positivistic language of 'experiments' and 'testing', the evaluators did not have access to any of the appropriate tools. Rigorous impact assessment proved impossible because there was no randomisation nor any form of control, save the history of what had gone before which could only be established *ex post facto*. Moreover, projects were responsible for supplying most of the data for evaluation. Furthermore, the twin objectives of assessing the impact of projects and evaluating the organisational model required different evaluative methodologies, although no such distinction seems to have been made.

Many of the standard definitional problems went unresolved: the meanings of poverty and social exclusion, how they differ, and how they manifest themselves in different contexts. But, of even more importance, Poverty 3 was hi-jacked by the understandable enthusiasm of those involved to do something, however limited, about the plight of the poor. As a consequence, sight was lost of the primary objective of learning what measures might best help poor people. Limited resources for evaluation were siphoned off to support implementation, monitoring took the place of evaluation, and 'coal-face' considerations took precedence over the need to produce generalisable insights.

Duffy notes that much was gained by sensitising staff involved in implementation to the importance of evaluation, and individual projects did, apparently, make constructive use of monitoring data to improve the focus and delivery of services. Maybe the initiative did succeed in keeping the issue of poverty, or at least social exclusion, alive within the European Union, another worthwhile achievement, but it is doubtful whether the policy community is better informed about policies to assist poor people as a result of Poverty 3.

The recurring themes of great expectations, limited resources and impossible time horizons are also evident in Rubery's account of the European Commission's network of experts on women's employment. Again, the administrative model is one of a spider sitting at the centre of a web of informants rapidly collating information and distilling insights for policy-makers in Brussels. Luck is the main defence against serious error, since there is little time for checking interpretations, and no one person can be adequately informed about all member states. On this occasion, however, the 'spider' is at least in a position clearly to define the questions asked of informants, and even to impose a common theoretical framework.

Rubery offers a number of important reflections which warrant further expansion. Her role, as co-ordinator, was to make information comprehensible and accessible to the Brussels bureaucrat. But information is seldom neutral, and so she was also a lobbyist, promoting the cause of women and counteracting the corrosive effects of gender-blind statistics and analysis. In this process, she had to be careful to highlight women's issues while avoiding pressures to ring-fence and perhaps ghettoise them. In seeking to influence policy, she was an active agent who needed to know how to ensure that the output of the network achieves maximum effect. This may well involve making information acceptable as well as accessible and, in this sense, burden the scientific with the problems and responsibilities of a gatekeeper, determining what should and what should not be known.

Harding's chapter addresses different issues, perhaps the most important of which is whether local developments can be better understood, firstly, by asking whether similar things are happening in different places and, secondly, by questioning whether the identical or disparate developments that may be observed are connected. If so, and Harding is convincing on this point, then all research and evaluation needs to build in an international comparative perspective. Precisely how this can be achieved raises innumerable questions most of which Harding, not surprisingly, either fails to address or resolve.

Although a deep vein in all four chapters, none effectively confronts the issue of how to evaluate the validity and reliability of cross-national comparisons. Instead, the theme looming large is the feasibility of cross-national policy evaluation. Evaluation in this sense is more than simple research; the task is to find things out. It is the application of social science, usually at the request of institutions with policy responsibility, to answer the question: Does it (policy) work? Transposed to a cross-national context, the question becomes: Does it work better in one country than in another? The chapters offer much evidence to date of failure and little of success.

However, the vast literature on policy and programme evaluation that has developed in the last three decades reveals the enormous achievements at local and national level, which have to be transferred to the supranational arena. While the authors demonstrate here that this will not be easy, social scientists must accept the challenge if policy-makers are ever to learn from other countries or determine whether supranational institutions function effectively.

13 Evaluating European Observatories and Networks on Social Policy

Bernard Simonin

Most European observatories and networks on social policy were established in the late 1980s at the initiative of the European Commission. They now cover a number of policy areas including: employment, family policy, social exclusion, older people, minimum income, and the development and convergence of social protection policies. Generally, an observatory comprises a national expert from all the member states and a co-ordinator responsible for producing synthesis reports. Originally, their approach was primarily descriptive. They were given the task of collating administrative documents on policy, as well as basic information on socio-economic and demographic indicators. Some observatories have assumed a more evaluative role, requiring the collection, analysis and interpretation of information about the implementation and impact of measures with a view to providing an informed judgement on the value of such policies.

The chapter is based on a report prepared for the European Commission (DGV) and presented at a seminar in Pavia on the theme of evaluation of social policy (Ferrera, 1993). The seminar brought together researchers and academics who were members of observatories and networks on social policies as well as representatives of governments in member states. The report was intended to provide a framework for debate about methods.

A large number of studies have been produced on the methodology of evaluation. Journals such as *Evaluation Review*, or more recently *Evaluation*, published by Sage, focus on evaluation studies, as do a number of other works from the same publisher. In France, the Research Council for Evaluation (Conseil Scientifique de l'Évaluation) produces an annual methodological report. It is worth asking to what extent these studies are relevant to the work of the observatories. The chapter will also be considering whether observatories should go further down the route of evaluation. If so, are the necessary resources and methodological tools available to enable them to assume a more evaluative role?

The problems of adopting an evaluative approach

Effective evaluation demands that a balance be maintained between three complementary activities: firstly, specific questions need to be asked about the objectives of a particular policy or about their appropriateness in a given context; secondly, the net effects of programmes set up to achieve these objectives need to be measured; thirdly, the appropriateness of the administrative apparatus established to respond to and implement policy objectives needs to be analysed.

Doubts may be expressed about the ability of observatories to undertake all of these activities, because the outcomes of programmes run under their auspices are difficult to measure. The Poverty Programmes (described by Duffy in her chapter) afford a good example. The difficulties of measuring the effects of the programmes on social exclusion are apparent from the national and consolidated reports prepared for the observatory. Depending on the areas under study, authors were forced to adopt varying definitions of exclusion. In programmes concerned with employment, exclusion was coterminous with unemployment; in the case of housing, it was synonymous with homelessness. It was therefore impossible to capture the multidimensional nature of exclusion which was of interest to the Commission.

Observatories are faced with all the problems that are seen as preventing effective evaluation: the excessively high costs of evaluation which are beyond the budgets allocated to observatories; the unreliable and sometimes contradictory findings, depending upon the methods adopted, making it impossible to draw conclusions about the effectiveness of a particular programme; the length of time needed to produce results, which is incompatible with the timetable for taking decisions (for example, the results of evaluations generally become available only when a programme has either disappeared or changed direction); and the inability to take account of unexpected outcomes which may be a critical factor in understanding a particular policy.

Policy evaluation, then, requires a clear definition and delineation of policy objectives. All observatories are facing similar difficulties, which can be summarised under four headings: delimiting the policy area, establishing boundaries, defining objectives and data management.

As an example, a number of studies have shown how difficult it is to reach agreement over the definition not only of family policy but also of the family itself (Hantrais and Letablier, 1996). Definitions of older people vary according to administrative decisions about retirement age (Hantrais, 1995). Social exclusion is a term originating in French but over which no two French people seem able to agree (a view attributed to Graham Room).

By confining observation to public policy, as in the case of the family or older people, observatories may not be able to understand the totality of a policy. The programmes within their remit are often administered by a great variety of poorly co-ordinated services, each of which may have its own definition of the field. The measures implemented may, therefore, be juxtaposed without any attempt to assess their combined impact.

Evaluation involves making a judgement based on a set of criteria. But in cases where the explicit aims differ from one country to another, as for example in the case of family policy, the criteria may be difficult to operate at European level (Gauthier, 1993). A distinction can usefully be made between observatories and networks, according to whether or not they are dealing with programmes that have received official recognition at European level and have been approved by national governments. But even when common objectives do exist, they are often ill-defined, making evaluation more difficult.

Despite the efforts made by Eurostat and the progress accomplished, the co-ordinators of observatories continue to bemoan the fact that they do not have available a body of comparable data for all the countries in the European Union. The ability of a European statistical system to respond to the demand is dependent on the good will of member states in developing their own survey systems and nomenclatures, a process which is advancing only very slowly.

An observatory, whose function is essentially descriptive, like the Mutual Information System on Social Protection in the Community (MISSOC) can, in some circumstances, have a very positive effect on European objectives for the convergence of social policies. All the member states are required to provide reliable information to MISSOC, which produces comparative tables on the situation in member states. The information is validated and widely disseminated.

The question remains as to whether the many factors inhibiting evaluation and restricting the value of descriptive accounts of systems and policy measures prevent observatories from fulfilling their evaluative function. From the researcher's point of view, evaluation would seem to come up against insuperable methodological problems, but from the policy-maker's perspective, it is clear that it is vital to progress down this route (Bouget and Nogues, 1993), a view shared by the Commission. One of the arguments frequently produced for opposing the extension of pilot programmes is the lack of proper evaluation.

Since observatories are themselves engaged in debate about the need for evaluation, it is timely to consider their evaluative function. The requirements and limitations of evaluation are clearly recognised, and there appears to be widespread consensus about the role hitherto played by observatories. Previously, they did not carry out policy evaluation; their purpose was rather to elucidate policy, to analyse some aspects of it in more detail and to identify the underlying rationale of national social protection systems. But even though it would be misleading to claim that they have achieved the objective of evaluation, the progress made is not to be underestimated (Walker, 1993).

Methodological questions in evaluating observatories

Much methodological discussion about observatories concerns some of the standard themes in evaluation, such as the use of indicators or the timing of evaluation.

Indicators

For the purposes of evaluation, an indicator can be defined as a unit of statistical information applied to an interpretative hypothesis and with the aim of providing a judgement about an action or a situation. The problems already mentioned with regard to the collection and interpretation of statistical data mean that caution has to be exercised in using indicators. An important objective for observatories is to gain a better understanding of the rationale underlying national policies, and to identify their similarities and differences. But by placing undue emphasis on indicators, comparisons of policies tend to be reduced to consideration of only a limited number of criteria, thereby preventing a full understanding of the content of a particular measure. The outcome may even be counterproductive if governments use the methodological weaknesses of particular indicators to question the value of the total work of an observatory.

Another primary objective of observatories is to participate in the construction of a European 'social space' from which to observe national policies. Indicators play a key role in the process if they can summarise the main characteristics of national policies in a straightforward way and make the information accessible to a wide public. A country needs to be able to locate its policies in relation to those of other EU member states; indicators are a key instrument in the process. They are therefore indispensable for observatories, but they need to be accompanied by explanatory notes providing contextual information and making explicit the conclusions that can legitimately be drawn from them. The indicators must be chosen with care so as to eliminate those which are derived from unreliable national data. It is also important not to construct indicators that cannot be linked to well-defined interpretative hypotheses.

Given the constraints on the availability of data, these prerequisites considerably reduce the number of indicators that can be used by each observatory. Even when indicators are technically feasible, they may not be appropriate for the main policy objectives under study. Regular contact with Eurostat can help to improve data collection and enhance its reliability. Other solutions include carrying out more systematic analyses using performance indicators or relying on European population panels. Statistical or econometric methods have long been used in evaluations to assess the impacts of policy on the groups concerned. Panels, as envisaged by the Commission, are representative samples of households in the different member states. Each respondent is questioned at regular intervals (every two years for example) about their current situation and about events they have experienced since the previous interview. The composition of panels and the tracking of the individuals belonging to them present a number of problems: the extent to which they are representative in the first instance; the management of changes in the composition of the household which make it difficult to know who should be tracked; and the means to exploit the large amount of unwieldy data collected over a long period of time. The advantage of using panel data is that they yield information about causal relationships between access to social policy programmes and changes in the situation of households.

The need for evaluation is linked to the Commission's long-held aim of building up a European panel responsible for monitoring living conditions and analysing certain aspects of national social policies. It may be no coincidence that progress has been slow: all manner of technical difficulties have arisen, combined with the high costs of launching and maintaining such a venture and exploiting the results. A carefully managed panel could make an important contribution to evaluation, but it is by no means certain that it could be properly managed or that the political will exists to support it. The stress on the need for evaluating social policies may, however, provide a unique opportunity for progress in this area.

Timing

In the case of observatories, the question of timing cannot be dealt with as it normally is in evaluation. One of the basic precepts in evaluation – to set up the assessment procedure when the programme to be evaluated is launched – does not apply for observatories. Nor do changes in policy happen at the same time in each country. The criticism often made of evaluation, that the results are produced too late to help with decision-making, cannot be applied in the case of observatories. They were not established with the explicit objective of evaluating new programmes which are then only pursued if they have proved worthwhile. Unlike procedures for evaluation, observatories do not have to make their timetable coincide with the timing of policy decisions.

There are many instances, which are common in evaluation work, where short, medium and long-term objectives may conflict and where the time schedule of those commissioning a study does not match the rate of production of knowledge by researchers. It is clearly not appropriate to map the production of observatories onto the annual scheduling of administrative contracts. A longer term perspective is needed, providing opportunities to review developments in the medium term, to take account of delays in analysing information that arrives late and to devote several years to studying certain aspects of policies so as to assess their impact.

Reinforcing the credibility of observatories

One of the peculiarities of evaluation as compared to other research activities is also characteristic of observatories and networks: evaluation implies an iterative process of knowledge and action. Knowledge is produced not only with a view to improving public policy as far as the decision-making process is concerned, but also as a way of stimulating and enriching public debate. Particular care therefore needs to be taken in examining the operation of observatories and in exploiting their findings.

Authors writing on the subject provide many insights into what has been called 'the quality of evaluation'. They are referring to the procedures and methods most likely to make the evaluation credible for those sponsoring the work. The search for credibility is not confined to the scientific value of evaluation, but also extends to its capacity to be recognised outside the research environment by policy-makers and, more generally, by public opinion as a serious exercise capable of producing new and rigorous conclusions contributing to the policy-making process.

The credibility of observatories, as far as evaluation is concerned, is far from being a foregone conclusion for a number of reasons. Authors of national reports rarely have access to evaluations that have already been validated by official organisations (commissions, public evaluation agencies), covering the whole, or at least a major part, of the policy area being studied, such as the Commission on Evaluation of the Minimum Income in France, which was in operation between 1990 and 1993. They are therefore dealing with fragmentary information from a wide range of scientific sources to which they have little access. Simply trying to recapitulate the main events occurring during the year presupposes that national informants have to make their own judgement on hidden priorities (Dumon, 1993). It is extremely difficult to choose between contradictory or incoherent elements of evaluation without giving precedence to one's own discipline. National representatives have to provide a meta-evaluation; they are expected to express a view on the validity of the information and to comment on individual policy measures or part of them, which is a very complex task.

Co-ordinators of the European synthesis reports are faced with similar difficulties and have the added problem of not being familiar with the context of each member state, which increases the risk of wrongly interpreting national information.

Evaluation is being undertaken in a situation where the operating principles on which the observatories are based do not closely follow the same procedures that are used for piloting observatories. A paradoxical situation therefore arises, as far as evaluation is concerned, where the body commissioning and piloting the observatories (the Commission) is not responsible for policy, which is within the remit of member states. The Commission's partners, in particular national or local governments, are therefore unlikely to endorse the conclusions produced by the observatories. They do not generally know the person responsible for the consolidated report; yet the credibility of any evaluation at national or local level may often rest on the reputation of the author.

As already mentioned, governments are under no obligation to change their policy direction in accordance with the results of observatory reports, contrary to what happens with the formal evaluation procedures set up in some countries (Vanlerenberghe, 1993). Observatories are only one source of information among many, and their impact on policy choices is far from being automatic; their influence can only be achieved by negotiation.

If the work of observatories is to gain greater credibility, a number of issues need to be addressed: transparency, organisation, the form and dissemination of work, and their mutual reinforcement.

An important question is how to distinguish between different levels of knowledge: what is known with a high degree of certainty, what is not certain, what is not known at all. Chelimski (1992) has suggested four concepts that may be helpful in ensuring transparency, while remaining alert to the problems inherent in the development of all knowledge. She also proposes ways of overcoming these problems at the same time as making clear to readers how much effort is involved in evaluation to determine the accuracy of the information gathered. The four concepts are: methodological self-criticism to anticipate potential gaps in an evaluation; a taxonomy identifying problem areas to offer alternative explanations in respect of the findings; attention to plausibility which reduces the number of interpretative hypotheses for the findings; and triangulation of methods, starting from a statement that every evaluative method has weaknesses and that the simultaneous use of a number of different evaluative approaches is a way of reducing them.

Most of these principles of rigorous methodology are likely to be applied spontaneously, although triangulation of methods is too seldom used because it entails disciplinary rigour. In addition, because observatories are so concerned about transparency, they tend to be very restrained in making their objectives known.

A number of questions arise about the way observatories are organised: What is the place assigned to the Commission's partners in defining the content of observatories and their priorities? What should be their involvement with the various stages of the observatories' work so that they are not simply the passive recipients of reports? How can greater collaboration be achieved between the researchers associated with observatories? The relationship between members of the scientific community and representatives of governments is another tricky question that has to be addressed: while researchers need to be completely independent of politicians, national experts cannot afford to be isolated from the concerns of national decision-makers. The question is well rehearsed in evaluation, but a balance remains to be found between the two pressures.

With regard to the form and dissemination of the observatories' work, the problem is to identify the main recipients, other than the Commission. One possible response is that the observatory is aiming at all possible users of the information. Experts in evaluation can readily show that, even if there is general agreement over target readers, it is not easy to adapt outputs of evaluation work to the objectives of sponsors.

Observatories can be perceived primarily as an internal negotiating tool between the Commission and national governments enabling the Commission to make proposals, surreptitiously, for improving a particular aspect of social policy in a member state. Another possible objective could be to provide social partners, non-governmental organisations and public opinion at large with information that they did not previously possess and which will enable them, if necessary, to exert pressure on governments to ensure that their policies achieve the objectives of a Social Europe. From this perspective, the comparative nature of observatories and, especially, the application of indicators could well be reinforced. More attention could also be paid to the dissemination of reports and their readability.

The danger of the various observatories analysing the same topics and producing contradictory results points to the need for greater co-ordination to avoid repetition and minimise incoherence. In particular, the more descriptive observatories could supply information to other observatories and networks. The possibility should not be excluded of several observatories with different objectives tackling common topics from a different perspective, in accordance with their individual analytical requirements (Tricart, 1993).

Evaluating evaluation

This chapter has shown how the development of the evaluative role of observatories and networks presupposes a major effort to develop appropriate instruments. It requires improved statistical sources, more appropriate use of indicators and of methods suited to comparative evaluation of policies. Given the amount of intellectual and financial investment involved if any significant progress is to be made in these areas, the co-ordination of efforts can only be applauded. It is also worth stressing that most observatories have been engaging with the same issues, with the result that they are tending to adopt research themes which cut across disciplinary boundaries. For example, social isolation concerns family policy (the breakdown of the traditional family unit), older people and policies to combat social exclusion. A new theoretical perspective on justice and equity has emerged, which may allow social policy-making to be grounded in principles which have greater legitimacy (Guillemard, 1993, on intergenerational equity, or Le Grand, 1993, on the reform of health care). The evaluative role of observatories is, thus, becoming much more readily accepted as their methodological base and theoretical underpinning are reinforced, thereby offering a greater guarantee of quality. Clearly, observatories cannot improve the quality of their output simply by making reference to methods of evaluation, but they do need to take account of theory and introduce new theoretical perspectives which cut across different areas of social policy.

14 Evaluating Social Action Programmes

Katherine Duffy

This chapter reviews the scope and limitations inherent in evaluating complex and experimental social action programmes. An assessment of the process and impact of programme evaluation in 'Poverty 3' (the third European action programme to foster the social and economic integration of the least privileged groups, 1989-1994) is offered as a means of drawing lessons for future evaluations of cross-national programmes. To some extent, the chapter is an assessment of programme evaluation in Poverty 3. This retrospective evaluation represents the author's judgement based on her own experience of the programme, including site visits and a review of some key literature. Therefore it can be classed with what Rossi and Freeman (1993) have referred to as evaluation by 'connoisseurs', described by them as 'the shakiest of all impact assessments' (Rossi and Freeman, 1993, p. 252). The chapter discusses the extent to which the conditions and structures necessary for programme evaluation were present in Poverty 3, and the effect on the evaluation process of the particular management strategies chosen. After an attempt to define evaluation, the focus is on design and implementation. The final section discusses two elements of the context – political and research support – which can influence the effective delivery of programme evaluation.

Monitoring and evaluation

> Evaluation research is the systematic application of social research procedures for assessing the conceptualisation, design, implementation and utility of social intervention programmes.
>
> (Rossi and Freeman, 1993, p. 5)

There is considerable debate about the distinction between monitoring and evaluation. A number of authors have identified monitoring with continuous assessment, and evaluation with analysis of outputs and outcomes. Bowden (1988) has convincingly argued that no clear boundary can be drawn between the two functions, but he has distinguished monitoring from evaluation in the following way. Monitoring is concerned with routine reporting of information on the progress and achievements of projects under implementation, including initial assessment of actions to be taken. Evaluation, on the other hand, is a study employing either monitoring data or data separately collected to assess the achievements (impact) and efficiency of implementation (process) of the project.

Evaluation involves two dimensions: first, a set of tools which operate as a means of information generation, reduction and synthesis; and second, the application of a set of criteria with which to make judgements concerning the worth of that which is being evaluated.

The tools and criteria can be brought to bear on three classes of evaluation activity: analysis of conceptualisation and design; monitoring of programme implementation; and assessment of programme effectiveness and efficiency (Rossi and Freeman, 1993).

Criteria for evaluation

Foley (1994) has outlined the Audit Commission criteria in the United Kingdom as the three 'E's of economy, efficiency and effectiveness. These are concerned with absolute cost, cost benefit and the extent to which policy objectives are achieved. Administrative and financial criteria alone are rather narrow for assessing social programmes, where the methods of implementation as well as the goals may involve ethical or political/policy choices. For example: there should be participation of the least advantaged in decision-making at every level of the project; the most important requirement for an evaluator or other staff member is local knowledge or personal experience of poverty or discrimination. These kinds of principles suggest that process is integral to the desired impact.

Evaluation for whom

Foley (1994) identifies the reasons for undertaking evaluation as promoting accountability, and assessing cost efficiency, effectiveness and policy impact. While accountability is a principal reason for undertaking evaluation, a key question concerns accountability to whom. Most evaluations are carried out for programme managers and sponsors. Yet the merit of the project may be varyingly assessed by different actors in the programme. In designing the evaluation and making the choice of tools, there are more considerations than cost and technical merit. The lesson from the Poverty 3 Programme is that it is important to be explicit at the outset, about ethics, about the criteria for merit, and about who are the owners and end-users of the evaluation. But even in programmes in which the least advantaged are expected to participate in decision-making, they are least likely to be involved at the outset, and programme designers must rely on representatives of organisations trusted by these groups to speak for them. The flexibility that would enable the least advantaged to change project goals and direction makes the programme more difficult to evaluate in a rigorous social scientific manner. Nevertheless, without this flexibility the programme cannot be said to meet the expressed, as opposed to the assumed, needs of least advantaged groups.

Evaluation at programme level

It is common, for the purpose of evaluation, to distinguish between a project and a programme. The former is a discrete activity, whereas a programme might be an ongoing activity with developmental objectives.

A structure for monitoring and evaluation of a multi-site programme probably requires an administrative unit, an information system, a methodology (or methodologies), political and administrative support for the analysis, and an 'evaluation capability' in the system (Bowden, 1988). In the author's view, the structures put in place in Poverty 3 to encourage and assist the transfer and absorption to European level of the very rich and detailed local project experience were less successful than those put in place to ensure project self-evaluation.

Two conditions are necessary for programme impact evaluation. The first is that aims and objectives should be sufficiently precise and practicable for the specification of operational measures of achievement. The second condition is that the project or programme should be sufficiently well implemented, so that it has actually directed its impact to the appropriate targets (Rossi and Freeman, 1993, p. 220).

Specific objectives are more difficult to achieve for complex social programmes, because the problem under review is also complex. This is exacerbated by the negotiated agenda required of partnership approaches. As well as offering possibilities for developing improved policies and generating consent for them, partnerships may also produce a 'fudge' to maintain consent; with consequent difficulties for evaluation. Poverty 3 experienced all of these problems, compounded by its experimental nature and cross-national scope.

Aims and objectives of Poverty 3

Poverty 3 was a small, direct action programme of 41 projects across the twelve member states. Apart from budgetary considerations, it was constrained in size to experimental status by the limitations of Commission competence in the social field. The general aims expressed by the European Commission were to promote locally based experiments in positive change in the lives of the poor and those at risk of becoming poor, and to stimulate the debate on poverty and exclusion. Key objectives were the development of preventative and corrective measures, and implementation of an innovatory organisational structure to promote social change. The action model to be implemented by the projects was based on three principles: partnership of agencies, participation of the least advantaged and a multidimensional approach to combating social exclusion, for which partnership is assumed to be a pre-condition.

Design

Poverty 3 was innovative at the level of its concepts and, in part, in its delivery system (partnership, participation and multi-dimensionality), and in the targets of its action (people in their own space). It can be argued that not only was Poverty 3 designed in a way that made impact evaluation difficult, but that the current evaluation tool kit is not designed to assess innovative programmes.

A future programme could make greater use of research and technical skills in the design as well as implementation of the programme. For impact assessment, it has to be possible to relate programme outputs and impact to the actions implemented. If impact is to be replicable, as it must be for policy relevance, then action must be linked to a coherent conceptual apparatus and must be measured with reliable instruments.

Construct validity concerns the extent to which a variable reflects the concept it is intended to measure. The lack of conceptual clarity with regard to aims inhibited assessment of the impact of the models implemented for the programmes' higher level objectives: namely testing its delivery mechanism for combating social exclusion and identifying its specific contribution to the development of initiatives and policies at national or Commission level.

Room (in Dennett *et al.*, 1982, p. 18) has cited ill-defined questions at programme level as one of the obstacles to evaluation experienced in Poverty 1. Despite this, the Poverty 3 Programme was given the task of testing a model to combat social exclusion when the concept's meaning, boundaries and operationalisation were still under development. Though the Commission's definition of social exclusion is in terms of participation in normal life, the operational definition is (still) a measure of relative poverty, that is households or persons on half or less of average income in the member state (Commission of the European Communities, 1993b). It cannot just be assumed that a definition of relative poverty is a good proxy for social exclusion. Yet many projects made no distinction between the concepts when determining their action strategies.

One key research question for the programme should have been to develop and test the boundaries, operability and policy relevance of a working definition of social exclusion. Otherwise, the programme goal of developing models and methods of best practice in combating exclusion is meaningless.

Besides problems in operationalising the concept of social exclusion, no programme perspective focused on the links between local geographic space, community and exclusion, which was the terrain of intervention.

Measurement reliability concerns the possibility of repeating the same results. Unreliability in the measuring instruments prevents accurate assessment of a programme's true effects. Among other reasons, the lack of specificity in the concepts and precision in the objectives has meant that only interpretative and judgemental assessments of the impact of the total programme are possible. While these may well produce *Verstehen*, they are, as cautioned at the outset, unreliable.

Nor were there adequate instrumental means to identify the presumed impact of the delivery mechanism, that is the gains of a partnership approach and a territorial remit.

Many projects were unable to specify in any detail the nature of the 'social gain' expected from some actions. Social gain could be specified at the level of direct impact on individual beneficiaries and changes in the strength and resilience of family and personal networks; changes in the density of community and social infrastructure, changes in policies of various actors at various levels, and so forth. Without such specification, it is difficult for evaluators to distinguish unintended and intentional impacts, and to relate any outcome to a particular cause.

Implementation of the programme

Uncontrolled selection is a problem for impact evaluation. The Poverty 3 Programme was a Commission initiative, and as a programme rather than a fund was meant to exhibit a high degree of coherence. But the principle of subsidiarity meant that national governments selected the projects. As well as affecting the coherence of the programme directly, this aspect of a Commission programme had an indirect impact on coherence because of the time taken for information to filter through to the local level. In many countries, potential primary partners (usually municipalities) became aware of the programme only a short time before the closing date for applications. This limited the scope for discussion about concepts, or indeed about any other aspects of the programme, either between national and local level or between municipalities and local communities or other local interests.

Therefore, in many countries, the Research and Development Units (RDUs) and the Central Unit (CU) began their task of implementing the experimental action without any specific requirements or expectations from national governments. Equally, they were not able to compensate once the programme began because of the pressure to put structures into place 'on the ground'.

As a means of progressing through its fixed life, the programme was organised into 'definition', 'implementation' and impact' (including 'exit') phases. Initially of six months duration, the 'definition' phase of the projects was intended as a period in which the full partnership could be established in its legal form, premises could be found, staff could be recruited and objectives clarified, so that the project strategies could be launched 'on the ground'. This timetable for implementation proved to be too ambitious. Pressure to spend the first year budget and the need to establish local credibility through 'early action' restricted the time that projects could devote to clarifying concepts and objectives, with consequent impact on the possibilities of evaluation.

In addition, it does not appear that projects utilised planning techniques, such as Gantts Charts, that might identify bottlenecks, and which could distinguish between the kind of events affecting only a minor part of a project and major setbacks that would block all further project development.

The evaluation budget was largely devolved to projects. While this assisted in developing evaluation skills and culture at local level, the devolution of the budget, powers and responsibilities for the projects, removed the incentive to meet any programmatic demands that did not have sanctions. There were, however, no sanctions for poor performance except where they had resulted either in failure to submit a project report and accounts, or in underspending of budget (the latter meant loss of matching Commission funding).

Further, in a 'bottom-up' evaluation system, one relies on the quality of local evaluators and locally generated data. Project evaluators mostly had little opportunity to 'get to know' the programme, its structure and goals, as opposed to those of the project which contracted them.

Consequent to Poverty 1, Room (Dennett *et al.*, 1982) proposed a decentralised network of researchers and evaluators with a central facilitating agency. He believed this was necessary to overcome the relative isolation experienced by the central agency (ESPOIR) which undertook external evaluation in Poverty 1.

In Poverty 3, RDUs were situated so that they constituted a pivotal link between the various actors in the programme, and they offered a means of filtering the mass of detailed information about the projects. However, no horizontal interaction was provided between the RDUs or local evaluators other than *ad hoc*, and therefore no means were available for maximising the evaluation resources and intellectual coherence of the programme. Thus, the 'vacuum of communication' described by Room (Dennett *et al.*, 1982, p. 20) persisted in other forms in Poverty 3, despite the implementation of a rather more decentralised network.

The Poverty 1 evaluators also suggested that the programme animation functions (such as organisation of cross-project meetings), undertaken by ESPOIR, were costly in terms of the team's resources, yet a necessary precondition for systematic evaluation of the programme. In Poverty 2, Room indicated that the team's approach to evaluation was still complicated by its responsibilities for both monitoring and animation; for example, financial certification, technical support and mediation (Room, 1993, p. 167).

The scope for a contribution to project or programme development was limited by the weight of the monitoring role. These functions conflicted, at least from the point of view of projects, with a role in support or animation and, therefore, in access to detailed information about 'problems'. A number of projects felt that the opportunities for the support function were eroded by fear of the monitoring function of the RDUs. Despite this, many RDUs negotiated quite open access to information from projects, often by reaching agreement concerning the use to which material might be put, or the degree of intervention acceptable in terms of an animation or monitoring function.

The context for programme evaluation

Without a budget or a line management role, persuasion and exhortation were the only routes open to individual RDUs in any attempt to get common research questions raised, or national perspectives addressed, or data collected that might aid a programme rather than a project evaluation. This applied just as much to their relations with the actors at the programme level as to those at the project level.

Their role in developing the national dimension of the programme was made difficult because the national level had been 'designed out' rather than 'designed in' to the programme.

Despite being the programme sponsors and the ultimate source of much of the matched funding, the relevant departments of national governments did not set objectives, nor did they automatically receive results. This reduced the relevance of the programme to the national level. The relative autonomy from national government increased the scope for experimentation, but it was bought at the cost of national influence and, more important, from the point of view of evaluation and transferable methods and models, at the cost of national relevance.

Although dominance by national agendas may weaken the opportunities for cross-national learning, given the oft-repeated Commission demand for 'national visibility' and 'national impact', there were very limited means of developing national government awareness of, and involvement in, the goals and methodologies of the programme. It also meant that, at national level, political support was lacking for the evaluation process, which allowed projects to downgrade the priority they needed to accord to this process.

The importance of theory in relation to action and measurement

This chapter has pointed to two flaws in the evaluation structure of Poverty 3 which weakened the possibility of providing an evaluation of the programme. The first was the lack of clarity concerning the higher level goal (combating social exclusion). The second flaw lay in the inadequate implementation of structures for transferring to other levels project evaluation material useful to an assessment of the programme. A third weakness might possibly be lack of political support for the evaluation at various levels: one has to question why the national and CU evaluation structures were so weak in resources and influence. However, it is more likely that the reason is the Poverty 3 'grass-roots' approach of self-evaluation, developed in contrast to the more 'top-down' experience of Poverty 2.

Odile Quintin (the responsible official in Directorate-General V of the Commission) asserted that the programme would 'allow the Community to have a first debate on these issues and to test the ground for further proposals' (Cram, 1993, p. 144). We may conclude that the evaluation of Poverty 3 has been sufficient to do that, despite the fact that a proposal for a successor programme has not been approved.

If any future programme is to take forward the debate and development of policies and practices, it will need to strengthen the programme evaluation structure, drawing on the lessons gained from Poverty 3.

Among these lessons is the need for a checklist of questions that can be asked by those planning an evaluation system. Such a list might include the following questions: What is the nature and scope of the problem? How can the problem be operationalised? What are the aims of the programme? What are the testable objectives? How does the nature and scope of the proposed intervention relate to the analysis of the problem? Who is the monitoring and the evaluation for? Why will it be done? When will it be done? How will it be done? Against what criteria? What skills and resources will be required? How will information be communicated? Who owns the evaluation? What control mechanisms will operate?

It will also be necessary to pay closer attention to the lessons of previous programmes regarding structure, content and implementation. Poorly defined objectives, rushed implementation, the complexity of the problem, the impact of the processes, political interference and the importance of training for 'poverty warriors' were all identified in the programmes following the 'Great Society' of Kennedy and Johnson (Zurcher, 1970, chapter 16).

Anti-poverty action and evaluation tools have developed together, both taking a substantial leap forward during the 'War on Poverty'. However, just as it has been necessary to refine the structure and content of programmes, it is also necessary to refine the approach to evaluation of innovative social programmes in a volatile external environment. During and after the operation of both the 'War on Poverty' and the much smaller European anti-poverty programme, there was criticism of their limited impact. However, the lesson of the Topeka programme is, for example, that the Target Neighbourhood Committees 'became social processes in themselves' (Zurcher, 1970, p. 316), just as in Poverty 3 the lesson has been the process by which the partnerships developed into entrepreneurial social agencies, capturing 'bits' of cash and policy.

This may be indicative of the fact that the programmes are more effective at combating exclusion than combating income poverty, and underlines the importance of clarity in the design at the level of concepts, aims and objectives. Programmes should be grounded in a clear and specific theoretical framework, with goals that are operational and testable objectives. However, it is not only the weaknesses in design and implementation of scattered fixed-life projects which may mask the true impact of anti-poverty action. The current evaluation approach assumes a fixed goal and assesses progress and achievement in relation to this goal. It is concerned with measurement, and it does not capture the dynamics of the intervention itself in creating or destroying the conditions for change. Analyses within the theoretical frameworks of social sciences such as politics or sociology may prove more fruitful in this respect; the 'one-club' economist's approach to comparative statistics and a measuring tool kit may have been too long dominant to the detriment of an understanding of the dynamics of poverty and social exclusion.

15 'Mainstreaming' Gender in Labour Market Policy Debates

Jill Rubery*

The function of the European Commission network referred to in this chapter is primarily to provide the Equal Opportunities Unit of the European Commission with background research information on women's employment in Europe. It is distinct from many of the other networks attached to the Equal Opportunities Unit, which are more policy orientated, and more concerned to provide information on or stimulate activity within the member states (see Simonin's chapter in this volume). The competences in the area of gender discrimination, which the European Commission derives from the Treaty of Rome and subsequent treaties generate a need to monitor and evaluate progress towards equal treatment in the labour market and the effectiveness of various equality policy measures. However, the tasks undertaken by the network should not be considered as research in the narrow sense of evaluation of specific equal opportunities programmes. The remit is wider: to evaluate the impact of national systems and changes within them on gender equality.

The activities of the network can, thus, be seen as primarily to provide information to help the Commission's understanding of the nature and extent of gender discrimination and the need for new policy initiatives. To generate a gender perspective on European labour markets and associated policy requires both the collection of information on trends and patterns within member states and a synthesis of this information across Europe. Thus, the task of the network extends beyond the objectives of the European Commission employment observatories, which focus mainly on the collection of national information to identify relations between gender inequality

---

*   The chapter draws extensively on the work undertaken by the author in her role as the co-ordinator of the European Commission's Network of Experts on the Situation of Women in the Labour Market. However, the paper is written in a personal capacity and does not necessarily reflect the views either of the European Commission or the network experts.

and labour market systems within member states and for Europe as a whole.

In synthesising this material, the search for a clear perspective on gender issues becomes more complicated, as the patterns which emerge from the member states cannot be simply categorised along a spectrum of high to low degrees of gender equality; nor, indeed, even by stages of integration of women into the wage labour market (see Dex and Sewell, 1995, for a study which uses different measures of gender equality to make cross-national comparisons). Instead, the process of comparison and synthesis reveals an altogether more complex picture, in which labour market and social institutions play a key role in shaping gender relations; women's integration into the wage labour force is influenced not only, or even mainly, by the stage of economic development, but by the historical evolution of the welfare state, the family and the system of labour market organisation; and the differences in gender roles and relations extend beyond differences in material outcomes or employment patterns to the key values or key objectives of policies to promote equal opportunities in specific member states.

On a purely political level, at first sight these findings create problems for EU equality policy. Gender inequality is a phenomenon that reproduces itself in all periods and countries and, as such, there are strong temptations to formulate universal policies to deal with a universal and persistent problem. Indeed, anything less than a simple position on many European-level labour market policy debates – such as whether part-time work is a good or a bad thing – could be regarded as likely to marginalise the issue of gender within policy debates in the future. When incorporating a gender perspective is complex, it is so much easier not to bother.

Yet the insights which derive from the process of comparison and synthesis can be regarded as, in fact, assisting in the determination of the appropriate level or form of European-wide intervention. The problem of simple assumptions of universality of cause and effect within European labour markets is by no means confined to the issue of gender, but focusing on this issue may reveal some of the deficiencies in statements about the European labour market at a highly aggregated level that is demonstrably inappropriate, even if convenient for EU researchers and policy-makers. Research can also help identify how institutions and regulations – defined in their widest sense and not simply focused on gender equality polices – can modify or reduce gender inequality. However, these results do not necessarily suggest that policies or institutions are transferable between member states, for reasons which are discussed further below.

By collecting data on gender differences within member states, the research also demonstrate how all institutional arrangements still give rise to gender inequality, albeit to different degrees and with different manifestations. While this finding at one level may also appear to detract from the usefulness of policy formation to promote gender equality, it nevertheless serves to highlight that gender inequality is a continuing problem which may not disappear but, in fact, could even increase over time. The reasons for persistent gender inequality are not, however, a direct subject of the research. The likelihood of unequal treatment by gender has also been taken as a given and goes unexplained within European treaties. The research follows this approach, focusing instead on the extent and form of differentiation.

The research methods

The research of the network is based on a range of methods, operating at several different levels. The network includes a national expert working in every member state and a research team based at the co-ordinator's own university. All the experts involved are academic researchers[1].

The research topic is determined by consultations between the network and the European Commission's Equal Opportunities Unit. It is an iterative process with the Equal Opportunities Unit indicating the areas where it would be useful, in view of current Commission concerns, to have information. The network (primarily here the co-ordinator) puts forward more detailed proposals as to how these interests could be converted into a work programme. The network of national experts are also asked for suggestions for broad areas of research, and are then consulted over the content of the work programme. The process takes place about six months before the network starts to examine the new research topic, while the previous research report is being completed. All reports have to begin and be completed within a twelve month programme. As this involves the translation of the main report, the actual time for research is considerably shorter: ten months at the most. Annual contracts are the norm in the European Commission and clearly constrain the extent to which comparative and evaluative research can be fully developed. The system also rules out the possibility of original data collection (which is also not allowed for in budgets). The research therefore draws exclusively on secondary data sources, both quantitative and qualitative. Since the research and intelligence needs of the European Commission's Equal Opportunities Unit change relatively rapidly, according to the priorities and activities of the Commission, the work of the network is more closely related to these priorities by being organised on an annual cycle.

The initial stage in a research programme involves the collection of national data and information by national experts, according to a common work programme, and the collection and analysis of existing harmonised data and cross-national studies by the co-ordinating team. These two parts of the research programme are conducted relatively separately in the initial months. Then, in the final stages of the preparation of the report, the co-ordinating team receives the national reports and undertakes the process of integrating the national information with the cross-national data and studies. In doing so, they aim not only to collate but also to synthesis, compare and, to a limited extent, evaluate the national and cross-national findings. This last stage of the research is the most difficult but also the most important, since by comparing the findings, for example from the Eurostat harmonised information on employment and earnings with the detailed national data and with information on national institutions, further insights can be gained into the factors that may account for the differences in outcomes in measures of gender equality. The national reports also provide a means of investigating the meaning and significance of the findings: for example the extent to which part-time work has the same implications for labour market status and career in all EU member states.

The main elements that determine success in integrating a national system perspective with cross-national harmonised data include the quality and availability of good secondary sources, both quantitative and qualitative, in the member states; the extent to which national reports effectively focus on the significant characteristics, from a comparative perspective, of each member state; the availability of relevant cross-national comparative and evaluative studies which can provide information on institutional and systemic differences, even if these studies do not have a gender perspective; the co-operation of the national experts in responding to queries on the interpretation of their reports or in providing additional information where this is missing, both during the initial writing of the report and when commenting on the first draft. The network does not perform the same function as the employment observatories, where information on policies is checked meticulously, often by government officials. However, these observatories usually do not comment on their findings and, as such, may have less value than research which tries, albeit with perhaps more sketchy information, to identify the key research and policy issues for the EU and for member states.

Theoretical approach

The theoretical underpinnings of the research reflect primarily the interests and perspectives of the co-ordinator of the network, although debates are held within network meetings as to how to interpret results in theoretical as well as empirical terms. The theoretical framework for the research is based around three principles. The first is the belief that labour markets tend to be segmented (Doeringer and Piore, 1971), and that segmentation along gender lines provides one of the more significant cleavages within employment systems. The second is that labour markets have to be understood within a broad societal perspective (Maurice *et al.*, 1986; Rubery, 1988b), whereby the organisation of the labour market is the outcome of the interactions between, for example, the industrial system, the legal and regulatory system and the social reproduction system. The third is the recognition of the problems arising from the societal approach.

It is from the broad perspective on labour markets that we can derive both the proposition that gender is likely to generate labour market divisions within all employment systems and the proposition that social and economic institutions and values may affect the extent and form of gender inequality. The tendency towards universal gender differences can be argued to arise out of the social construction of gender relations and attitudes, the organisation of society into households and the division of labour between paid and unpaid work. Gender segregation in employment may be the outcome both of the gendering of the demand side of the labour market and of gender differences in labour supply conditions relating to gender roles in the home. Three main bases for gender segregation can be identified: differences in 'appropriate' gender roles or skills; differences in working time; and differences in pay. The latter two dimensions reflect assumptions of different responsibilities towards the household, with women taking responsibility for care and domestic work and men for being the main income provider, while the first dimension – roles and skills or attributes – is more cultural and not related to a specific domestic division of labour, although it is clearly important in underpinning the prevailing system of household organisation.

The societal approach takes into account cultural values and, indeed, household organisation and, thus, provides a basis for understanding the prevalence and persistence of gender differences. At the same time, it also provides a basis for the analysis of how different societies may give rise to different degrees of gender differentiation. These may arise from different social and welfare systems (Esping-Andersen, 1990), that is the extent to which they reinforce or modify the notion of a male breadwinner (Lewis, 1992; Sainsbury, 1994); from differences in labour market regulations, which may modify or reinforce gender divergence in working time or in pay levels; and from patterns of industrial organisations which may promote or reduce the tendencies towards gender segregation by industry, occupation or organisation. It is from this perspective also that we can recognise the potential differences in values and priorities which may underpin moves towards gender equality in various countries. In particular, it becomes essential within this perspective to consider policy within a broad framework, to realise that general labour market policy is likely to have more impact than specific gender equality policy in determining gender equality outcomes, and also to take into account the ramifications on the overall societal system of importing new policies which have perhaps aided gender equality elsewhere, but which within a different social and economic context may have unintended and perhaps undesirable outcomes.

The third principle driving the research is the need to recognise the dangers as well as the benefits of a societal-level approach (Rubery, 1992). These dangers arise from three factors; first the danger that the universality of gender inequality may be lost sight of in the exploration of between-country differences, leading to a false view that specific policy measures have solved problems of gender equality; second, the danger that the analysis of the role of gender relations in the maintenance of the societal system may lead, almost by definition, to a focus on the harmony between the current gender order and the societal arrangements, such that the inequalities which the system imposes on women are played down and, instead, the compatibilities between current arrangements and current social values are emphasised; and thirdly, the danger that a societal based approach will emphasise differences between women from one country to another but neglect differences in the interests and fortunes of women within nation states. This issue has particular relevance to the work within the European Union where evidence is emerging of some convergence between higher educated women across EU member states, while more major differences between countries can be found for women with lower qualifications.

Thus, in developing the research of the network, a delicate balance had to be found between, on the one hand, explaining differences between member states by reference to different societal systems and, on the other hand, providing an evaluation of the extent to which the societal system could be regarded as 'female friendly'.

Problems of monitoring and evaluating societal systems

The research that the network undertakes has a distinct policy orientation. There is no requirement to propose specific measures, but the work is undertaken within a policy focus and the national experts are concerned both with policy at a nation-state and a European level. This remit has been strengthened as a consequence of the more focused approach to labour market policy within the European Union following the Delors White Paper on Growth, Competitiveness and Employment and the conclusions of the Essen summit in December 1994 (see OECD, 1994d, for a similar attempt to 'mainstream' gender). The work of the network has contributed to the mainstreaming of gender issues but has also revealed some of the complexities of integrating gender because of the differences between member states in not only specific employment patterns but also values and aspirations. Each of the reports we have completed has raised issues relating to the problems of formulating either common objectives or common policy initiatives across all member states. These findings suggest that the European Commission should act as a catalyst for national level policy, and, indeed, should have a monitoring and evaluative role (Rubery and Fagan, 1994a), but policies also need to be developed and implemented at the national level so that they can be better targeted at the key problems confronting women within EU member states.

Gender segregation in context

Research has shown that, despite declining segregation in higher level jobs, and the maintenance or increase in segregation within lower level clerical and manual jobs, European labour markets are strongly segregated by gender (Rubery and Fagan, 1993; Rubery and Fagan, 1995b). The similarity of patterns across member states has not, however, resulted in the identification of clear or universal policy prescriptions as to how to change the segregated nature of European labour markets.

The types of factors which affect the appropriateness and priority accorded to desegregation over reducing the penalties of segregation include the level of relative pay in women's jobs, the level of employment and unemployment among women and the range of jobs in which women are employed. Issues of pay dominate over those of segregation in countries such as the United Kingdom where there is an extreme dispersion of pay rates and low relative pay levels for women; 'horizontal' desegregation takes on greater importance in some Southern European countries where women are still excluded from many service sector jobs and where unemployment rates are high and employment rates low; while vertical desegregation becomes the main focus in some Northern countries where women are already concentrated in the expanding lower level job areas.

The choice between acting on training and education or through employer policies is again influenced by whether access to jobs is strongly regulated by qualifications, whether through vocational training, as for example in Germany (Maier, 1995), or the educational system, as for example in Denmark. Even in these countries, employers can still deny women access to jobs, but acquiring qualifications is an essential prerequisite to breaking down segregation. However, in other countries such as the United Kingdom, a more flexible system of access prevails in many job areas, which means that there is no recognised system of job grading based on skills and qualifications. Thus, there is more scope in the United Kingdom, than in countries where job and pay grading structures are based on qualifications, for those jobs which become feminised to move down the pay and job status hierarchy.

Finally, the introduction of family-friendly policies is likely to be perceived as more useful to women in countries where constraints on part-time work or parental leave opportunities are seen as major barriers to continuous participation. Under these conditions, such policies may help women retain their position in the job market hierarchy. In other countries where women are already integrated more on a full-time basis into the labour market, such policies may be regarded as retrograde, unnecessarily reinforcing women's position as homemakers.

Contexts for wage determination and sex segregation

The most controversial policy issue to emerge out of the analysis of the impact of wage determination systems on gender pay equity was whether it was appropriate to advocate a move towards the use of job evaluation to implement the principle of equal pay for work of equal value. Analytical job evaluation has come to be seen in many Anglo-Saxon countries as a major means by which existing pay differentials between men's and women's work can be challenged, and also as a means of making visible the skills employed in women's jobs.

The research programme was also carried out to coincide with the preparation of a memorandum on equal pay for work of equal value by the Equal Opportunities Unit which implicitly endorses job evaluation as the main technique for implementing equal value, although some of the potential pitfalls are also recognised.

The cross-national research revealed a common problem of the undervaluation of women's jobs in EU countries, although the extent of the problem varied according to the degree of wage dispersion and the existence or otherwise of formal pay structures (Rubery and Fagan, 1994b; Rubery and Fagan, 1995a). More controversial was the determination of the appropriate policy response to the problem. There were concerns that to embrace the principle of job evaluation might undermine and destabilise the system of collective bargaining or formal pay determination within the private and/or the public sectors, and *de facto* may provide greater power to management in the determination of pay differentials. The long-term impact of such changes could be negative for women. Such concerns have been echoed in fact in some of the studies of comparable worth in the United States (see Acker, 1989). The effectiveness and use of a payment system has to be situated within the broader economic, social and political context. In Greece, for example, job evaluation was primarily found in multinationals who were trying to break away from the collective bargaining system, and in Italy seniority pay, often regarded in countries where women have interrupted career patterns as a blatant form of sex discrimination, was argued to have done much in Italy to bring about equalisation of pay between the sexes. The strategy which would do most to narrow the gender pay gap in the longer term was recognised to depend on the social, economic and indeed political context.

Contextualising changes in work patterns and working time

An equally contentious issue for determining EU policy arises in the study of work patterns and working time, namely that of part-time work. The network study (Rubery *et al.*, 1995a) clearly showed that part-time work was not an essential prerequisite for women to enter or remain in wage work, even when they had responsibility for children, but nevertheless part-time work remains primarily a female preserve and is strongly associated with the segregation of women into lower paid and lower skilled jobs. On these grounds, the case could clearly be made that the Delors White Paper advocacy of part-time work as a form of work sharing without an analysis of its implications for gender segregation and for the continuing subordination of women within the labour market and the household was unacceptable. The gendered nature of part-time work needs to be identified and its consequences for issues of gender equality weighed against other forms of work sharing such as short full-time weeks which were ruled out of consideration in follow-up to the White Paper.

Critiques of existing policy perspectives tend to be straightforward; a more difficult issue is to develop a working-time policy for gender equality (Fagan *et al.*, 1994). Two types of problems can be identified; the first relates to the longer term vision of what constitutes a society where there is gender equality. To some, and in particular the debate in the Netherlands can be identified, a gender equal society is also one in which both partners have time for care work, that is a 'caring model' of work patterns and not a 'careless' pattern. For others, and here the French debate on part-time work can be cited, the more important factor is to minimise the identification of women with a specific care role, so that policies which may reaffirm women's role as carers by providing opportunities for part-time or interrupted work should be recognised as harmful to gender equality. This model would also espouse a move towards a shorter working week for all, but the need not to differentiate by gender is given priority over the need to facilitate care.

A second type of problem relates to the practicalities of policy positions. In a society where men work very long hours, is it practical or possible to oppose part-time work? To what extent should policy reflect the existing norms and values of the women concerned in societies where mothers express preferences for part-time work? Is it possible or appropriate to regard these preferences as simply the effect of lack of publicly provided childcare or are there different value systems which need to be taken into account?

Public policy and employment rates

One aspect of the research into the role of women and the European employment rate involved the consideration of public policy in shaping women's participation patterns (Rubery *et al.*, 1995b). Here the research aimed to distinguish between strong and weak breadwinner models of household organisations (Lewis, 1992) and to identify the role of the welfare system in shaping and reinforcing household organisation, and in limiting women's independent access to resources. These policy concerns necessarily led to a consideration of the case for individualisation of rights in the welfare system, a principle called for in the Delors White Paper and at the Essen summit.

The research indicated that the extent to which individualisation can and would benefit women depends on their position in the labour market, the particular form of the benefit system and the number of women who have entered into a gender contract where they have assumed that they would be provided for by their partners.

Methods and management: an agenda for improvement

The research work undertaken by the network of experts on the situation of women in the labour market is necessarily constrained by its remit to provide timely information on an annual cycle to the European Commission's Equal Opportunities Unit. The needs of the European Commission within a rapidly changing policy environment may preclude a lengthening of the time period available for the research. However, the work of the network could be greatly eased and improved if the now numerous reports on labour market developments adopted a gender perspective. If all EU publications and reports contained information broken down by gender, and if comparisons of industrial relations systems paid attention to what is occurring in service sectors and among part-time as well as full-time workers, fewer gaps would exist in the information base that need to be filled before the work of the comparison and evaluation can begin (see CERC, 1991, for an example of a report which did provide a gender dimension). Because of the gender blindness of many reports, gender research has often to start from almost a blank sheet. Where gender is taken into account the results are often inadequate. For example, the OECD Jobs study (OECD, 1994b) attempts to look at differences in receipt of unemployment benefits for men and women but only takes into account the fact that men are more likely to have a dependent spouse and not that they tend to earn more and on a more continuous basis than women. Even worse, many data, for example on benefit entitlements for people on average earnings in reports by the OECD and the EU, do not even state whether they are using male or male and female combined categories (reports referred to here include some tables in OECD, 1995, and Commission of the European Communities, 1995). Choice of examples for considering gender issues are also often inappropriate; for example in looking at the effect of part-time work on pension entitlements, the EU report on social protection (Commission of the European Communities, 1993c) assumed, for illustrative purposes, that the person worked half time when in a part-time job and returned to full-time work 20 years before retirement. Under these conditions, part-time work has little effect on pension entitlement, but under assumptions of either shorter than half-time working or continuing in part-time work up to retirement the situation would be very different.

Thus, the main way to assist the efforts of the network to improve the quality and the depth of its work would be to expand the comparative information base from a gender perspective. Mainstreaming of gender cannot be left to one group of experts but needs to be adopted across the board within the EU policy-making and research community.

Note

1. Many of the individual experts draw upon the help of other researchers to assist in their work for the network, and in some cases two national experts effectively share the work, taking it in turns for one to be nominated as the named expert. All member states receive the same funding for the research, irrespective of either size of country or number of experts involved. Full meetings of the network are held twice a year in Brussels, hosted by the Commission, with the co-ordinator travelling more frequently to Brussels to consult over the research and present results.

16 Cross-National Research and the 'New Community Power'

Alan Harding

The conceptual and methodological aspects of a research project entitled 'Coalition-Formation and Urban Redevelopment: a Cross-National Study' forms the basis of the present discussion. The project was part of a wider programme of research which focused primarily on Britain. Cross-national comparison was, nonetheless, encouraged under the programme's objectives which were: firstly, to analyse the fragmentation of decision-making within the United Kingdom and the transition from local government to multi-institutional local governance; secondly, to assess the strengths and weaknesses of current theoretical approaches from an interdisciplinary perspective; and thirdly, to compare the system of British local governance with international trends. The project concentrated upon urban development and regeneration policies and activities. The degree of flux, fragmentation and experimentation apparent within British local governance in this field created an interesting canvass on which to test the first of the empirical concerns of the wider research programme. But it was progress with regard to the other two concerns that offered the greatest potential advance in British analysis and posed the most interesting challenges for cross-national research.

Analysis of British experience has predominantly assumed that recent change is driven by the politics of Conservative governments (Barnekov *et al.*, 1989; Deakin and Edwards, 1994), the institutional changes they induced (Brindley *et al.*, 1989; Atkinson and Moon, 1994) and the reactions they triggered in the wider policy community (Jacobs, 1992; Thornley, 1992). Whilst not exactly wrong, this analysis tends, firstly, to rest upon a narrow political-administrative analysis, and applies only to a relatively brief time period; secondly, to make implicit judgements about British exceptionalism without the benefit of any structured comparison with other countries; and, thirdly, to operate in a theoretical vacuum. The dominant approach in the United Kingdom was, therefore, vulnerable to criticisms that it exaggerated the difference between the pre- and post-1979 periods, overstressed the particularism of the British experience and suggested the range of available alternative approaches was perhaps wider than it was in reality.

The project challenged the implicit basis of much British research in allowing for three rather different possibilities. First, that the process of coalition-formation for urban redevelopment might be a response to global rather than domestic factors and that the experience of other countries might be more similar and more relevant to that of the United Kingdom than was often assumed. Second, that 'foreign' approaches to the study of accommodations between levels of government and between public and private sectors, though generally regarded suspiciously, might, suitably adapted, be useful in developing concepts and methods for analysing the European experience. Thirdly, that comparative analysis within Europe would help put the British experience into perspective.

Substantively, the project assessed whether the formation of subnational development coalitions, a long-standing phenomena in the United States, had become common in Europe and how much change there had been in recent years. It asked if recent changes were significant, what lay behind them and whether they were broadly caused by international, national or subnational factors. It examined what forms coalitions took, who the key players within them were, what motivated these players and how such motivations had changed. It also assessed how different public and private sector interests co-operated on specific projects and with what results.

A number of cross-national research issues had to be addressed in order to examine these questions adequately. The substantive objectives of the project were: to synthesise two potentially complementary theoretical approaches to the study of decision-making on urban redevelopment; to develop a research methodology, drawing on these two approaches, which could be applied on a cross-national basis; to collect a new body of research information by applying this methodology to studies of five Northern European cities; and to further understanding of new forms of urban redevelopment decision-making which are likely to be of increasing importance in a more unified Europe.

The cross-national research challenge was theoretical and methodological. At the theoretical level, it meant creating a viable set of research questions which could be tested in a European context from two previously unlinked and contrasting literatures, each operating at very different levels of generality. At the methodological level, the challenge was to develop research tools that could adequately address the key research questions in each national context whilst also minimising the impact of language barriers. The way the project attempted to cope with these challenges is described in the next two sections.

From theoretical eclecticism to a structured research framework

The purpose in synthesising the two literatures alluded to above was to give fresh conceptual insight to the traditional community power debate, which has long been an essential reference point within British urban studies but has never made any appreciable impact on the methods or objects of British research (Saunders, 1979; Dunleavy, 1980; Harding, 1995; Judge, 1995). The project proposed a modernised approach to community power which transcended conceptual and methodological limitations and distinguished between power within communities and the power of communities.

Although tracing patterns of power and influence within communities was a central concern of the original community power schools, the project considered the literature that evolved from them – recent North American work on urban political economy – to be conceptually more relevant to contemporary study. The project drew upon urban regime theory (Elkin, 1987; Stone and Sanders, 1987; Stone, 1989), the growth machine thesis (Molotch, 1976, 1990; Logan and Molotch, 1987) and related writings (Cox, 1989; Cox and Mair, 1988), all of which essentially examine and explain who, working within or on behalf of particular localities, has influence or power over the decisions which result in their physical reproduction and modification. They argue that electoral coalitions rarely govern in more than a narrow sense. Rather than concentrate on formal local politics, therefore, they are concerned to analyse how the power to achieve certain development objectives is fused together by public and private sector organisations and interests which are independent of each other but incapable of bringing about desired changes alone.

The key to utilising the American literature for comparative work in Europe lay in overcoming its tendency to take important characteristics of North American social, economic and politico-administrative structures for granted and to assume that the way they predisposed different interest groups into particular forms of behaviour were common. While there has been significant interest in applying insights from this literature to empirical study beyond the United States (Harding, 1991; Levine, 1994; Caulfield and Wanna, 1995), the tendency is to overlook differences between American circumstances and those in other countries. As a result, scepticism has been expressed about the value of such efforts and about the literature's ethnocentricity (Shaw, 1993; Stoker and Mossberger, 1994). The key to overcoming these reservations is not to reject the literature wholesale, but to take from it what is widely applicable, to use work whose general applicability is questionable as a basis for research hypotheses that are amenable to empirical verification and actually to test whether the underlying conditions that promote subnational coalitions in the United States are also found in Europe.

The project's other theoretical component helped in the latter task by highlighting ways in which national experiences might become more similar as a result of global level influences. The project assessed two key ways that supranational forces have been argued to affect national and subnational decision-making, privileging the latter by examining economic geography and the politics of globalisation (Harding and Le Galès, 1996). The first meant consulting a wide range of literature analysing localised sources of dynamism within the global economy and the factors that appear to influence them (Castells, 1989; Storper and Walker, 1989; Beccatini and Sengenberger, 1990; Ohmae, 1990). The second, concentrating on regulation theory (Aglietta, 1979; Boyer, 1986; Jessop, 1994; Mayer, 1994), which involved unravelling the various ways subnational institutional structures and policies delivered subnationally might be affected by national adjustments to new global economic circumstances.

Neither literature was ideal for the task in hand. With regulation theory, the main problem was the highly abstract level at which argument is pitched and the apparent reluctance to apply it to detailed analyses of particular national experiences. The theory had to be 'filled out' before some tangible implications could be drawn from it and research questions generated for empirical analysis. The opposite problem applied to the economic geography literature. Here, because analyses are largely deductive, the list of factors said to 'cause' changes in locational decision-making and high rates of local economic growth is bewilderingly long and relatively few attempts have been made to prioritise them. Where analysis has been conducted, notions such as 'institutional thickness' are used to explain variations in the innovative development capacities of localities. Such concepts are seen as 'very general, even vague . . .

liminal concepts', including by their proponents (Amin and Thrift, 1993, p. 16), and they clearly require further elaboration before they could form a basis for research.

Ultimately, theoretical formulations were used parsimoniously to support the particular needs of the project. The weaknesses of the literatures were isolated and their strengths used to generate useful hypotheses against which empirical results could be tested. This demanded building up a strongest case scenario as to what sorts of institutional and policy changes were likely in situations where generalised, cross-national changes are leading to a strengthening of subnational autonomy. Further, it requires the assembling of a list of research questions which would enable comparisons and contrasts to be made between the United States and Europe and among European countries.

The more general, globalisation literature suggested a number of possible scenarios: for example, change in the mode of governance, from welfare/distributive to developmental/supply-side orientations and from nationally based, process orientated arrangements to ones that are locally based and product orientated; encouragement of more 'entrepreneurial' subnational decision-making intended to make urban regions more competitive in global markets; flexibility and experimentation in the design and delivery of policy initiatives, decentralisation to subnational institutions and non-governmental interests who know localities best; and greater use of national government sanctions and incentives to improve mobilisation and capacity building at subnational level and more intergovernmental development partnerships.

The urban political economy literature, on the other hand, suggested a clear focus on the interaction of politics and markets at subnational level. It helped frame several useful questions: for example, who the key coalition builders were likely to be and what would motivate them; how business leaders' motivations might be affected by their level of dependence on local markets, the sectors they operate in and their membership of business networks; how the various interests, formally or informally, go about 'gaining and fusing a capacity to act' (Stone, 1989, p. 229); and how the propensity of public authorities to support development coalitions might be affected by intergovernmental financial transfers, proportionate reliance on local business taxes, patterns of business mobilisation within formal local politics and their powers in the development field, as dictated by the various resources over which they have influence or control.

Out of the library and into the field

The conceptual phase also generated key questions to guide the detailed case study research. Had the promotion of urban development and regeneration become more important as a result of the recent history of national, regional and local policy change? What institutional changes, if any, had been associated with policy change? Had interest in urban–regional economic fortunes, and in redevelopment initiatives, grown within the private sector, and was there evidence of greater self-organisation among business leaders? And, which key projects characterised intergovernmental and public–private sector partnerships in particular cities, and how were they developed and delivered?

The research was comparative in various ways. Minimally, it compared nations, in that it examined the way national policy change and institutional restructuring affected the nature and incidence of development coalitions; it looked at cities and city-regions as the primary analytic objects, and institutions and inter-organisational relations, since the powers, resources and structures of public and private agencies and the formal interactions between them were important to case study observations. Policy and strategy formation were relevant in so far as they provided the focus through which the roles and behaviours of different actors and interests were analysed, as was networking behaviour, in that the case study method tried to identify informal as well as formal channels of communication and coalition building.

The study was also wide ranging in that it attempted to analyse key inputs to policy formation, coalition-building and project delivery, the processes themselves and both the outputs (as measured by the success or otherwise in delivering project goals) and certain outcomes (in terms of changing the way outputs were attained). The project's mode of enquiry was analytic in that certain research questions were prioritised over others as a result of the conceptual phase, descriptive in so far as the compilation of case study narratives was essential to the final product, and evaluative in that case study evidence was used to compare different national/subnational experiences and to refer back to conceptual antecedents and assess their explanatory power.

The empirical part of the project was managed in two phases. They differed in the balance of data sources and data gathering methods used, but one general, overriding requirement was to surmount language barriers. This meant choosing case study areas carefully, balancing the ideal in terms of comparison with pragmatic 'deliverability' criteria. The non-UK case study cities were chosen on the basis of the author's previous knowledge and friendly contacts within them, the English-speaking prowess of their policy communities, the density of English-language secondary sources available, the likelihood of certain primary materials being available in translation and the need to minimise the use of interpreters. Ultimately, the project focused upon five Northern European cities, a choice that offered the additional advantage of limiting the degree of socio-cultural variation while at the same time ensuring a good degree of constitutional and politico-administrative contrast. They were Amsterdam, Copenhagen, Edinburgh, Hamburg and Manchester.

The cities are similar in the way that all reasonably large, well-established cities in Northern Europe are similar. But they were not chosen for their similarities, not least because one of the claims from the globalisation literature that the research wished to test was whether urban experiences became more similar as the result of changes that applied irrespective of national location. The cities and their regions vary, for example, in size, degree of centrality/ peripherality in Europe, city-regional economic structures and trajectories and local patterns of political domination and change.

The need to minimise the impact of language barriers had implications for the choice of research methods, too. It meant opting for an interview based approach, supplemented by easily translated data. In total, the project involved extensive interviews with government and quasi-public organisations, the non-statutory (mainly private) sector and with academic contracts. Developing this approach presented few practical difficulties, but it did not flow straightforwardly from the conceptual phase because the one thing that neither of the theoretical literatures could do was suggest in detail how empirical study might be operationalised. This was particularly surprising in the case of American urban political economy where, paradoxically, there is heavy reliance on arguments built up from case study evidence but very little discussion of research methodology. Only Stone (1989, pp. 254–60) deals overtly with methods and sources, and then only briefly in an appendix.

Therefore, the project ultimately returned to the original community power school in the search for appropriate research tools. It adopted a methodologically individualist approach that built on the three main methods used – which are rarely combined, but defended vigorously as alternatives – within the community power debate.

The three approaches used were reputational, positional and decisional analysis. The reputational method, as favoured by elite theorists, relies on evidence about the reputation for power or influence commanded by certain key individuals. The positional approach also sees power as being the property of individuals in the last instance but argues that it depends upon the nature of the organisation or group to which individuals belong, the assets at the organisation's disposal and the extent to which the individual concerned can command their deployment.

These two approaches can usefully be combined as an *entrée* into empirical work in that they pose questions along the lines of 'Who cares? Who is active? Who could achieve?'. They cannot satisfactorily answer questions of 'Who achieves and how?', as neither the expectation that certain individuals or groups will have power and influence in particular circumstances because of their status and roles, nor second-hand assessments of their importance comprise compelling evidence in themselves. Such questions are best approached through some form of decisional analysis, as traditionally favoured by pluralists, which demands more direct observation of who has influence and power in actual decision-making situations.

The first phase of the empirical work combined desk work and introductory interviews. A trawl was made through various social science databases in order to assemble appropriate English-language secondary material, where available, on each of the key topics generated in the conceptual phase, for example on relevant national and local policy changes, patterns of institutional restructuring, and subnational business mobilisation. Then, a number of statistical snapshots, which together described changes in appropriate economic, social, political and demographic conditions within the case study areas over the relevant time period, were assembled by exploiting various published and on-line sources (for British cities) and specialist statistical yearbooks (for non-British comparators).

Subsequently, work began on a reputational analysis. Preliminary case study visits were used, in part to probe knowledgeable interviewees with a good overview of the politics of development within their areas – between four and six people, drawn from academia, the media, key business organisations and the local public authority – about useful data sources and the key networks within which individuals interested in development issues operate. On the basis of such information, two separate listings were conducted. One, using international business databases, generated lists of individuals who were senior executives and directors within the largest companies (by turnover) in each city. This list delimited an economic elite and made it possible, by checking multiple/overlapping directorships, to identify powerful business leaders. The other involved assembling a list of individuals who served in similar positions within various partnership organisations active in the development field and in other civic organisations. By combining and comparing these two lists, it was possible to identify overlap between economic and civic elites and to select influential individuals, who might be invisible in other research methods, but who were most active within developmental debates, strategies and projects.

In case the listings approach proved ineffective, and to cross-verify its findings, a more subjective form of network analysis was attempted. This meant repeating, in a very limited form, the reputational technique of elite theorists, essentially asking initial interviewees to name key individuals who were interested and active within development politics, arranging further interviews for the main case study visit, repeating the questions and so generating a snowballing effect. The knowledgeable contacts within each city were also useful in two other ways. They aided positional analysis by identifying key interviewees within the public sector. Such individuals are, of course, much more visible and accessible to the researcher simply because of their formal statutory roles and responsibilities, but the initial interviews enabled the project to 'get at' key figures quickly and often helped with introductions. The knowledgeable contacts were also able to point to a number of major projects that illustrated processes of intergovernmental and public–private sector partnership operating within their areas. A series of interviews followed up the general agenda generated by the conceptual phase and concentrated upon the pattern of public and private sector involvement in redevelopment and associated activities, individual and organisational motivations for becoming involved and perceptions of what had caused them to change, and the formal and informal ways in which collaboration was organised, resources assembled and actions co-ordinated. The bulk of decisional analysis was based around two key projects within each city. One project was 'internationalist' while the other sought to alleviate specific local problems. The projects exemplified some of the principal processes operating within the cities. For each, the research probed the background to the initiative, how and why it came about, the contributions of the various partners and the reasons they were made, the decision-making structures developed for realising the project, and the broad costs and benefits of the initiative for the partners themselves and for other interest groups.

Evaluating the project: wisdom after the event?

Methodologically, the project was reasonably successful. It would have helped to have been able to translate larger amounts of primary and secondary material. But such was the nature of the study, and of the information that interviews tried to unearth, that written materials could only have played a minor part. On one hand, the concerns of the project were very specific and relatively little secondary analysis was likely to have been undertaken in the same field. On the other, the bulk of primary documentation tends either to serve public relations goals or simply to record, usually in rather deadpan and opaque fashion, compromises made behind the scenes between powerful decision-makers. It was the process of compromise, rather than the document that noted it, that was central to the research.

Not being able to use primary documentation in this way in the non-British cases simply meant that more questions had to elicit factual description as opposed to analysis and evaluation. Since time constraints were rarely an issue, though, this posed few problems. The one methodological component of the study which only performed well in some cases was the listings process. Business listings sources were easily traceable, but the variation in the extent to which development related and civic networks were formalised on the emerging British model made comparison difficult. Although the listings procedure helped in all cases – it tended to highlight interesting cultural and political differences, as well as identify key interviewees – it had to be backed up by the more subjective network analysis in all non-British cases.

Most project tasks were performed by the author, with limited support in gathering statistical and listings data from colleagues. This had its drawbacks but also avoided the disadvantages that can arise from various researchers or teams ostensibly sharing a common methodology but in reality approaching case studies very differently. If mistakes were made within the project, they were made consistently, in all places. An important advantage in each of the non-UK case study visits was the resort to a base within a supportive academic environment which not only helped overcome routine logistical problems but provided a constant stream of low level intelligence which was vital in developing a more nuanced understanding of each place.

Overall, the project managed to achieve the cross-national research objectives initially set for it. It successfully synthesised the two sets of . theoretical literature and generated a reasonably consistent set of research questions against which empirical observations could be tested, thus making structured, cross-national comparison possible. It made good the methodological deficiencies and limitations of the theoretical literatures by seeking out other appropriate empirical research tools and combining them into a methodology that worked more powerfully than any one of them could independently, was consistent with the concepts derived from the theoretical literature, and minimised the potential impact of language barriers. It generated a body of comparative empirical work which avoids tendencies toward insularity and ethnocentricity on the one hand, and a simplistic approach to cross-national comparison on the other.

Acknowledgements

This paper is based on work undertaken for a research project entitled 'Coalition-Formation and Urban Redevelopment: a Cross-National Study', financed through the UK Economic and Social Research Council's Local Governance Programme (Project L311253002).

Departure Points for Further Reading

Introduction to cross-national research

The literature treating cross-national methods in the social sciences is superabundant. Reference is, therefore, made here to a highly selective list of readings, which provide an orientation to the field.

For readers seeking detailed treatment of specific methods in quantitative, qualitative and evaluative research, Sage has published an extensive series, although the books are not necessarily presented within a cross-national focus. The edited collection by Kohn (1989) provides a useful analysis of the case for carrying out cross-national research in sociology, while the text by Johnson and Tuttle (1989) looks at the problems of intercultural research. The contributors to the volume edited by Øyen (1990) examine the strengths and weaknesses of using different concepts, theories and methods within cross-national contexts. Sage has also launched a methods database on CD-Rom.

Jones (1985, new edition 1996) has provided a highly accessible source book for comparative social policy analysis. Another preliminary contribution is that of Dogan and Pelassy (1984), which covers relevant material from within the perspective of comparative politics. More advanced readers should consult the seminal works of Przeworski and Teune (1970), Smelser (1976) and Ragin (1987, 1991).

Quantitative methods

The literature on quantitative methods is more advanced for the universal, scientific dimension than for the national, administrative one. The history of statistics as cognitive and mathematical techniques is described, for example, by Porter (1986), Stigler (1986) and Hacking (1990). The national development of statistical administrations is described for Britain by Szreter (1991), for the United States by Anderson (1988) and Duncan and Shelton (1978), and for France by INSÉÉ (1987). Desrosières (1993) synthesises two dimensions up to 1940. No comprehensive comparative international description of statistics exists for different countries and, in particular, on questions of harmonisation.

Hyman (1972), Hakim (1982) and Grémy (1989) explore the research areas and issues where secondary analysis of primary data can usefully be exploited. Dale *et al.* (1988) discuss the potential of secondary analysis for testing theoretical perspectives, and Arber and Ginn (1991), and Dale (1993) examine how the approach can be applied in the analysis of sub-populations.

Summers *et al.* (1993) have edited a collection of contributions on large-scale comparative analysis of policy on urban change in the United States and Western Europe. Cheshire and Hay (1989) have published an economic analysis of urban problems in Western Europe.

Large-scale, quantitative, comparative studies of social security provision are well established (for example Gordon, 1988). A large-scale historical study of the evolution of social security, making extensive use of quantitative data, is provided by the Study Group on Historical Indicators of West European Democracies (HIWED) and is published in a collection by Flora and Heidenheimer (1981). Fridberg (1993) has compared provision in the Nordic states, while Øverbye (1994) has looked at the ways different European countries have combined insurance and assistance schemes. Berghman and Cantillon's (1993) edited collection covers social security systems in Europe, including analysis of the legal and structural features of social assistance schemes in selected countries, and Mitchell (1991) focuses on income transfers. The Welfare State Programme of the Suntory-Toyota International Centre for Economics and Related Disciplines has used social security and taxation data to examine distributional impacts and has extended their models to Eastern Europe (see for example Atkinson, 1992; Atkinson and Mickelwright, 1992; Gardiner *et al.*, 1995). The European Commission's MISSOC project includes descriptive tables on minimum income schemes for the EU member states, which can be used for an initial comparative analysis.

The policy simulation technique was first developed by Kamerman and Kahn (1978) in international comparisons of family policy. It was used by Bradshaw and Piachaud (1980) to study child support in Europe and was further elaborated in the study of child support packages in fifteen, and then eighteen countries by Bradshaw *et al.* (1993) and Bradshaw (1995). This approach is used routinely in OECD studies (for example OECD, 1990) and has also been applied by Whiteford and Bradshaw (1994) in a study of the structural and incentive effects of benefit policies for lone parents, and by Shaver and Bradshaw (1995) to examine support for married women who stay at home to look after children.

Qualitative methods

The most instructive reading on systems approaches, normative models, and the application of normative criteria shows these approaches in practice. The analysis of systems is more usually undertaken by using descriptive empirical categories rather than normative criteria. The most notable examples of normative analysis of systems are Esping-Andersen (1990) and Korpi and Palme (1994), though the latter has still to be published more widely. The analyses of Rueschemeyer *et al.* (1992) and the collection by Castles (1993) consider methodological issues in relation to model building in comparative contexts. For the development of models, which is an aspect of more general consideration of systems, accessible examples are Mishra (1981) and Palme (1990). In relation to the application of normative criteria, Spicker (1993) is unusual in referring to a wide range of issues; it is more typical to see studies based on a particular criterion, like equality, and analysed in quantitative terms.

The issues raised by qualitative comparative analysis of education and training are developed in Jobert *et al.* (1995). Ryan (1991) brings together an interesting collection of papers on various aspects of vocational training, while Chisholm (1992) examines the diversity of national education and training systems, and Drake (1995) identifies different forms of linkages between schools, firms and labour markets in an OECD study.

Themes and findings which raise new questions for qualitative, comparative research into elder care can be found in the European observatory study report (Walker *et al.*, 1993), the OECD elder care series (OECD, 1994; with two further volumes forthcoming) and Alber (1995). New approaches to the comparative analysis of welfare regimes with particular attention to informal care and the position of women are proposed by Chamberlayne (1993) and Ostner (1994). Room and 6 (1994) focus on the role of the third sector as a central dimension of comparative welfare state analysis.

The Narrative Study of Lives by Josselson and Lieblich (1993) provides a good and accessible introduction to the use of hermeneutic and related methods, and includes a chapter which demonstrates a key aspect of Rosenthal's case reconstruction method. For an overview of developments and issues in qualitative methods in

Germany in the 1970s and 1980s, see Gerhardt (1988). A comparable and more recent account of developments in English-speaking life-history methods is given by Thomson *et al.* (1994). Contradictions between the public and private spheres in welfare of East and West Germany are discussed by Chamberlayne (1995), whereas Balbo (1987) provides a stimulating starting point for consideration of the modernisation of women's roles through the mediation of welfare.

Accessing information

The literature on accessing information is less abundant. The early studies by Maurice (1979) and Maurice *et al.* (1996) established the importance of gaining access to detailed knowledge about the societal contexts in which well-defined phenomena are located within the context of industrial sociology. Hyman's (1994) work has also helped to raise awareness of issues for comparative researchers studying industrial relations, while Heidemann *et al.* (1994) have looked at vocational training as a component of the social dialogue. Hannerz (1992), a Swedish social anthropologist, examines the problems of understanding cultures in a global perspective, thus contributing to the discussion of foundations of cross-cultural research.

Some of the specific problems arising in the use of different types of vignette techniques are discussed by Alexander and Becker (1978), Burstin *et al.* (1980), Stillion *et al.* (1984), including qualitative and quantitative aspects of the method and experience of using vignettes to gain insights into culturally determined social attitudes.

The problems encountered by historians engaged in cross-national comparisons, particularly of political change, are covered by Lijphart (1971), and by Rustow and Paul (1991). Issues arising in urban history are addressed by Dyos (1976), and the oral history method is analysed by the contributors to Grele's (1975) edited collection.

The focus in Engbersen *et al.* (1993) is on conceptualising the cultures of unemployment.

Evaluation

Definitions of evaluation and the issues raised by attempts to evaluate European projects and programmes are examined by Bowden (1988), Cram (1993), Foley (1994), and Rossi and Freeman (1993). Ferrera (1993) brings together several contributions evaluating the operation of the European observatories and networks.

A number of evaluative studies have examined poverty and social exclusion from a comparative perspective. Of particular interest are those by Deleeck *et al.* (1992), Rodgers *et al.* (1995) and Room (1995). The Luxembourg Income Study by Smeeding *et al.* (1989) compares income distribution across nations, and Heidenheimer *et al.* (1990) assess public policy in widely differing welfare contexts.

Evaluation of the gender dimension of the labour market is the focus of the comparative studies reported in the collection edited by Rubery (1988) on women and recession, using the societal systems approach. The collection of articles edited by Sainsbury (1994) explores the same topic from a comparative perspective, involving both detailed bilateral comparisons and attempts to develop indices. The OECD (1994d) looks at the role that women's employment has played in the structural changes taking place within OECD countries. For information on comparative labour market trends readers should also refer to regular reports by the OECD, *Employment Outlook*, and by the European Commission, including *Employment in Europe* and *Social Protection in Europe*.

The edited collection by Alterman and Cars (1991) provides a useful contextualisation of issues concerning local area regeneration in a series of evaluative European case studies. Evaluation of urban policy is the subject of works by Robson (1994). Hambleton and Thomas (1995) assess urban policy evaluative approaches, mostly from a UK focus but with some international comparisons.

Bibliography

Abrahamson, P. (1991) 'Welfare and poverty in the Europe of the 1990s: social progress or social dumping?', *International Journal of Health Services*, vol. 21, no. 2, pp. 237–64.

Acker, J. (1989) *Doing Comparable Work: Gender, Class and Pay Equity* (Philadelphia: Temple University Press).

Aglietta, M. (1979) *A Theory of Capitalist Regulation* (London: New Left Books).

Alber, J. (1994) 'Paying for long-term care in a social insurance system'. Paper presented at the OECD meeting on Caring for Frail Elderly People: Policies for the Future, 5–6 July, Paris.

Alber, J. (1995) 'A framework for the comparative study of social services', *Journal of European Social Policy*, vol. 5, no. 2, pp. 131–49.

Alexander, C.S. and Becker, H.J. (1978) 'The use of vignettes in survey research', *Public Opinion Quarterly*, vol. 42, pp. 93–104.

Alterman, R. and Cars, G. (eds) (1991) *Neighbourhood Regeneration: an International Evaluation* (London: Mansell).

Amin, A. and Thrift, N. (1993) 'Globalisation, institutional thickness and local prospects'. Paper to the seminar on Challenges in Urban Management, 25–27 March, Newcastle University.

Anderson, M.J. (1988) *The American Census. A Social History* (New Haven and London: Yale University Press).

Anttonen, A. and Sipilä, J. (1995) 'Five regimes of social care services'. Paper presented at the 8th Nordic Social Policy Research Seminar, 9–11 February, Stockholm.

Arber, S. and Ginn, J. (1991) *Gender and Later Life* (London: Sage).

Atkinson, A.B. (1992) 'The welfare experience with social safety nets', *STICERD Welfare State Programme Working Paper*, no. 80 (London: STICERD).

Atkinson, A.B. and Mickelwright, J. (1992) 'The distribution of income in Eastern Europe', *STICERD Welfare State Programme Working Paper*, no. 72 (London: STICERD).

Atkinson, R. and Moon, G. (1994) *Urban Policy in Britain: the City, the State and the Market* (London: Macmillan).

Back, L. and Solomos, J. (1993) 'Doing research, writing politics: the dilemmas of political intervention in research on racism', *Economy and Society*, vol. 22, pp. 178–99.

Baglioni, G. and Crouch, C. (1990) *European Industrial Relations. The Challenge of Flexibility* (London: Sage).

Baker, J. (1986) 'Comparing national priorities', *Journal of Social Policy*, vol. 15, no. 4, pp. 421–42.

Balbo, L. (1987) 'Family, women and the State: notes toward a typology of family roles and public intervention', in C. Maier (ed.), *The Changing Boundaries of the Political* (Cambridge: Cambridge University Press), pp. 201–19.

Baldock, J. and Evers, A. (1991) 'Citizenship and frail old people: changing patterns of provision in Europe', in N. Manning (ed.), *Social Policy Review 1990–91* (London: Longman), pp. 101–27.

Baldock, J. and Evers, A. (1992) 'Innovations and care of the elderly: the cutting-edge of change for social welfare systems. Examples from Sweden, the Netherlands and the United Kingdom', *Ageing and Society*, vol. 12, pp. 289–312.

Baldock, J. and Ungerson, C. (1994) *Becoming Consumers of Community Care: Households within the Mixed Economy of Welfare* (York: Joseph Rowntree Foundation).

Barnekov, T., Boyle, R. and Rich, D. (1989) *Privatism and Urban Policy in Britain and the United States.* (Oxford: Oxford University Press).

Barro, R.J. and Sala-i-Martin, X. (1991) 'Convergence across states and regions', *Brookings Papers on Economic Activity*, no. 1, pp. 107–82.

Beccatini, G. and Sengenberger, W. (1990) *Industrial Districts* (Geneva: ILO).

Bell, C. and Roberts, H. (eds) (1984) *Social Researching: Politics, Problems, Practice* (London: Routledge & Kegan Paul).

Benhabib, S. (1990) 'Epistemologies of postmodernism: a rejoinder to Jean-François Lyotard', in L. Nicholson (ed.), *Feminism/ Postmodernism* (London: Routledge), pp. 107–32.

Berry, B.J.L. (1973) *Growth Centres in the American Urban System* (Cambridge, Massachusetts: Ballinger).

Berry, B.J.L. (ed.) (1976) *Urbanization and Counter-Urbanization* (London: Sage).

Berting, J. (1987) 'The significance of different types of cultural boundaries in international comparative and cooperative research in the social sciences', *Cross-National Research Papers*, vol. 1, no. 3, pp. 1–13.

Björnberg, U. (ed.) (1991) *European Parents in the 1990s: Contradictions and Comparisons* (London: Transaction).

Bobeck, H. (1969) 'Über einige funktionelle Stadttypen und ihre Beziehungen zum Lande', in P. Schöller (ed.), *Allgemeine*

Stadtgeographie (Darmstadt: Wissenschaftliche Buchgesellschaft) pp. 269–88.

Bolderson, H. and Mabbett, D. (1995) 'Mongrels or thoroughbreds: a cross-national look at social security systems', *European Journal of Political Research*, vol. 28, no. 1, pp. 119–39.

Born, C. and Krüger, H. (eds) (1993) *Erwerbsverläufe von Ehepartnern und die Modernisierung weiblicher Lebensläufe* (Berlin: Deutscher Studien Verlag).

Bornat, J. (1994) *Reminiscence Reviewed* (Milton Keynes: Open University Press).

Bornat, J. and Middleton, D. (1994) 'Context and interpretation in accounting for experience: two case studies relating to biographical work'. Paper presented at Cultures of Care Anglo-German seminar on Biographical Methods for Comparative Social Policy, April, London.

Bouget, D. and Nogues, H. (1993) 'L'évaluation des politiques de lutte contre les exclusions sociales', in M. Ferrera (ed.), *The Evaluation of Social Policies: Experiences and Perspectives* (Milano: Casa Editrice Dott. A. Giuffrè), pp. 73–92.

Bowden, P. (1988) *National Monitoring and Evaluation* (Aldershot: Gower).

Boyer, R. (1986) *La théorie de la régulation: une analyse critique* (Paris: La Découverte).

Bradshaw, J. (1994) 'Simulating policies: an example in comparative method', in B. Palier (co-ordinator), *Comparing Social Welfare Systems in Europe*, vol. 1 *Oxford Conference, France – United Kingdom* (Paris: MIRE), pp. 439–60.

Bradshaw, J. (1995) 'The level of social assistance in 18 countries', *Benefits*, no. 12, pp. 16–20.

Bradshaw, J. and Piachaud, D. (1980) *Child Support in the European Community* (London: Bedford Square Press).

Bradshaw, J., Ditch, J., Holmes, H. and Whiteford, P. (1993) *Support for Children: a Comparison of Arrangements in Fifteen Countries*, DSS Research Report, no. 21 (London: HMSO).

Brindley, T., Rydin, Y. and Stoker, G. (1989) *Remaking Planning: the Politics of Urban Change in the Thatcher Years* (London: Unwin Hyman).

Bruer, W. (1994) 'Revenu minimum garanti et politiques d'insertion sur le marché de l'emploi: le cas de l'Allemagne', in CERC, *Le traitement de la pauvreté en Europe: revenu garanti et politiques d'insertion sur le marché de l'emploi* (Paris: CERC/DARES).

Burgess, R. (1984) *In the Field. An Introduction to Field Research* (London: Allen and Unwin).

Burstin, K., Doughtie, E.B. and Raphaeli, A. (1980) 'Constrastive vignette technique: an indirect methodology designed to address reactive social attitude measurement', *Journal of Applied Social Psychology*, vol. 10, no. 2, pp. 147–65.

Cass, B. and Freeland, J. (1994) 'Social security and full employment in Australia', in J. Hills, J. Ditch and H. Glennerster (eds), *Beveridge and Social Security* (Oxford: Clarendon Press), pp. 220–41.

Castells, M. (1989) *The Informational City* (London: Edward Arnold).

Castles, F. (1994) 'Comparing the Australian and Scandinavian welfare states', *Scandinavian Political Studies*, vol. 17, no. 1, pp. 31–46.

Castles, F. (ed.) (1993) *Families of Nations: Patterns of Public Policy in Western Democracies* (Aldershot: Dartmouth).

Caulfield, A. and Wanna, J. (eds) (1995) *Power and Politics in the City: Brisbane in Transition* (Melbourne: Macmillan Australia Educational).

CEDEFOP (1994) *European Journal of Vocational Training*, no. 1 (Berlin: European Centre for the Development of Vocational Training).

CERC (1991) *Les bas salaires dans les pays de la CEE*, V/20024/91-Fr. (Paris: Centre d'Études des Revenus et des Coûts).

CERC (1994a) *Le traitement de la pauvreté en Europe: revenu minimum garanti et politiques d'insertion sur le marché de l'emploi* (Paris: CERC/DARES).

CERC (1994b) *Les revenus des Français 1993* (Paris: La Documentation Française).

Chamberlayne, P. (1993) 'Models of welfare and informal care', in J. Twigg (ed.), *Informal Care in Europe* (York: University of York, SPRU), pp. 71–87.

Chamberlayne, P. (1994) 'Women and social policy in Germany', in J. Clasen and R. Freeman (eds), *Social Policy in Germany* (London: Harvester), pp. 173–90.

Chamberlayne, P. (1995) 'Gender and the private sphere – a touchstone of misunderstanding between Eastern and Western Germany?', *Social Politics*, vol. 2, no. 1, pp. 25–36.

Chelimski, A. (1992) 'La transparence de l'évaluation', in Conseil Économique et Social et Observatoire de la Décision Publique, *First National Conference on Evaluation of Public Policies* (Paris: Conseil Économique et Social et Observatoire de la Décision Publique), pp. 52–60.

Cheshire, P.C. (1979) 'Inner areas as spatial labour markets: a critique of the inner area studies', *Urban Studies*, vol. 16, no. 2, pp. 29–43.

Cheshire, P.C. and Hay, D. (1989) *Urban Problems in Western Europe: an Economic Analysis* (London: Unwin Hyman).

Cheshire, P.C., Camagni, R.P., de Gaudemar, J-P. and Cuadrado Roura, J.R. (1991) '1957 to 1992: moving towards a Europe of regions and regional policy', in L. Rodwin and H. Sazanami (eds), *Industrial Change and Regional Economic Transformation: the Experience of Western Europe* (London: Harper Collins Academic), pp. 268–300.

Chisholm, L. (1992) 'A crazy quilt: education, training and social change in Europe', in J. Bailey (ed.), *Social Europe* (London and New York: Longman), pp. 123–46.

Collier, D. (1991) 'The comparative method: two decades of change', in D.A. Rustow and K. Paul (eds), *Comparative Political Dynamics: Global Research Perspectives* (New York: Harper Collins), pp. 28–59.

Collins, R. (1992) 'Pursuing errant fathers: maintenance systems in three countries', in P. Close (ed.), *The State and Caring* (Basingstoke: Macmillan), pp. 72–85.

Commission of the European Communities (1993a) *Community Structural Funds 1994–1999: Regulations and Commentary* (Luxembourg: Office for Official Publications of the European Communities).

Commission of the European Communities (1993b) 'Medium term action programme to combat exclusion and promote solidarity. A new programme to support and stimulate innovation (1994–1999) and report on the implementation of the Community programme for the social and economic integration of the least privileged groups (1989–1994)', COM (93) 435.

Commission of the European Communities (1993c) *Social Protection in Europe* (Luxembourg: Office for Official Publications of the European Communities).

Commission of the European Communities (1994a) *Competitiveness and Cohesion: Trends in the Regions*, 5th Periodic Report (Luxembourg: Office for Official Publications of the European Communities).

Commission of the European Communities (1994b) *Growth, Competitiveness, Employment. The Challenges and Way Forward into the 21st Century* (Luxembourg: Office for Official Publications of the European Community).

Commission of the European Communities (1995) *Employment in Europe* (Luxembourg: Office for Official Publications of the European Communities).

Cornwell, N. (1992) 'Assessment and accountability in community care', *Critical Social Policy*, vol. 36, pp. 40–52.

Cox, K.R. (1989) 'Book review essay: urban growth machines and the politics of local economic development', *International Journal for Urban and Regional Research*, vol. 13, no. 1, pp. 137–46.

Cox, K.R. and Mair, A. (1988) 'Locality and community in the politics of local economic development', *Annals of the Association of American Geographers*, vol. 78, no. 2, pp. 137–46.

Cram, L. (1993) 'Calling the tune without paying the piper', *Policy and Politics*, vol. 21, no. 2, pp. 135–44.

Crouch, C. (1993) *Industrial Relations and European State Traditions* (Oxford: Clarendon).

Cseh-Szombathy, L. (1985) 'Methodological problems in conducting cross-national research on life styles', *Cross-National Research Papers*, vol. 1, no. 1, pp. 56–63.

Dale, A. (1987) 'Occupational inequality, gender and life-cycle', *Work, Employment and Society*, vol. 1, no. 3, pp. 326–51.

Dale, A. (1993) 'Le rôle de l'analyse secondaire dans la recherche en sciences sociales', *Sociétés contemporaines*, nos 14–15, pp. 7–22.

Dale, A. and Glover, J. (1989) 'Women at work in Europe', *Employment Gazette*, June, pp. 299–308.

Dale, A. and Glover, J. (1990) *An Analysis of Women's Employment Patterns in the UK, France and the USA*, Department of Employment Research Paper, no. 75 (London: Department of Employment).

Dale, A., Arber, S. and Procter, M. (1988) *Doing Secondary Analysis* (London: Unwin Hyman).

Dalley, G. (1988) *Ideologies of Caring* (Basingstoke: Macmillan).

Davis, J. and Jowell, R. (1989) 'Measuring national differences: an introduction to the international social survey programme (ISSP)', in R. Jowell, S. Witherspoon and L. Brook (eds), *British Social Attitudes Survey: Special International Report* (Aldershot: Gower), pp. 1–13.

Deakin, N. and Edwards, J. (1993) *The Enterprise Culture and the Inner City* (London: Routledge).

Deleeck, H., van den Bosch, K. and de Lathouwer, L. (1992) *Poverty and the Adequacy of Social Security in the EC* (Aldershot: Avebury).

Dennett, J., James, E., Room, G. and Watson P. (1982) *Europe against Poverty; the European Poverty Programme 1975–80* (London: Bedford Square Press).

Denzin, N.K. (1989) *Interpretative Biography* (London: Sage).

Denzin, N.K. and Lincoln, Y.S. (eds) (1994) *Handbook of Qualitative Research* (Thousand Oaks: Sage).

Department of the Environment (1983) *Urban Deprivation*, Information Note 2, Inner Cities Directorate (London: HMSO).

Desrosières, A. (1993) *La politique des grands nombres. Histoire de la raison statistique* (Paris: La Découverte).

Desrosières, A., Goy, A. and Thévenot, L. (1983) 'L'identité sociale dans le travail statistique', *Économie et statistique*, no. 152, pp. 55–81.

Dex, S. and Sewell, R. (1995) 'Equal opportunities policies and women's labour market status in industrialised countries', in J. Humphries and J. Rubery (eds), *The Economics of Equal Opportunities* (Manchester: Equal Opportunities Commission), pp. 367–92.

Dex, S., Walters, P. and Alden, D. (1993) *French and British Mothers at Work* (Basingstoke: Macmillan).

Doeringer, P.B. and Piore, M.J. (1971) *Internal Labour Markets and Manpower Analysis* (Lexington: Heath).

Dogan, M. and Pelassy, D. (1984) *How to Compare Nations* (Chatham, USA: Chatham House Publishers).

Doron, A. (1985) 'The Israeli welfare state at crossroads', *Journal of Social Policy*, vol. 14, no. 4, pp. 513-26.

Doyal, L. and Gough, I. (1991) *A Theory of Human Need* (London: Macmillan).

Drake, K. (1994) 'Policy Integration and Co-operation: a Persistent Challenge', in L. McFarland and M. Vickers (eds), *Vocational Education and Training for Youth: towards Coherent Policy Practice* (Paris: OECD), pp. 143–68.

DSS (1994a) *Tax Benefit Model Tables, April 1994* (London: Analytical Services Division, DSS).

DSS (1994b) *Income Support Statistics: Annual Enquiry 1993* (London: DSS).

DSS (1995) *The Government's Expenditure Plans 1995/96 to 1997/98* (London: HMSO).

Dufour, C. and Hege, A. (1993) 'Les instances de représentation des salariés dans l'établissement: comparaison France/Allemagne'. Unpublished Convention, Ministère du Travail, IRES.

Dumon, W. (1993) 'The European Observatory on National Family Policies', in M. Ferrera (ed.), *The Evaluation of Social Policies: Experiences and Perspectives* (Milano: Casa Editrice Dott. A. Giuffrè), pp. 5–8.

Duncan, J.W. and Shelton, W.C. (1978) *Revolution in United States Government Statistics 1926–1976* (Washington: US Department of Commerce).

Dunleavy, P. (1980) *Urban Political Analysis* (London: Macmillan).

Duriez, B., Ion, J., Pinçon, M. and Pinçon-Charlot, M. (1991) 'Institutions statistiques et nomenclatures socio-professionnelles', *Revue française de sociologie*, vol. 32, pp. 29–59.

Dyos, J.J. (ed.) (1976) *The Study of Urban History* (London: Arnold).

Eardley, T., Bradshaw, J., Ditch, J., Gough, I. and Whiteford, P. (1996) *Social Assistance Schemes in OECD Countries*, vol. 1 *Synthesis Report*, DSS 1283 (University of York: Social Policy Research Unit).

Economic and Social Consultative Assembly (1989) *Poverty* (Brussels: European Communities Economic and Social Committee).

Elkin, S.L. (1987) *City and Regime in the American Republic* (Chicago, IL.: University of Chicago Press).

Engbersen, G., Schuyt, K., Timmer, J. and Van Waarden, F. (1993) *Cultures of Unemployment* (Boulder, Colorado: Westview Press).

Engeli, C. and Matzerath, H. (eds) (1989) *Moderne Stadtgeschichtsforschung in Europa, USA und Japan* (Stuttgart: Kohlhammer).

Erben, M. (1993) 'The problem of other lives: social perspectives on written biography', *Sociology*, vol. 27, no. 1 (Special Issue on Auto/Biography in Sociology), pp. 15–25.

Esping-Andersen, G. (1990) *The Three Worlds of Welfare Capitalism* (Cambridge: Polity).

Eurostat (1988) *Labour Force Survey Methods and Definitions* (Luxembourg: Office for Official Publications of the European Communities).

Euvrard, F. (1989) 'Minimum income schemes: practical lessons'. Proceedings of the European Conference on Basic Incomes, 15–17 November, Cumberland Lodge, UK.

Evers, A. and Nowotny, H. (eds) (1987) *The Changing Face of Welfare* (Aldershot: Gower).

Evers, A. and Svetlik, I. (1991) *New Welfare Mixes in the Care for the Elderly* (Vienna: European Centre for Social Welfare Policy and Research).

Evers, A., Leichsenring, K. and Pruckner, B. (1992) *Pflegegeldregelungen in ausgewählten europäischen Ländern* (Vienna: European Center for Social Welfare Policy and Research).

Evers, A., Leichsenring, K. and Pruckner, B. (1993) *Alt genug um selbst zu entscheiden* (Freiburg i. B.: Lambertus).

Fagan, C., Rubery J. and Plantenga, J. (1994) 'Part-time work and inequality? Lessons from the Netherlands and the UK', in R. Hoffman and J. Lapeyre (eds), *A Time for Work, a Time for Living* (Brussels: ETUC and ETUI), pp. 129–56.

Ferrera, M. (ed.) (1993) *The Evaluation of Social Policies: Experiences and Perspectives* (Milano: Casa Editrice Dott. A. Giuffrè).

Ferner, A. and Hyman, R. (1992) *Industrial Relations in the New Europe* (Oxford: Blackwell).

Finch, J. (1987) 'Research note: the vignette technique in survey research', *Sociology*, vol. 21, no. 1, pp. 105–14.

Foley, P. (1994) 'Local economic policy and job creation: a review of evaluation studies', *Urban Studies*, vol. 29, nos 3–4, pp. 557–98.

Flora, P. and Heidenheimer, A.J. (eds) (1981) *The Development of Welfare States in Europe and America* (New Brunswick: Transaction Books).

Freeman, M. (1993) *Rewriting the Self: History, Memory and Narrative* (London: Routledge).

Fridberg, T. (ed.) (1993) *On Social Assistance in the Nordic Capitals* (Copenhagen: Danish National Institute for Social Research).

Gabanyi, M., May, S. and Schneider, M. (1992) 'Absicherung des Pflegerisikos am Beispiel ausgewählter europäischer Länder', *Forschungsbericht 218 Sozialforschung* (Bonn: Bundesminister für Arbeit und Sozialordnung).

Gardiner, K., Hills, J., Falkingham, J., Lechene, V. and Sutherland, H. (1995) 'The effects of differences in housing and health care systems on international comparisons of income distribution, *STICERD Welfare State Programme Working Paper*, no. 110 (London: STICERD).

Gauthier, A.H. (1993) 'Family policies in the EC countries', in M. Ferrera (ed.), *The Evaluation of Social Policies: Experiences and Perspectives* (Milano: Casa Editrice Dott. A. Giuffrè), pp. 55–72.

Gearing, B. and Coleman, P. (1995) 'Biographical assessment in community care', in J. Birren, G. Kenyon, J.E. Ruth, J.J.F. Schroot, J. Svensson (eds), *Ageing and Biography: Explorations in Adult Development* (New York: Springer).

Gerhardt, U. (1988) 'Qualitative sociology in the Federal Republic of Germany', *Qualitative Sociology*, vol. 11, nos 1–2, pp. 29–43.

Gibbon, E.G. and Lincoln, Y.S. (1994) 'Competing paradigms in qualitative research', in N.K. Denzin and Y.S. Lincoln (eds), *Handbook of Qualitative Research* (Thousand Oaks: Sage), pp. 1259–62.

Glendinning, C. and McLaughlin, E. (1993) 'Paying for care: lessons from Europe', *Social Security Advisory Committee*, Research Paper, no. 5 (London: HMSO).

Glover, J. (1989) 'The classification of occupations in cross-national research: issues relating to the secondary analysis of large national data sets', *Cross-National Research Papers*, Special Issue, pp. 80–2.

Glover, J. (1991) 'French and British women in employment'. Unpublished PhD thesis presented to the University of Surrey.

Glover, J. (1993) 'Analyse secondaire et recherche comparative internationale: problèmes et résultats', *Sociétés contemporaines*, nos 14–15, pp. 93–112.

Goldfarb, R.S. and Yezer, A. (1987) 'Interregional wage differentials dynamics', *Papers of the Regional Science Association*, no. 62, pp. 45–56.

Gordon, I.R. and Lamont, D. (1982) 'A model of labour-market interdependencies in the London region', *Environment and Planning A*, no. 14, pp. 238–64.

Gordon, M. (1988) *Social Security Policies in Industrial Countries. A Comparative Analysis* (Cambridge: Cambridge University Press).

Görres, S. (1992) *Geriatrische Rehabilitation und Lebensbewältigung* (Weinheim und München: Juventa).

Grele, R.J. (ed.) (1975) *Envelopes of Sound. Six Practitioners Discuss the Theory, Method and Practice of Oral History and Oral Testimony* (Chicago: Precedent).

Grémy, J-P. (1989) 'Problèmes de l'analyse secondaire', in A. Girard and E. Malinvaud (eds), *Les enquêtes d'opinion et la recherche en sciences sociales* (Paris: L'Harmattan), pp. 51–87.

Guillemard, A-M. (1993) 'L'équité entre générations dans les sociétés démographiquement vieillissantes: un problème d'évaluation des politiques publiques', in M. Ferrera (ed.), *The Evaluation of Social Policies: Experiences and Perspectives* (Milano: Casa Editrice Dott. A. Giuffrè), pp. 93–116.

Hacking, I. (1990) *The Taming of Chance* (Cambridge: Cambridge University Press).

Hakim, C. (1982) *Secondary Analysis in Social Research* (London: Allen & Unwin).

Hall, P. and Hay, D. (1980) *Growth Centres in the European Urban System* (London: Heinemann).

Hall, P., Gracey, H., Drewett, R. and Thomas R. (1973) *The Containment of Urban England* (London: Allen & Unwin).

Hambleton, R. and Thomas, H. (eds) (1995) *Urban Policy Evaluation: Challenge and Change* (London: Paul Chapman).

Hamel, P. (1995) 'Collective action and the paradigm of individualism', in L. Maheu (ed.), *Social Movements and Social Classes: the Future of Collective Action* (London: Sage), pp. 236–57.

Hannerz, U. (1992) *Cultural Complexity. Studies in the Social Organization of Meaning* (New York: Columbia University Press).

Hantrais, L. (1995) *Social Policy in the European Union* (London and New York: Macmillan).

Hantrais, L. and Ager, D.E. (1985) 'The language barrier to effective cross-national research', *Cross-National Research Papers*, vol. 1, no. 1, pp. 29–40.

Hantrais, L. and Letablier, M-T. (1996) *Families and Family Policies in Europe* (London and New York: Longman).

Harding, A. (1991) 'The rise of urban growth coalitions, UK-style?', *Government and Policy*, vol. 9, no. 3, pp. 295–317.

Harding, A. (1995) 'Elite theory and growth machines', in D. Judge, G. Stoker and H. Wolman (eds), *Theories of Urban Politics* (London: Sage), pp. 35–53.

Harding, A. and Le Galès, P. (1996) 'Globalisation, urban change and urban policy', in A. Scott (ed.), *The Limits of Globalisation* (London: Routledge).

Hauser, R. (1993) 'Approaches to comparative social policy analysis', in J. Berghman and B. Cantillon (eds), *The European Face of Social Security* (Aldershot: Avebury), pp. 79–93.

'Health and Welfare' (1995) *Oral History*, Special Issue, vol. 23, no. 1.

Heidemann, W., Kruse, W., Paul Kohlhoff, A. and Zeuner, C. (1994) *Social Dialogue and Further Education and Training in Europe. New Challenges for the Trade Unions* (Berlin: Sigma).

Heidenheimer, A., Heclo, H. and Adams, C. (1990) *Comparative Public Policy*, 3rd edn (New York: St Martin's Press).

House of Commons Trade and Industry Committee (1994) *Competitiveness of UK Manufacturing Industry* (London: HMSO).

Hugman, R. (1994) *Ageing and the Care of Older People in Europe* (New York: St Martin's Press).

Hyman, H. (1972) *Secondary Analysis of Sample Surveys: Principles, Procedures and Potentialities* (New York: Wiley).

Hyman, R. (1994) 'Introduction: economic restructuring, market liberalism and the future of national industrial relations systems', in R. Hyman and A. Ferner (eds), *New Frontiers in European Industrial Relations* (Oxford: Blackwell), pp. 1–14.

Hyman, R. and Ferner, A. (1994) *New Frontiers in European Industrial Relations* (Oxford: Blackwell).

ILO (1988) *ISCO–88 International Standard Classification of Occupations* (Geneva: International Labour Office).

INSÉÉ (1983a) *Guide des catégories socioprofessionnelles* (Paris: INSÉÉ).

INSÉÉ (1983b) *PCS (Nomenclature des professions et catégories socioprofessionnelles)* (Paris: INSÉÉ).

INSÉÉ (1987) *Pour une histoire de la statistique*, vol. 1, *Contributions*; vol. 2, *Matériaux* (Paris: Economica).

Iribarne, P. d' (1991) 'Culture et effet sociétal', *Revue française de sociologie*, nos 32–4, pp. 599–614.

ISSA (1990) 'The social protection of the frail elderly', *Studies and Research*, no. 28 (Geneva: International Social Security Association).

Jacobs, B.D. (1992) *Fractured Cities: Capitalism, Community and Empowerment in Britain and America* (London: Routledge).

Jamieson, A. (1991a) 'Community care for older people', in G. Room (ed.), *Towards a European Welfare State?* (Bristol: SAUS Publications), pp. 107–26.

Jamieson A. (ed.) (1991b) 'Home care for older people in Europe', *Health Service Research Series*, no. 7 (Oxford: Oxford University Press).

Jani-Le Bris, H. (1993) *Family Care of Dependent Older People in the European Community* (Dublin: European Foundation for the Improvement of Living and Working Conditions).

Jessop, B. (1994) 'Post-Fordism and the State', in A. Amin (ed.), *Post-Fordism: a Reader* (Oxford: Blackwell), pp. 251–79.

Jobert, A., Marry, C. and Tanguy, I. (eds) (1995) *Éducation et travail en Grande-Bretagne, Allemagne et Italie* (Paris: Armand Colin, Bibliothèque Européenne des Sciences de l'Éducation).

Johnson, J.D. and Tuttle, F. (1989) *Problems in Intercultural Research* (Newbury Park: Sage).

Jones, C. (ed.) (1985) *Patterns of Social Policy: an Introduction to Comparative Analysis* (London: Tavistock).

Josselson, R. and Lieblich A. (eds) (1993) *The Narrative Study of Lives* (London: Sage).

Judge, D. (1995) 'Pluralism', in D. Judge, G. Stoker and H. Wolman (eds.), *Theories of Urban Politics* (London: Sage), pp. 13–34.

Judge, D., Stoker, G. and Wolman, H. (eds) (1995) *Theories of Urban Politics* (London: Sage).

Kaelble, H. (1993) 'Vergleichende Sozialgeschichte des 19. und 20. Jahrhunderts: Forschungen europäischer Historiker', *Jahrbuch für Wirtschaftsgeschichte*, no. I.II, pp. 173–200.

Kamerman, S.B. and Kahn, A.J. (1983) *Income Transfers for Families with Children* (Philadelphia: Temple University Press).

Kamerman, S.B and Kahn, A.J. (1989) 'Single parent, female-headed families in Western Europe: social change and response', *International Social Security Review*, no. 1/89, pp. 3–34.

Kamerman, S.B. and Kahn, A.J. (eds) (1978) *Family Policy: Government and Families in Fourteen Countries* (New York: Columbia University Press).

Karger, H. (1991) 'The radical right and welfare reform in the United States', in H. Glennerster and J. Midgley (eds), *The Radical Right and the Welfare State* (Hemel Hempstead: Harvester Wheatsheaf), pp. 63–78.

King, D. (1993) 'The Conservatives and training policy 1979–1992: from a tripartite to a neo-liberal regime', *Political Studies*, vol. 41, no. 2, pp. 214–35.

King, G., Keohane, R.O. and Verba, S. (1994) *Designing Social Inquiry* (Princeton: University Press).

Kinnear, R. (1987) 'Interference from the researcher's background in comparisons across the ideological divide', *Cross-National Research Papers*, vol. 1, no. 4, pp. 9–14.

Kohler Riessman, C. (1994) *Qualitative Studies in Social Work Research* (London: Sage).

Kohn, M.L. (ed.) (1989) *Cross-National Research in Sociology* (Newbury Park: Sage).

Korpi, W. and Palme, J. (1994) 'The strategy of equality and the paradox of redistribution'. Paper presented to the Social Policy Association Conference, University of Liverpool.

Kraan, R., Baldock, J., Davies, B., Evers, A., Johansson, L., Knaper, M., Thorslund, M., and Tunissen, C. (eds) (1991) *Care for the Elderly* (Frankfurt a. M. and Boulder: Campus Verlag and Westview).

Lammers, C. and Hickson, D. (eds) (1979) *Organisations Alike and Unlike: International and Interinstitutional Studies* (London: Routledge & Kegan Paul).

Landesarchiv Berlin und Arbeitsgemeinschaft Berliner Archivare (eds) (1992) *Berliner Archive* (Berlin: Landesarchiv).

Le Grand, J. (1993) 'The evaluation of health care system reforms', in M. Ferrera (ed.), *The Evaluation of Social Policies: Experiences and Perspectives* (Milano: Casa Editrice Dott. A. Giuffrè), pp. 33–54.

Leibfried, S. (1992) 'Towards a European welfare state? On integrating poverty regimes into the European Community', in Z. Ferge and J.E. Kolberg (eds), *Social Policy in a Changing Europe* (Frankfurt-a.-M. and Boulder: Campus Verlag and Westview Press), pp. 245–79.

Leibfried, S. (1993) 'Towards a European Welfare State', in C. Jones (ed.), *New Perspectives on the Welfare State in Europe* (London: Routledge), pp. 133–56.

Leira, A. (1993) 'Concepts of care: loving, thinking and doing', in J. Twigg (ed.), *Informal Care in Europe*, Conference Report (York: University of York – SPRU), pp. 23–39.

Lenoir, D. (1994) *L'Europe sociale* (Paris: Éditions la Découverte).

Levine, M.A. (1994) 'The transformation of urban politics in France: the roots of growth politics and urban regimes', *Urban Affairs Quarterly*, vol. 29, no. 3, pp. 383–410.

Lewis, J. (1992) 'Gender and the development of welfare regimes', *European Journal of Social Policy*, vol. 2, no. 3, pp. 159–73.

Lijphart, A. (1971) 'Comparative politics and comparative method', *American Political Science Review*, vol. 65, no. 3, pp. 682–98.

Lisle, E. (1985) 'Validation in the social sciences by international comparison', *Cross-National Research Papers*, vol. 1, no. 1, pp. 11–28.

Lisle, E., Machin, H. and Yasin, S. (eds) (1984) *Traversing the Crisis: the Social Sciences in Britain and France* (London: ESRC).

Lødemel, I. and Schulte, B. (1992) 'Social assistance: a part of Social Security or the Poor Law in new disguise?'. Proceedings of the Conference, Social Security Fifty Years after Beveridge, 27–30 September, University of York.

Logan, J. and Molotch, H. (1987) *Urban Fortunes: the Political Economy of Place* (London: University of California Press).

Lorenz, W. (1994) 'Personal social services', in J. Clasen and R. Freeman (eds), *Social Policy in Germany* (New York: Harvester Wheatsheaf), pp. 148–69.

McGlone, F. and Cronin, N. (1994) 'A crisis in care?', *Occasional Paper*, no. 19 (London: Family Policy Studies Centre).

Maheu, L. (1995) 'Collective action and the paradigm of individualism, in L. Maheu (ed.), *Social Movements and Social Classes: the Future of Collective Action* (London: Sage), pp. 236–57.

Maier, F. (1995) 'Skill formation and equal opportunity. A comparative perspective', in J. Humphries and J. Rubery (eds), *The Economics of Equal Opportunities* (Manchester: Equal Opportunities Commission), pp. 203–18.

Majnoni d'Intignano, B. (1993) *La protection sociale* (Paris: Éditions de Fallois).

Masprone, B. (rapporteur) (1989) 'Opinion on poverty', *Official Journal of the European Communities*, C221, pp. 10–15.

Matthes, J. (1992) 'The operation called "Vergleichen"', in J. Matthes (ed.), *Zwischen den Kulturen* (Göttingen: Schwartz), pp. 75–99.

Maurice, M. (1979) 'For a study of the "societal effect": universalism and specificity in organization research', in C.J. Lammers and D.J. Hickson (eds), *Organizations Alike and Unlike: International and Inter-Institutional Studies in the Sociology of Organizations* (London: Routledge & Kegan Paul), pp. 42–60.

Maurice, M., Sellier, F. and Silvestre, J-J. (1986) *The Social Foundations of Industrial Power* (Cambridge, Mass: MIT Press).

Mayer, M. (1994) 'Post-Fordism in city politics', in A. Amin (ed.), *Post-Fordism: a Reader* (Oxford: Blackwell), pp. 316–37.

Micklewright, J. (1993) review of D. Mitchell, 1991, *Income Transfers in Ten Welfare States* (Aldershot: Avebury), in *European Sociological Review*, vol. 9, no. 1, pp. 99–100.

Mishra, R. (1981) *Society and Social Policy* (Basingstoke: Macmillan).

MISSOC (1993) *Social Protection in the Member States of the Community* (Brussels: Commission of the European Communities).

Mitchell, D. (1991) *Income Transfers in Ten Welfare States* (Aldershot: Avebury).

Molotch, H. (1976) 'The city as growth machine', *American Journal of Sociology*, vol. 82, no. 2 , pp. 309–55.

Molotch, H. (1990) 'Urban deals in comparative perspective', in J. Logan, and T. Swanstrom (eds), *Beyond the City Limits: Urban Policy and Economic Restructuring in Comparative Perspective* (Philadelphia, PA.: Temple University Press), pp. 175–98.

Moore, C. and Richardson, J.J. (1989) 'The politics of unemployment: the national context', in C. Moore and J.J. Richardson (eds), *Local Partnership and the Unemployment Crisis in Britain* (London: Unwin Hyman).

Norman, A. (ed.) (1968) *Memory and Attention. An Introduction to Human Information Processing* (New York: Freeman).

O'Connor, J. (1993) 'Gender, class and citizenship in the comparative analysis of welfare state regimes: theoretical and methodological issues', *British Journal of Sociology*, vol. 44, no. 3, pp. 501–18.

OECD (1990) *Health Care Systems in Transition: the Search for Efficiency* (Paris: OECD).

OECD (1994a) 'Caring for frail elderly people', *Social Policy Studies*, no. 14 (Paris: OECD).

OECD (1994b) *The OECD Jobs Study* (Paris: OECD).

OECD (1994c) *Quarterly Labour Force Statistics*, June (Paris: OECD).

OECD (1994d) *Women and Structural Change: New Perspectives* (Paris: OECD).

OECD (1995) *Employment Outlook*, no. 3 (Paris: OECD).

Offen, K. (1992) 'Defining feminism: a comparative historical approach', in G. Bock and S. James (eds), *Beyond Equality and Difference: Citizenship, Feminist Politics and Female Subjectivity* (London: Routledge), pp. 70–88.

Ogborn, K. (1988) *Workfare in America: an Initial Guide to the Debate* (Canberra: Social Security Review).

Ohmae, K. (1990) *The Borderless World* (London: Collins).

Oliver, M. (1989) 'Disability and dependency: creation of industrial societies?', in L. Barton (ed.), *Disability and Dependency* (London: The Falmer Press), pp. 6–22.

OPCS (1980) *Classification of Occupations 1980* (London: HMSO).

OPCS (1990) *Standard Occupational Classification* (SOC), vols 1–3 (London: HMSO).

Osgood, C.E., Suci, G.J. and Tannenbaum, P.H. (1957) *The Measurement of Meaning* (Urbana: The University of Illinois Press).

Ostner, I. (1994) 'Independence and dependence', *Women's Studies International Forum*, vol. 17, nos 2–3, pp. 129–39.

Øverbye, E. (1994) *Comparative Review of Social Insurance and Social Assistance Schemes in Europe* (Oslo: National Institute of Social Research).

Øyen, E. (1990) 'The imperfections of comparisons', in E. Øyen (ed.), *Comparative Methodology: Theory and Practice in International Social Research* (London: Sage), pp. 1–18.

Øyen, E. (ed.) (1990) *Comparative Methodology: Theory and Practice in International Social Research* (London: Sage).

Palme, J. (1990) 'Models of old age pensions', in R.E. Goodin and A. Ware (eds), *Needs and Welfare* (London: Sage), pp. 104–25.

Passerini, L. (1987) *Fascism in Popular Memory: the Cultural Experiences of the Turin Working Class* (Cambridge: Cambridge University Press).

Platt, J. (1992) 'Case study in American sociological thought', *Current Sociology*, vol. 40, no. 1, pp. 17–48.

Porter, T. (1986) *The Rise of Statistical Thinking* (Princeton: Princeton University Press).

Prais, S. (ed.) (1990) *Productivity, Education and Training: Britain and other Countries Compared* (London: National Institute for Economic and Social Research).

Przeworski, A. and Teune, H. (1970) *The Logic of Comparative Social Enquiry* (New York: Wiley).

Ragin, C. (1987) *The Comparative Method: Moving beyond Qualitative and Quantitative Strategies* (Berkeley: University of California Press).

Ragin, C. (1991) *Issues and Alternatives in Comparative Social Research* (Leiden: Brill).

Riemann, G. and Schütze, F. (1991) '"Trajectory" as a basic theoretical concept for analysing suffering and disorderly social processes', in D. Maines (ed.), *Social Organisation and Social Processes* (New York: de Gruyter), pp. 333–57.

Roback, J. (1982) 'Wages, rents and quality of life', *Journal of Political Economy*, vol. 90, no. 6, pp. 1257–78.

Roberts, H. (ed.) (1981) *Doing Feminist Research* (London: Routledge & Kegan Paul).

Robson, R. (1994) *Assessing the Impact of Urban Policy* (London: HMSO).

Rodgers, G., Gore, C. and Figueredo, J. (eds) (1995) *Social Exclusion: Rhetoric, Reality, Response* (Geneva: ILO).

Room, G. (1995) *Beyond the Threshold: Measurement and Analysis of Social Exclusion* (Bristol: Policy Press).

Room, G. (ed.) (1993) *Anti-Poverty Action Research in Europe* (Bristol: SAUS).

Room, G. and 6, P. (1994) 'Welfare states in Europe and the third sector', in P. 6 and I. Vidal (eds), *Delivering Welfare* (Barcelona: CIES), pp. 39–67.

Roos, P. (1987) 'From farm to office: family, self-confidence and the new middle class', *Récits de vie*, no. 13, pp. 7–20.

Rosanvallon, P. (1988) 'The decline of social visibility' in J. Keane, (ed.), *Civil Society and the State* (London: Verso), pp. 199–220.

Rose, M. (1985) 'Universalism, culturalism and the Aix Group: promise and problems of a societal approach to economic institutions', *European Sociological Review*, vol. 1, no. 1, pp. 65–83.

Rosen, S. (1979) 'Wages-based indexes of urban quality of life', in P. Mieszkowski and M. Straszheim (eds), *Current Issues in Urban Economics* (Baltimore: Johns Hopkins University Press), pp. 74–104.

Rosenthal, G. (1993) 'Reconstruction of life stories: principles of selection in generating stories for narrative biographical interviews', in R. Josselson and A. Lieblich (eds), *The Narrative Study of Lives* (London: Sage), pp. 59–91.

Rosenthal, G. and Bar-On, D. (1992) 'A biographical case study of a victimizer's daughter's strategy: pseudo-identification with the victims of the Holocaust', *Journal of Narrative Life-History*, vol. 2, no. 2, pp. 105–27.

Rossi, P.H. and Freeman, H.E. (1993) *Evaluation: a Systematic Approach* (London: Sage).

Rubery, J. (1988a) 'Women and recession: a comparative perspective', in J. Rubery (ed.), *Women and Recession* (London: Routledge & Kegan Paul), pp. 253–86.

Rubery, J. (ed.) (1988b) *Women and Recession* (London: Routledge & Kegan Paul).

Rubery, J. (1992) 'Productive systems, international integration and the Single European Market', in A. Castro, P. Méhaut and J. Rubery (eds), *International Integration and Labour Market Organisation* (London: Academic Press), pp. 244–62.

Rubery, J. and Fagan, C. (1993) 'Occupational segregation of women and men in the European Community', *Social Europe Supplement*, no. 3/93 (Luxembourg: Office for Official Publications of the European Communities).

Rubery, J. and Fagan, C. (1994a) 'Equal pay policy and labour market regulation: the scope for European, national and organisational-level initiatives', *Industrial Relations Journal*, vol. 25, no. 4, pp. 281–92.

Rubery, J. and Fagan, C. (1994b) 'Wage determination and sex segregation in employment in the European Community', *Social Europe Supplement*, no. 4/94, CE-NC-94-004-EN-C (Luxembourg: Office for Official Publications of the European Communities).

Rubery, J. and Fagan, C. (1995a) 'Comparative industrial relations research: towards reversing the gender bias', *British Journal of Industrial Relations*, vol. 33, no. 2, pp. 209–36.

Rubery, J. and Fagan, C. (1995b) 'Gender Segregation in Societal Context', *Work, Employment and Society*, vol. 9, no. 2, pp. 213–40.

Rubery, J., Fagan, C. and Smith, M. (1995a) 'Changing patterns of work and working time in the European Union and the impact on gender divisions', Report to the European Commission, DGV – Equal Opportunities Unit (Brussels: European Commission).

Rubery, J., Smith, M., Fagan, C. and Grimshaw, D. (1995b) 'Women and the European employment rate: the causes and consequences of variations in female activity and employment patterns in the European Union', Report to the European Commission, DGV – Equal Opportunities Unit (Brussels: European Commission).

Rueschemeyer, D., Stephens, E.H. and Stephens, J. (1992) *Development and Democracy* (Cambridge: Polity).

Rustow, D.A. and Paul, K. (eds) (1991) *Comparative Political Dynamics: Global Research Perspectives* (New York: Harper Collins).

Ryan, P. (ed.) (1991) *International Comparisons of Vocational Education and Training for Intermediate Skills* (London and New York: Falmer).

Sainsbury, D. (ed.) (1994) *Gendering Welfare States* (London: Sage, Modern Politics Series, no. 35).

Saldern, A.v. (1991) 'Die Stadt in der Zeitgeschichte', *Die alte Stadt*, no. 18, pp. 127–53.

Samuel, N. (1985) 'Is there a distinct cross-national comparative sociology, method and methodology?', *Cross-National Research Papers*, vol. 1, no. 1, pp. 3–10.

Samuel, N. (1989) 'The value of cross-national comparisons', *Cross-National Research Papers*, Special Issue, pp. 1–8.

Sanders, D. (1993) 'Methodological considerations'. Paper presented to the Cross-National Comparative Resource Workshop, ESRC Data Archive, May.

Saunders, P. (1979) *Urban Politics: a Sociological Interpretation* (London: Hutchinson).

Schneider, G. (1994) 'Sozialwissenschaftliche Hermeneutik und "strukturale" Systemtheorie. Zu den Grenzen und Entwicklungs-möglichkeiten der "objektiven Hermeneutik"', in D. Garz and K. Kraimer (eds), *Die Welt als Text: Theorie, Kritik und Praxis der objektiven Hermeneutik* (Frankfurt a. M.: Suhrkamp), pp. 153–94.

Schulte, B. (1989) 'Minimum income strategies'. Proceedings of the European Conference on Basic Incomes, 15–17 November, Cumberland Lodge, UK.

Schulte, B. (1993) 'Minimum income policy in Europe', in J. Berghman and B. Cantillon (eds), *The European Face of Social Security* (Aldershot: Avebury), pp. 321–36.

Schütze, F. (1992) 'Pressure and guilt: the experience of a young German soldier in World War II and its biographical implication', Part 1, *International Sociology*, vol. 7, no. 2, pp. 187–208.

Sen, A. (1993) 'Capability and well-being', in M. Nussbaum and A. Sen (eds), *The Quality of Life* (Oxford: Clarendon Press), pp. 30–53.

Shaver, S. and Bradshaw, J. (1995) 'The recognition of wifely labour by welfare states', *Social Policy and Administration*, vol. 29, no. 1, pp. 10–25.

Shaw, K. (1993) 'The development of a new urban corporatism: the politics of urban regeneration in the North East of England', *Regional Studies*, vol. 27, no. 3 , pp. 251–86.

Smeeding, T., O'Higgins, M. and Rainwater, L. (eds) (1989) *Poverty, Inequality and Income Distribution in Comparative Perspective* (London: Harvester Wheatsheaf).

Smelser, N. (1976) *Comparative Methods in the Social Sciences* (Englewood Cliffs, NJ.: Prentice Hall).

Soydan, H. (1995) 'A cross-cultural comparison of how social workers in Sweden and England assess a migrant family', *Scandinavian Journal of Social Welfare*, vol. 4, no. 2, pp. 85–93.

Soydan, H. and Stål, R. (1994) 'How to use the vignette technique in cross-cultural social work research', *Scandinavian Journal of Social Welfare*, vol. 3, no. 3, pp. 75–80.

Spicker, P. (1993) *Poverty and Social Security* (London: Routledge).

Stanley L. and Wise, S. (1993) *Breaking Out Again* (London: Routledge).

Stigler, S. (1986) *The History of Statistics. The Measurement of Uncertainty before 1900* (Cambridge: Harvard University Press).

Stillion, J.M., McDowell, E.E. and Shamblin, J.B. (1984) 'The suicide attitude vignette experience: a method for measuring adolescent attitudes toward suicide', *Death-Education*, vol. 8 (Supplement), pp. 65–79.

Stjernø, S. (1995) *Mellom Kirke og Kapital* (Oslo: Universitetsforlaget).

Stoker, G. and Mossberger, K. (1994) 'Urban regime theory in comparative perspective', *Environment and Planning C: Government and Policy*, vol. 12, no. 2, pp. 195–212.

Stone, C.L. (1989) *Regime Politics: Governing Atlanta 1946–1988* (Lawrence: University Press of Kansas).

Stone, C.L. and Sanders, H.T. (eds) (1987) *The Politics of Urban Development* (Lawrence: University Press of Kansas).

Storper, M. and Walker, R. (1989) *The Capitalist Imperative: Territory, Technology and Industrial Growth* (Oxford: Basil Blackwell).

Summers, A.A., Cheshire, P.C. and Seen, L. (eds) (1993) *Urban Change in the United States and Western Europe: Comparative Analysis and Policy* (Washington D.C.: The Urban Institute Press).

Szreter, S. (ed.) (1991) *The General Register Office of England and Wales and the Public Health Movement 1837–1914, a Comparative Perspective, Social History of Medicine*, Special Issue, vol. 4, no. 3.

Sztompka, P. (1990) 'Conceptual frameworks in comparative inquiry: divergent or convergent?', in M. Albrow and E. King (eds), *Globalization, Knowledge and Society* (London: Sage), pp. 47–58.

Tester, S. (1996) *Community Care for Older People* (London: Macmillan).

Thomas, R. and Elias, P. (1989) 'The Development of the Standard Occupational Classification', *Population Trends*, vol. 55, Spring, pp. 16–26.

Thompson, C. and West, P. (1984) 'The public appeal of sheltered housing', *Ageing and Society*, vol. 4, no. 3, pp. 305–26.

Thomson, A. (1994) *Anzac Memories: Living with the Legend* (Oxford: Oxford University Press).

Thomson, A., Frisch, M. and Hamilton, P. (1994) 'The memory and history debates: some international perspectives', *Oral History*, vol. 22, no. 2, pp. 33–43.

Thornley, A. (1992) *Urban Planning Under Thatcherism: the Challenge of the Market* (London: Routledge).

Titmuss, R. (1974) *Social Policy* (London: George Allen and Unwin).

Tonkin, E. (1990) 'History and the myth of realism', in R. Samuel and P. Thompson (eds), *The Myths we Live by* (London: Routledge), pp. 25–35.

Touraine, A. (1992) 'Two interpretations of contemporary social change', in H. Hafercamp and N.J. Smelser (eds), *Social Change and Modernity* (Berkeley: University of California Press), pp. 57–77.

Tricart, J-P. (1993) 'Le réseau sur le revenu minimum', in M. Ferrera (ed.), *The Evaluation of Social Policies: Experiences and Perspectives* (Milano: Casa Editrice Dott. A. Giuffrè), pp. 29–31.

Ungerson, C. (1990) 'The language of care: crossing the boundaries', in C. Ungerson (ed.), *Gender and Caring: Work and Welfare in Britain and Scandinavia* (Hemel Hempstead: Harvester Wheatsheaf).

van den Berg, L., Drewett, R., Klaassen, L., Rossi, A. and Vijverberg, C.H.T. (1982) *Urban Europe: a Study of Growth and Decline* (Oxford: Pergamon).

van Gunsteren, H. and Rein, M. (1984) 'The dialectic of public and private pensions', *Journal of Social Policy*, vol. 14, no. 2, pp. 129–50.

van Parijs, P. (1994) 'Au delà de la solidarité', *Futuribles*, no.184, February, pp. 5–30.

Vanlerenberghe, P. (1993) 'Impact de l'évaluation sur les politiques publiques', in M. Ferrera (ed.), *The Evaluation of Social Policies: Experiences and Perspectives* (Milano: Casa Editrice Dott. A. Giuffrè), pp. 139–47.

Vilrokx, J. and Van Leemput, J. (1992) 'Belgium. A new stability in industrial relations?', in R. Hyman, and A. Ferner (eds), *New Frontiers in European Industrial Relations* (Oxford: Blackwell), pp. 357–92.

Walker, A. (1993) 'A cultural revolution? Shifting the UK's welfare mix in the care of older people', in A. Evers and I. Svetlik (eds), *Balancing Pluralism* (Aldershot: Avebury), pp. 67–88.

Walker, A. (1993) 'The European Observatory on Ageing and Older People', in M. Ferrera (ed.), *The Evaluation of Social Policies: Experiences and Perspectives* (Milano: Casa Editrice Dott. A. Giuffrè), pp. 15–20.

Walker, A., Alber, J. and Guillemard, A-M. (1993) *Older People in Europe: Social and Economic Policies*, The 1993 Report of the European Observatory (Brussels: Commission of the European Communities, Directorate General V).

Walker, R. (1991) *Thinking about Workfare* (London: HMSO).

Wetzel, J. (ed.) (1992) *Das Landesarchiv und seine Bestände* (Berlin: Landesarchiv).

Whiteford, P. (1995) 'The use of replacement ratios in international comparisons of benefit systems', *Social Policy Research Centre Discussion Paper*, no. 54 (Sydney: University of New South Wales).

Whiteford, P. and Bradshaw, J. (1994) 'Benefits and incentives for lone parents: a comparative analysis', *International Social Security Review*, nos 3–4/94, pp. 69–89.

Wilensky, H. and Lebeaux, C. (1958) *Industrial Society and Social Welfare* (New York: Free Press).

World Bank (1990) *World Development Report 1990* (Oxford: Oxford University Press).

Zurcher, L. (1970) *'Poverty Warriors', the Human Experience of Planned Social Intervention* (Austin: University of Texas Press).

Index

academic traditions 114
accessibility 103
accessing data 8, 29, 32, 105–6,
138
accessing information 198
accountability 149, 163
accuracy 109, 159
action model 165
administrative correspondence
133
administrative data 33, 143
administrative model 150
agencies 89
aggregates 130
aggregate data 62, 63, 89
analysis
  see decisional, discourse,
    empirical, hermeneutic textual,
    historical, micro-, network,
    normative, regime, secondary,
    sequential, socio-linguistic,
    units of analysis
anonymity 109
approach(es)
  see biographical, conceptual,
    culture-free, Gestalt,
    juxtaposition, mixed, model
    case, multidisciplinary,
    positional, societal, system-by-
    system, systems, theoretical
    approach(es)
archives 31, 133
archiving 29
assessment 89, 92, 162–3, 166,
170
assumptions 59–61, 92, 114, 122,
131, 173, 176
attitudes 105–6
audio-visual material 135
availability of data 87, 156
availability of material 89, 107,
175

Bayesian statistics 15
best practice 166
bias 121
bibliographic searches 112
biographical approaches 95–104
biography/ies 97, 133
budget(s) 86, 168, 175

care regimes 88
case reconstruction(s) 98–102,
197
case study/ies 5, 107, 132, 149,
189, 191–3
case-oriented comparative
methodology 85
cataloguing of data 23
categorisation 65
category/ies 74, 76–7, 80, 87, 107,
183
classification(s) 26, 30, 66–7, 71–
2, 74, 76, 87, 108, 130, 132, 139
see also functional, occupational,
organisational classification(s)
co-ordination 114, 160
co-ordinator(s) 149–50, 154, 158,
176, 183
codebooks 29
codes 35
coding 9, 13, 21, 34
coherence 167
collaboration 1–3, 7, 12, 33, 112,
100, 159
communication 107, 117–18
comparability 40, 46, 57, 60, 89,
116, 125, 132, 138, 141–3, 146
comparative model(s) 138, 144–6
comparative statistics 171
comparative tables 154
comparison(s)
  see diachronic, frame of, units of
    comparison
complexity 146